Penguin Education

Poverty

Edited by Jack L. Roach
and Janet K. Roach

Penguin Modern Sociology Readings

General Editor
Tom Burns

Poverty

Selected Readings

Edited by Jack L. Roach and Janet K. Roach

Penguin Books

Penguin Books Ltd, Harmondsworth,
Middlesex, England
Penguin Books Inc., 7110 Ambassador Road,
Baltimore, Md 21207, USA
Penguin Books Australia Ltd,
Ringwood, Victoria, Australia

First published 1972
This selection copyright © Penguin Books, 1972
Introduction and notes copyright © Penguin Books, 1972

Made and printed in Great Britain by
Cox & Wyman Ltd,
London, Reading and Fakenham
Set in Monotype Times

Contents

Introduction*

Sociological analysis and poverty

A voluminous literature on poverty has been produced by sociologists and others who write in a sociological vein. Very little of this writing, however, can be seen as contributing to a 'sociology of poverty' in the sense of providing the elements of a conceptual or theoretical framework. One reason for this lies in the relative recency of sociologists' attention to contemporary poverty. During the 1940s, the 1950s, and the first few years of the 1960s, the topic of poverty was virtually nonexistent in the sociological literature. For example, of eleven of the most widely used 'social problems' texts published in America between 1956 and 1964, eight had no comment on poverty, and only one (appearing in 1964) gave an account of poverty comparable to treatments in non-sociological sources. Poverty was 'rediscovered' in the United States by socialist 'non-professionals' such as Michael Harrington (1962) and Dwight MacDonald (1963). As late as 1963, a year after the appearance of *The Other America*, which stimulated public interest, a diligent search could uncover only a small handful of essays by sociologists. Most of them, as Harrington did, deplored the scandal of so much poverty in the most affluent society in the world. From that point on, sociological contributions accelerated rapidly – mainly following the fortunes of the War on Poverty – and now once again in the early 1970s they are showing signs of slackening off.

Why sociological interest followed rather than preceded public interest may be of greater significance for explaining the under-developed state of the sociology of poverty than the recency itself. Surely it was not because of a lack of pertinent data. The facts of entrenched poverty affecting millions of families were readily

* We wish to thank the staff of the Reference and Government Documents departments of the Wilbur Cross Library, The University of Connecticut. The compilation of this volume was eased considerably by their expert and friendly help.

available in government records. Continuing reports issued by Social Security officials and others throughout the 1940s and 1950s demonstrated that contrary to conventional opinion, large-scale poverty did not disappear after the Great Depression.[1]

It has been argued that a high level of sociological interest in poverty during this period was obscured by changing terminology and new frames of reference. Thus, it is claimed, the labels 'poor' and 'poverty' were replaced by such designations as the 'lower class' or the 'lower income group' or 'class V persons' in carrying out research bearing upon social problems and social stratification, the traditional areas in which the subject of poverty has been dealt with by the field. In brief, according to this view, the part of the population living in severe economic deprivation remained a focus of a great deal of sociological inquiry, but this fact was less evident because of new terms of reference.

An examination of the literature of the late 1940s and the decade of the 1950s suggests that this is a questionable contention. While some research was carried out on the poor, or using the preferred label, the 'lower class'[2] the concerns of sociologists, particularly during the 1950s, increasingly shifted away from those at the bottom to the middle class and its problems, for example, suburban life, the plight of the organization man, and the quest for identity.

This movement away from the poor and the growing preoccupation with the ways and woes of the middle class was partly a consequence of some of the basic conditions of modern social research which place restraints on the selection of topics to be investigated and on the preferred methods of study. The 1950s, for example, saw a proliferation of commercial sponsors who are interested in the behaviour of labour and consumers, not in the effects of poverty on behaviour. Moreover, the poor did not appear to be suitable subjects for the two most prestigious modes

1. In 1944, a point of peak employment of the labour force, Burns (1951) disclosed that nearly one quarter of urban families were living below the standard of a basic maintenance budget. In 1950 Heilbroner (1950, pp. 27–33) discussed the plight of 30 million impoverished Americans 'in the midst of plenty'.

2. In actuality most of this research was on groups *above* the poverty line, a segment of the population commonly referred to as the working class.

of research during the 1950s – the large-scale sample survey and laboratory experiments.

It seems likely, however, that a more important reason for the deflection of interest from the poor is the fact that sociologists appeared to have uncritically accepted the commonly held belief that the burgeoning postwar affluence had all but eliminated poverty in American society. For example, to the extent that sociologists had anything to say about the size and makeup of the group living in poverty during the 1950s (and even in the early 1960s) typically they depicted the poor as comprising less than 10 per cent of the population – a segment presumably consisting largely of Negroes, immigrants, rural residents, the aged, and the disabled.[3]

Such portrayals stood in embarrassing contrast to official statistics that became widely disseminated by 1963 (data as we have noted that were available long before this) indicating that over 20 per cent of Americans were poor, of which the majority were white, urban, native-born, and under sixty. By the mid 1960s a number of sociologists had managed to make the transition from ignorance or indifference to the reality of poverty and were busily engaged in adding to an already imposing bibliography on the topic which, up to that time, was largely the product of journalists, social philosophers, economists, and a variety of government officials.

Of importance to our purpose here, a perusal of the literature of the 1960s shows that the vast bulk of it is of very limited utility for a sociological analysis of poverty. Somewhere in the depictions of the life and ways of the poor which figure so prominently in the literature and in the innumerable essays bearing on the many facets of the War on Poverty there may be valuable data but it remains for them to be organized in a systematic way – a necessary first step toward a sociology of poverty.

Sociological perspectives or interpretive frameworks with an obvious sociological orientation are not completely absent from the literature on poverty. In the past four years an increasing number of sociologists have utilized various conceptual and theoretical schemes in carrying out research on poverty and the

3. See, for instance, Horton and Leslie (1960, p. 174) and Bergel (1962, pp. 268–9).

behaviour of the poor.[4] Generalizations from the field of formal organization, for example, have been employed in examining the functioning (or malfunctioning) of the welfare bureaucracy. Concepts and hypotheses stemming from research on community power are being tested with respect to the success or failure of the poor in participating in decisions affecting them. Perhaps the most notable example is the use of theoretical schemes from the field of deviance and social control. While other analytical models from this area of study have been employed,[5] 'labelling theory' is currently in vogue as an explanation of the plight and behaviour of the poor.[6] It is highly questionable, however, that the employment of theoretical schemes from traditional sociological specialties such as bureaucracy and formal organization or deviant behaviour has contributed, or will contribute, appreciably to a sociology of poverty. It would appear, in fact, that to the extent that theory is enhanced or conceptual tools are sharpened, the benefits will redound primarily to the further development of the sociology of formal organization or deviant behaviour, or whatever specialized area is tapped.

Assessed more broadly, what seems to be now taking place is a return to the use made of the lower class in research carried out during the 1950s. The material deprivation of the lower class was of less interest to sociologists than their desire to have data to compare or contrast with research findings on the middle class. The high incidence of social pathology (e.g. crime, family disorganization and mental illness), in the lower class also led sociologists to direct attention to this segment of the population in order to gain better understanding of the roots of such pathology.

Put somewhat differently, the phenomena commonly denoted

4. Many writers use the theme of a 'culture of poverty' as if it were a conceptual or even explanatory framework. The thesis of a culture of poverty is such a hazy notion that we have doubts as to its descriptive value, not to mention its explanatory significance. See Roach and Gursslin (1967).

5. A salient example is the 'status frustration thesis', stemming largely from the work of Robert K. Merton and Albert K. Cohen. Related to this thesis, although tangential to the field of deviant behaviour, is research on 'achievement motivation', most of which deals with comparisons between the middle and what is assumed to be the lower class.

6. A brief account of some of the perspectives of labelling theory and its applications is given in Simmons (1965, pp. 223–32).

by the words 'poor' and 'poverty' are again rapidly becoming transmogrified and muted into 'independent variables', into factors presumed to have 'explanatory power' for inquiries into a wide range of standard sociological concerns. In short, judging from recent trends in sociological writing on poverty, the poor are of interest to sociologists primarily because they represent an important 'subject group', often a 'captive population', for the enrichment of sociology as a scientific discipline.

To many sociologists this appraisal will appear unduly harsh. Many others, while perhaps preferring more euphemistic expressions, would argue that, 'in the long run', sociology can be much more effective in the analysis and amelioration of social problems (such as poverty) to the degree that it expands the quantity and quality of basic sociological knowledge.

Thus far our position that a sociology of poverty does not exist rests upon the claim that very little writing on the subject is 'theoretical' or 'conceptual' except that which is principally designed to expand the frontiers of knowledge in other special areas in the discipline. Those conceptual rudiments which do exist or can be extracted consist almost entirely of a particular, almost esoteric, approach to the *social psychology* of poverty (e.g. labelling theory). The most serious shortcoming is that this narrow brand of social psychology is essentially geared to the conditions of poverty in contemporary America. At the very most it is 'exportable' to other highly industrialized nations, especially those with socio-cultural settings similar to the United States. (For all practical purposes this means Canada and Great Britain.)

What would be the status of a sociological theory of bureaucracy or of deviant behaviour that was basically confined to American society, or at best generalizable to its British and Canadian cousins? Most sociologists would probably agree as to the 'low level' of such theory, or even question the use of the label 'theory' for explanations of such restricted scope.

Our conclusion is this: It may be possible to extract from the literature some facets of a *social psychology* of poverty but such a limited interpretive scheme – tied as it is to research almost exclusively on the American poor – would be of questionable value for a *sociology* of poverty that must encompass the forms and conditions of poverty prevalent in underdeveloped lands throughout the world as well as the poverty found in affluent societies.

Sociology and the analysis of world poverty

The past decade has seen a tremendous growth in literature bearing explicitly or indirectly on world poverty – a body of writing produced by a variety of scholars from the physical and social sciences, including economists, geographers, agronomists, nutritionists, and anthropologists.[7]

Sociologists should be capable of offering much more important contributions to the analysis of world poverty than they are now doing.[8] Given the limitations of space and objectives of this introductory survey, not to mention the many gaps and uncertainties in our own thinking at this stage, we cannot presume to set forth a full-blown conceptual framework for a sociology of poverty that is not so culture-bound nor so impoverished by the parochialism which now characterizes most sociological writing on poverty. We can, however, present, and comment briefly on, some of the directions, emphases, areas and levels of inquiry requiring far greater attention.

Focus on the political and economic institutions

What often passes for an 'institutional approach' in much of the current sociological writing on poverty is a preoccupation with 'institutions of the poor' such as informal networks of mutual help, or studies of welfare institutions. Such 'lower level' institutional analysis becomes so entangled in minutia that the basic operations of key social institutions in relation to poverty are obscured. What is called for is a comparative *macro-sociological*

7. The selections in this volume are a good example of the diverse backgrounds of those addressing themselves to the problem of world poverty.

8. One of the few noteworthy publications that provides some sociological perspectives on poverty beyond the confines of the United States is Bloomberg and Schmandt (1968).

analysis,[9] focusing on the organization of political and economic institutions[10] and their role in causing and perpetuating poverty.

Re-examination of the role of ideology[11]

Related as the subject is to such highly charged issues as power, exploitation, inequality, conflict, and human misery it is no surprise that discussions of the problem of poverty often turn into open polemics over conflicting political and economic values. Few sociologists would deny that there is some overlap between sociology and ideology.[12] The position commonly held is that a professionally trained sociologist should be, and usually is, cognizant of his basic ideological dispositions, thus helping to ensure a sociological, as distinguished from an ideological, analysis.

How close is the reality of sociological practice to this idealized state? This is not the place to deal with such a basic problem. But we can say that with respect to sociological approaches to the study of poverty the presumption of a scholarly separation of sociological and ideological modes of analysis would be ill-advised. The initial concurrence by sociologists with the belief that poverty was no longer a problem in postwar America, the emphasis on the psychology of poverty and a 'middle range' institutional analysis, the support of remedies such as job training programmes, and in general the focus on various plans for loosening up the 'opportunity structures' suggests the operation of ideology much more than that of a scholarly sociology.

9. While not directly or centrally concerned with poverty, the approaches used by Horowitz (1966) and Lenski (1966) illustrate the mode of analysis we have in mind.

10. Some would argue that a good deal of the literature does consist of basic institutional research in light of the attention given to the family as an institution in the perpetuation of poverty. While we would agree that research on the relations between the family and poverty is desirable, our position is similar to that of Ness (1970, p. xi) who gives a low priority to studies of family structure in his attempt to set forth a sociology of economic development.

11. Our usage of ideology here refers to a pattern of beliefs and attitudes, particularly those pertaining to political and economic values.

We suggest that the literature on world poverty provides one of the more notable illustrations of the absurdity of much of the 'end of ideology' thesis advanced a decade ago by a group of prominent sociologists.

12. Horowitz's observations on the 'interpenetration' between sociology

In practice, then, the separation of ideology from sociology in the study of poverty appears to be an illusion. This illusion is rendered the more impervious by the trappings of 'objective' methods of analysis, the dispassionate rhetoric of most sociological writing, and above all by the *professional* ideology of sociologists that they, more than most other scholars (not to mention the non-professional), can master their ideological biases. In our estimation, at least concerning the study of poverty, most sociologists are essentially circumspect ideologues for a more benevolent system of capitalism, but are either reluctant to acknowledge their advocacy of conservative social reformism or are oblivious to such a bias.

We are not arguing for a 'pure' sociology. We are simply contending that the current sociology of poverty is permeated by a particular set of political and economic values. For sociologists to be more fully aware of how much their approach to poverty rests upon such an ideology and on its implications is of course desirable, but such awareness may be of little consequence if it does not lead to the incorporation of viable alternative ideological frameworks.

Greater incorporation of Marxist perspectives

A dialectic between Marxist and non-Marxist thinking on the causes, persistence, and resolution of poverty underlies virtually all writing on world poverty and related areas of inquiry. Often it is explicit as seen in many of the selections in this volume.

As we noted above, most sociologists, particularly American scholars, are strongly influenced by an economic philosophy that is manifested in a more or less enlightened private enterprise system, often referred to as welfare capitalism. In view of this pervasive bias favouring schemes of capitalistic social organization it is not sufficient merely to be cognizant of the centrality and implications of the Marxist–non-Marxist controversy in the literature. Rather it is necessary that more sociologists build upon

and ideology are well taken, but we view the overlap as far greater than he does, and are much less certain about the possibilities of adequately distinguishing between them. See Horowitz (1966) chapter 22.

models of man and social systems reflecting Marxist perspectives[13] for the foundation of a sociological analysis of poverty.[14]

A more adequate social psychology of poverty

We have already observed that to the extent one can speak of a sociology of poverty it consists largely of social-psychological constructs and theories. Moreover, as we indicated, this pre-occupation with the social psychology of the poor is the more questionable because it leans so heavily on a few theoretical orientations coming mainly from the field of deviant behaviour.

Far from being opposed to research into the social psychology of poverty we urge its expansion so that it may become a more substantial and complementary part of a general sociology of poverty. More specifically, we urge that the 'thought', 'sentiments', and 'actions' of the poor be analysed and interpreted via conceptual frameworks other than the type represented by the 'status frustration' thesis, 'labelling' theory, and the 'achievement motivation' syndrome.

One path of inquiry into the attitudes and behaviour of the poor usually ignored by sociologists but not anchored to the American scene as are the schemes just alluded to, is briefly discussed next.

Attention to the material conditions of poverty

A commonly held sociological fiction is that the physical conditions of poverty (e.g. availability of food and shelter) are not significant determinants of behaviour, or at least that they are relatively unimportant for sociological analyses because of their 'non-social' character. This reduction of factors of physical deprivation to a minimal causal role in the behaviour of the poor stems from a rigid thesis of cultural determinism which takes a

13. Marxist perspectives entail of course a social psychology as well as a macro-sociological approach. As we note below, that which now passes for a social psychology of poverty seems to ignore the fact that man is a physical as well as a social creature. The emphasis in Marxism on the man–nature dialectic would be an important corrective.

14. The recent acceleration of interest in the contributions of Marxism to sociology has as yet had little discernible influence in how American sociologists discuss poverty and its resolution in the United States. Of those who appear to be moving in the direction of a Marxist analysis, virtually all stop far short of really using such a conceptual framework. Typically, they

very narrow view of the mainsprings of human motivation and behaviour.[15]

Persistence in the stance that sociologists need not be concerned with the possibility that social behaviour is vitally affected by the state of satisfaction of physical needs places strictures on potential sociological contributions to the study of poverty in at least two major ways:

1. It impedes the recognition by sociologists of the striking commonalities in the behaviour of the poor that cut across variations in cultural settings and especially of the *sources* of these commonalities.

2. It creates barriers to understanding and collaboration with scholars from other disciplines, especially from the biological sciences who, in their studies of poverty, are more cognizant of the role of physical privation in human conduct.

If directions and perspectives such as these are to be incorporated into a sociology of poverty, sociologists will find themselves increasingly using materials from other disciplines. Focusing on the economic institution implies some reliance on data from economics. Attention to the material conditions of poverty and their effects may require reference to studies ranging from those carried out by psychologists on stress to those on nutrition which analyse the effects of insufficient food on humans. Non-academic sources whether objective journalism or polemical tracts may suggest new hypotheses and potential frameworks worthy of consideration. This by no means exhausts the possible sources of information which exist outside sociology. Within the discipline, one may find relevant special areas such as rural and urban sociology, demography, social stratification, and especially the sociology of development.

Even when the pertinent aspect of the particular discipline or speciality has been identified, the sociologist may need considerable perseverence and imagination to ferret out the particular inform-

---

shift to critiques and proposals indicating a basic faith in the rationalism and goodness of welfare capitalism. In many ways their hybrid formulations are not unlike Myrdal's analysis of poverty in backward countries, which according to Mattick, stems from his quasi-socialistic sympathies. (See Paul Mattick, 'Gunnar Myrdal's Dilemma', in Part Four of this volume.)

15. For a fuller discussion of this issue see Roach (1965, pp. 68–77).

ation he needs. His task is further complicated by unfamiliar terminology and concepts and the presence of a great deal of highly specialized but irrelevant research. For example, the literature on economic development clearly has a bearing on poverty, but much of it would be peripheral, at best, to the sociologist's interest. The use of data from unfamiliar though related fields may expose the sociologist to charges that he has misunderstood or misused them. Even if such charges are occasionally correct, the resulting discussion and debate may help to open the way for interdisciplinary studies and cooperative programmes which are often called for but seldom carried out.

Sociologists have largely abandoned the Comtean notion of sociology as the capstone of the social sciences, but some continue to regard it as the *synthesizing* social science. Although this claim may seem grandiose or presumptuous, of all the social sciences sociology comes closest to being a general science of society. At the same time that sociologists have been moving more in the direction of creating highly specialized niches for themselves in the study of society and culture, scholars in other fields have expressed a need for sociologists to exercise their synthesizing abilities. This is particularly evident in analyses by economists of the success or failure of purely economic programmes which were instituted to reduce poverty.[16] Unsatisfactory results are often attributed to the operation of social and cultural factors. Which factors and how they operate are virtually unspecified or sketched in impressionistically. Such analyses often conclude that adequate planning can come only from a synthesis of social, cultural and economic considerations.

Poverty: dimensions, roots and remedies

The remainder of this introductory discussion is a bridge between the preceding commentary on the problems of a sociology of poverty and the articles selected for inclusion in this volume. It is organized under the headings, The Life of the Poor, Measurement, Incidence, and Characteristics of Poverty, and Problems of Roots and Remedies, which correspond to the principal sections of the book.

16. The same thing holds true for agricultural programmes designed to increase the food supply. See Scudder (1969).

The life of the poor

Thus far we have said nothing about the fact that the referent of the abstraction 'poverty' is the day-to-day living conditions of two-thirds of the world's people. Something of what poverty means to *them* is conveyed by the selections in Part One. These accounts should shock no one. The mass media have repeatedly made equally graphic depictions available to all. But knowledge of the plight of the world's poor has not led to sustained, well-supported efforts to alleviate poverty. Rather, after an initial furore, in which strenuous denials of the deplorable conditions presented vie with demands for their correction, a committee is appointed for further study, and very little happens to change the life of the poor.

The following excerpt from Robert Coles's testimony before the Select Committee on Nutrition and Human Needs of the United States Senate (1969) illustrates this process. His statement was made some months after a television documentary, 'Hunger in America' had created a stir among the American public.

[. . .] two years ago, with five other physicians, I helped present some observations we all made to the US Senate Subcommittee on employment, manpower, and poverty. We declared that we had seen in the State of Mississippi not only extreme poverty, but gross, clinical evidence of chronic hunger and malnutrition – evidence that we as doctors found it hard to deal with ourselves, let alone talk about, because we had been unprepared by our own medical training for what we saw. Today's American physicians are simply not prepared by their education to expect to find in this nation severe vitamin deficiency diseases, widespread parasitism, and among infants, a mortality rate that is comparable, say, to the underdeveloped nations of Asia or Africa [. . .]

In Mississippi, almost two years after this issue of hunger and malnutrition was first brought to the attention of the American public – I repeat 'almost two years later' – I saw once again in several counties, including ones visited by us six physicians in 1967, malnourished children, children who are not getting the right amount and kinds of food, who suffer from several diseases and see no physician, who indeed were born in shacks without the help of a doctor and under conditions that are primitive, to say the least, and to say it without the anger and outrage that are by any civilized standards utterly warranted. Why, two years later, must these children still go hungry, still be sick? Why must families essentially without money be asked to pay for food stamps with money they don't have? Why do American children get born without the help of a doctor, and never, never see a doctor in their lives? It is awful, it is humiliating for all of us that these questions still have to be asked in a nation like this, the strongest and richest nation that ever was [. . .]

I do not understand why these things have to persist and why we have to talk about this again and again and again, and people like me have to come and repeat all of these findings which have been buried in the medical literature for years and years.

Why, indeed, do these things have to persist? Why *do* we have to talk about this again and again? *Why* must we repeat findings which have been available for years? It is easy to become preoccupied with methodology, theories of causation, or the problem of competing ideologies to the point where studying poverty is more attractive than doing something about it. Answers to Coles's implied questions ought to be the goal of anyone who is interested in the sociology of poverty.

Measurement, incidence and characteristics of poverty

One who has been touched by the accounts of the life of the poor may feel that those who produce the extensive and highly technical literature on the definition, measurement and incidence of poverty are insensitive to the real problems of the poor. Do attempts to arrive at some answers to the questions of 'What is poverty?', 'Who is poor?' and 'How is poverty distributed?' represent indulgence in intellectual luxury in the face of suffering? Or can the answers and the debate and contention that lead up to them contribute to approaches for the elimination of poverty?

If one proposes to eliminate poverty he probably has some notion of what he proposes to eliminate. When he joins with others who have the same purpose he may find that while they agree on general goals, they do not share the same concept of poverty. Thus it becomes necessary for them to answer the question, 'What is poverty?' before they can go very far toward eliminating it.

Poverty is commonly defined as an insufficiency of basic needs. This definition leads immediately to two more questions: 'What are basic needs?' and 'How much satisfaction of them is "enough"?' We find a range of definitions in use which fall between an end-point which sets basic needs as that which is necessary to assure survival and one which defines needs in terms of the average standard of living of the particular society. Similarly, the meaning of 'enough' can range from just enough to a more generous estimate.

There will be little disagreement that persons who are so deprived that their physical survival is threatened are poor. There is much less agreement that everyone who is not so severely deprived is not poor. Most definitions of poverty move somewhat beyond this austere type. One reason may be that we have some vision of a minimal 'good life' which should be available to all of society's members. This vision, in turn, is influenced not only by a commitment to humanitarian values, but also by observation of things which are available to the 'average man'. As poverty comes to be defined in terms of how nearly the lowest segment of society approaches the average, we can see that we are coming close to defining it in terms of social inequality. In substance, such a definition assumes that as long as there is social inequality there will be poverty, since someone will always be below the average. Hence the question arises of how much inequality a society is prepared to tolerate.

Another reason for moving from a definition of poverty solely in terms of basic needs for physical survival lies in its inappropriateness for most of the world. This may sound contradictory in view of our knowledge that two-thirds of the world's people are hungry and uncounted numbers lack shelter and clothing to protect them from the elements. A few societies (e.g. Australian aborigines and other small tribal bands) remain in which we can consider that all a person's basic needs are met if he has enough food, clothing and shelter to assure his survival. However, virtually all nations throughout the world have moved away in varying degrees from the traditional agricultural subsistence form toward specialization, rationalization, urbanization – 'modernization'. This movement has created new needs and redefined old ones. City living, for example, requires that 'adequate' shelter not only protects one from the elements, but that it not present a fire hazard to others and that attention be paid to water supplies, sewage, and garbage disposal. These problems are simply met in rural situations and failure to meet them usually affects only one or two families. In the most modern societies 'adequate' clothing does not mean just enough to protect one from the sun or cold. His clothing must also be appropriate to the job he fills or hopes to fill. Employment away from home creates a need for a means of getting to it. The inventory of expanding material and social needs related to changing forms of social organization could be enlarged indefinitely. These few examples, however, at least suggest that the minimal definition of poverty may not be too useful. The factors related to the form of social organization are reinforced by what has been called the 'revolution of rising expectations', which suggests that the less-privileged will not be satisfied with measures which only protect them from starvation or death from exposure.

Whatever definition of poverty is chosen one is faced with the problem of measuring poverty, devising some kind of standard for distinguishing the poor from the non-poor. Until such a tool is available it is difficult convincingly to comment either on the magnitude of the problem or the success or failure of any remedial measures.

Two types of standards are found in the literature: the *absolute* and the *relative*. The former involves assigning a price tag to the necessities of life (the 'poverty line') and designating as poor those whose income falls below that figure. When the latter standard is used the bottom segment of the income distribution is the poverty group.

Since devising a standard of poverty involves objectifying particular definitions of poverty, the standards are subject to many of the same disagreements and problems as the definitions. The poverty line may be set high or low with a corresponding increase or decrease in the number of poor. (See Samuel Mencher's discussion of the use of a budget for 'temporary', and 'emergency' use as a poverty line in the United States in 'The Problem of Measuring Poverty' (page 77). Note also how a change of 10 per cent in the poverty line alters the number of poor in Canada in Albert Rose's, 'Poverty in Canada: An Essay Review' (page 126).) It should be readily apparent from our previous discussion, that wide disagreement is possible regarding what constitutes an acceptable minimum standard of living. It may not be so apparent that to the extent that the estimates of poverty are to be used as bases for ameliorative action, where to draw the line may be influenced by political considerations rather than an estimate of desirable living conditions. This is partly because the cost of ameliorative programmes rises as the numbers of poor increase. There is also some reluctance to accept a poverty line which would encompass a number of fully employed persons and their families, probably because poverty itself has long been a status of degradation which conflicts with the picture of the respectable working man. (In the selection from *The Poor and the Poorest* note that a family is ineligible for national assistance if the breadwinner is employed full time even though his earnings may be insufficient to meet the family's needs.)

While absolute standards of poverty are 'absolute' in the sense of denoting a specific standard of living, they are not absolute in the sense of being fixed in time or, more specifically, in denoting a set of needs which has some sort of inherent validity. (We are not referring here to the question of changing costs of the fixed items. Of course adjustments for these changes can be made. The problem is the one faced by Rowntree in his third survey of poverty in York, the changing conception of need. Rowntree and Lavers (1951).) 'Absolute standards' become 'contaminated' with notions of relativity as soon as the needs they encompass move beyond such indicators as protein and calorie intake. Whether or not a man 'needs' to visit the barbershop a particular number of times a year, a child 'needs' an allowance which will enable him to go to the movies, a family 'needs' a particular number of square feet of living space depends to some extent on what constitutes the average standard of living in his society. Necessities in one society may be luxuries in one whose members are encountering problems in bare survival. Just as the set of needs will vary from one society to another, it can vary in the same society as its standard of living changes.

The use of relative standards of poverty which has been proposed as a means of avoiding some of the problems encountered in establishing absolute standards also poses difficulties. Is it the bottom third, fourth, fifth, or tenth of the population that is to be called 'poor'? The reason for drawing the line at a particular point is likely to be related to what needs that segment of the population is able to satisfy with its income – some conception of an absolute standard. Indeed, the selection of the bottom quintile of income distribution in the United States as the poverty group by some writers may have been influenced by its congruence with a group arrived at through the employment of 'absolute' standards. Where to draw the line in poor nations would be similarly affected by an idea of an *adequate* standard. One could not sensibly set the bottom quintile as the poverty group if he found there were persons above this line who were in danger of starvation. Neither could a relative standard be used easily for a society which has large segments outside the money economy, since the usual index, income, cannot measure the well-being of those traditional sectors.

Use of a relative standard of poverty is no less immune from political considerations than the use of absolute standards. As we noted in our discussion of the definition of poverty, the concept of poverty as relative to an average standard of living converts poverty into an aspect of social inequality. When a relative standard is used, there will always be a bottom segment unless there is total equality. Elimination of poverty, then, may seem inordinately costly to those segments at and above the average. Mobilization of support for programmes for the reduction of poverty will probably rest for some time to come, on demonstrating that the bottom segment lacks items which the majority considers 'essential', not just that it is on the bottom. (This prediction assumes the continuation of the present allocation of power which makes relief of poverty a matter of how much the non-poor, particularly those in control of political and economic institutions, are willing to provide.)

The preceding discussion suggests that the standards of poverty in actual use represent some mixture of the absolute and relative in which one or the other will be predominant. The nature of the combination depends largely on its appropriateness to the society being investigated. The use of absolute standards will be more prominent in nations where much of the population suffers from severe physical deprivation. In these situations the 'average' standard of living may be so low that if one reached it he would still be the victim of serious deprivation of basic needs. As the average standard of living becomes higher, we find relative standards coming more into play, either implicitly as they affect the setting of the absolute standard to be used or explicitly in designating the bottom segment of the population 'poor'. As we have seen, even the latter represents a mix in which selection of the cutting point is guided by an implicit absolute standard.

In addition to raising these sorts of conceptual problems, the term measurement implies a quantification of poverty. If we ask, 'How much poverty is there?', it is convenient to be able to answer with a numerical figure. (We do not expect the answer to be as precise as the answer to 'What is two and two?' The answer may be analagous to an answer to the two and two question such as, 'more than three, but less than five', or simply, 'more than two'.) Therefore, the investigator must devise a set of indicators of poverty to which numerical values may be assigned. Indicators used in the selections in this book include: calorie intake, protein intake, life expectancy, infant mortality, housing (its own level indicated by the number of homes with water, electricity and plumbing), education (gauged by the level of literacy, newspaper circulation, and the number of students in higher education), unemployment, the Gross National Product (GNP), per capita income, per capita consumption (often measured through correlated phenomena such as the number of passenger vehicles, energy consumption and cement production), the share of total income in the nation which falls to quintile groups, the cost of a minimally adequate range of food, clothing and shelter compared to income.

What is the relationship of these indicators to poverty? Does the extent to which each varies in magnitude indicate variations in poverty? A brief discussion of a few of them may help to clarify the relationship. Low calorie and protein intake is evidence of hunger whose association with poverty is evident. Short life expectancy and high rates of infant mortality are associated with a number of conditions such as poor nutrition, poor sanitation, inadequate shelter experienced by people living in poverty. Low levels of education suggest poorly paid employment. Comparing actual income either to the costs of a minimum standard of living or to a household's expenditure for essentials indicates the household's ability to meet its needs. Gross National Product, per capita income, and per capita consumption are useful in making comparisons between nations on the assumption that low levels in these indicators will be reflected in a generally lower standard of living. The assumption is strengthened by the correlations among the indicators themselves.

The choice of indicators to be used in a particular study is influenced by many related factors: the extent to which they permit valid comparisons of the type one wishes to make, the nature of the society being investigated, and the availability of data (for the moment we are speaking of technical factors and excluding the role of ideology). Per capita income, for example,[17] is not a very reliable index of poverty in a country in which substantial segments of the population are not included in the money economy but provide for their own needs directly or through barter. (Note that in Rose (page 127) a different set of indicators is used to assess poverty in the Eskimo and Indian populations.) Or low per capita income may be supplemented by a wide range of government-financed services in which instance low per capita income would obscure a generally high standard of living. Two countries with similar per capita incomes may have considerable differences in the extent of poverty within them because of the actual distribution of income.

It is important to note that many of the indicators of poverty are also indicators of movement from a traditional form of social organization to modern forms. A key feature of the modernization process is the changeover to a money economy, and monetary indicators are among the most heavily used. Other features of modernization suggested by the indicators are industrialization (GNP and unemployment), specialization (education), urbanization (housing and its indicators), and increase in formal communication (literacy and newspaper circulation). Judging from their choice of indicators, it would appear that most researchers agree that the greater the degree of modernization, the less the poverty. Whether this proposition represents 'truth', the ideological biases of investigators or a mixture is a moot question.

Assertions about the incidence or distribution of poverty which can be found in the selections in Part Two of this book fall into two general categories. One is geographic (continent, region of

17. The figure itself is difficult to determine when census data are questionable. Similar difficulties arise with respect to other indicators as well.

the world, or nation); the other is the characteristics of the poor themselves (age, family size, place of residence,[18] education). Statements such as 'Latin America is not as poor as Africa or Asia,'[19] fall into the first category, while, 'Almost 20 per cent of the rural population was poor, compared with 14 per cent for the urban population,'[20] falls in the second. The types of statements made about the incidence of poverty are not entirely a function of the availability of data or the form of social organization. They are also affected by the magnitude of poverty. To attempt detailed descriptions of the characteristics of the poor in a nation whose per capita income is under $300 a year is analagous to measuring an elephant with a micrometer. Ordinarily, then, we find statements of incidence of the first sort (geographic) used with reference to nations whose poverty is extensive and severe. Statistical profiles of poverty are more common with reference to nations where poverty is confined to a relatively small segment of the population. Although poverty may not be as extensive in these countries, this should not obscure the fact that some portion of the population may suffer from deprivation as severe as that experienced in the poor countries. This can be seen in Part One of this book, The Life of the Poor.

An elaborate description of the characteristics of the poor may be useful in providing clues to the causes and solutions of their condition, but it may lead to a facile conversion of the characteristics into causes. Undue attention to the *characteristics* of the poor can preclude serious consideration of how the overall functioning of society has excluded certain categories of the population from its general prosperity. Efforts to reduce poverty in such instances may emphasize exhortation of the poor to lift themselves by their own bootstraps and occur in an atmosphere which blames the poor themselves.

The measurement of poverty is clearly an essential step in moving toward an understanding of the causes and effects of poverty and the development of ways to reduce or eliminate it. Charts, graphs, and assertions about the incidence of poverty are

18. This usually refers to rural or urban residence, although it may also refer to a region of the country.
19. Gerald Meier, 'Recent Indicators of International Poverty', p. 86.
20. 'Poverty Amid Plenty', p. 119.

useful aids. However, when we see them in their final form it is easy to forget that their objective appearance tends to mask all the subjective decisions about definitions, standards, and indicators that have been made along the line. These decisions rest, as we have seen, on the values of the investigator and his sponsor which may or may not coincide with our own values and on political feasibility. A degree of scepticism may be desirable, even as we use the data, in order that we not unwittingly be influenced by biases and decisions hidden in them.

Problems of roots and remedies
Some general roots

Once methods for measuring poverty which permit comparisons among nations are developed it is possible to analyse the differences between rich and poor nations which might account for the variation in poverty found in them. The terms used to describe what we have thus far called 'poor nations' suggest some differences which have seemed, to many observers, to have causal significance. These are 'non-industrial', 'underdeveloped', 'lesser-developed', and 'developing', in contrast to 'industrialized' and 'developed'. One can conclude that poor nations are poor because of inadequate industrialization or, more generally, their low level of economic development. Put simply, poor nations do not produce enough to permit all of their people to live much above the subsistence level.

Those who identify poor nations by the designation 'Third World' usually stress exploitation [21] as the main reason that they remain underdeveloped. In brief, the reasoning is as follows. The previous colonial status of poor nations limited both economic and social development and controlled them in the interests of the colonial powers. Political independence has not brought freedom from exploitation, since the affluent nations through foreign aid and investment, tariff, and purchasing policies are able to exert tremendous influence on economic development. This influence benefits people in Third World countries only when programmes

21. The use of this concept is not confined to underdeveloped lands. In the United States, for example, the term is commonly used in explaining the plight of Blacks, Puerto-Ricans, Mexican Americans, and other 'third-world' minority groups.

coincide with the objectives of the rich nations. Even then, the improvement accrues primarily to the small segment of the population which oversees the exploiting nation's interests in that country. Thus, the higher degree of income inequality in most poorer nations as compared to rich nations is seen largely as a consequence of external exploitation.

Income inequality itself is often viewed as a major factor contributing to continued national poverty. This is because resources for consumption are concentrated in a small group of people who spend conspicuously on imported luxury items. This spending diverts capital from domestic investment, retarding economic development. More equal distribution, it is argued, would not only directly benefit the rest of the population but would also increase demand for the nation's own products.

There is general agreement on the relationship between highly unequal income distribution and poverty, but there is less consensus on the relationship of exploitation to poverty. Many social scientists regard exploitation as a thesis appropriate in political arguments but of dubious scholarly value. In view of the number of studies that support the usefulness of the concept in research,[22] the continued resistance to its use is an unnecessary barrier excluding a significant range of phenomena. This resistance may be because arguments for redistribution of income can be made within the framework of welfare capitalism and the thesis of exploitation challenges that framework. Whatever bias is operative, a survey of the literature on world poverty reveals a far greater emphasis on the role of income distribution in poverty than on exploitation.

Another contrast between rich and poor nations is that 'the less developed areas of the world, containing two-thirds of the total population, are now the most rapidly growing regions of the world.'[23] This 'population explosion' in areas where per capita income is already low is regarded by many as crucial in maintaining poverty in these regions. Here the emphasis is not on the size of the pie (available resources), or the unequal division of it, but on the number of people it is expected to serve.

22. See, for example, such diverse analyses as Frank (1970); Kolko (1969); and Jalée (1970).

23. Philip Hauser, 'Population, Poverty, and World Politics', p. 204.

Lack of sufficient economic development, highly unequal distribution of income, and overpopulation are the most commonly advanced reasons for the poverty of nations. These causes are no less relevant to poverty *within* nations, including the industrialized countries, although the relative importance attributed to them may vary with the degree of development.

Remedies: industrialized nations[24]

Plans for the reduction of poverty in industrialized countries are based on a projected rate of *economic growth* and are often geared to programmes for increasing that rate. It is assumed that continued economic growth, particularly at an accelerated rate, will assure a high level of employment. In addition to its direct impact on poverty economic growth offers a means of financing other efforts to reduce its incidence, some of which are also concerned with economic development. Furthermore, paying for poverty programmes with the proceeds of economic growth avoids a reduction in the present standard of living of the non-poor. While it may slow down any increase in their standard of living, it offers at least the illusion of getting something for nothing.

Clearly, area development plans are intended to bring the benefits of industrialization to inhabitants of depressed areas. Education – literacy programmes, language skills, job-training, programmes to keep youngsters in school or to finance higher education – is proposed as an important means of enabling people who cannot meet job requirements to secure jobs or as a way to assure that future generations will be prepared for employment. Such efforts are futile if there are no available jobs or if the wages for these jobs are so low that employment does not provide sufficient income.

Industrialized nations also provide for the relief of the poor through some form of *income maintenance* (public assistance; old age, unemployment and disability insurance; family allotments; and guaranteed annual income) and *government-financed services* (low-cost housing, clinics, public education and school breakfast and lunch programmes). The first puts money directly into the hands of the needy, while the second increases their

24. One must often infer causes from the plans proposed for the reduction of poverty, although frequently causes are listed independent of planning.

limited resources by satisfying needs for which they would have to pay if no service programme existed. To the extent to which the money to support either kind of plan is derived from progressive taxation and they are available to anyone who is in need of them, they tend to have a redistributive effect. (See 'Social Policy and the Distribution of Income in the Nation' and Paukert's 'Social Security and Income Redistribution: A Comparative Study', both in Part Three of this volume.)

Despite much apparent interest in family planning and considerable public knowledge of the association between family size and poverty, *population limitation* usually has not been a highly visible approach to the reduction of poverty in industrialized countries.[25] However, the lack of visibility may not be a good index of its importance in these countries. Most comprehensive proposals for the relief of poor include the availability of birth control information through clinics. In the United States protests by minority groups suggest that, not only has contraceptive information been 'available', but that considerable pressure has been exerted on the poor to use it. A further indication of the salience of concern for population control in combating poverty is the vigorous opposition in the United States to children's allotments on the grounds that they will encourage the poor to have more children. This is a spurious argument. Data from countries which have had children's allotments for some years show no such relationship.

The persistence of poverty in some of the most modern, industrialized, developed nations of the world may lead one to question whether the relationship between increasing modernization and the reduction of poverty is as simple as might be supposed. Although modernization is associated with a rise of the average standard of living and a reduction of the per cent of the population living at or below the subsistence level, it also generates poverty-producing situations. Indeed it may be that the concept of poverty

25. Japan, where an abortion programme has been conducted is an exception to the generalization made above. Demands for legalized abortions in other industrialized countries are tied to womens' rights movements. The highly visible proponents of zero population growth emphasize the ultimate depletion of the earth's resources and might be viewed as working toward prevention of future poverty.

itself is only applicable in societies in which some degree of modernization has already occurred. Members of present-day hunting and gathering or subsistence agriculture societies (our closest approximation to 'ideal type' primitive societies) are not usually referred to as poor or living in poverty, although they exist at the subsistence level. References to poverty seem to come into use when some part of a society's population requires money to meet a portion of its needs.

In modern societies one's ability to satisfy his needs is contingent upon policy decisions made at a distance. Monetary and fiscal policies to slow inflation also raise unemployment rates.[26] Normal operation of capitalist economies is based on the availability of a pool of unemployed. Shifting national priorities, such as the United States' commitments to a manned space programme which has been recently cut back, motivate people to qualify for the jobs that are created, and then leave them unemployed. For example, in the states of Washington and California large numbers of highly-trained aerospace engineers and technicians have been jobless for some time, because their training qualifies them for no other kind of work. Corporate decisions to automate affect the job market and alter training requirements. Not only is the ability of people to provide for themselves affected by decisions such as these, but it is restricted by some of the very conditions which make the benefits of modernization available when one is employed. For example, deprived of money, urban residents cannot raise their own food, or provide shelter above the shanty-town level.

Nevertheless, most modern, industrial societies have the capacity to eliminate at least severe material deprivation. The financial resources exist, they have agencies and structures for distribution of money or provision of services, and there are means of assessing and mitigating the effects of policy decisions. Yet, poverty has not been eliminated in most industrialized nations. The underdeveloped nations lack, in varying degree, all

26. Partly as a result of such policies, the *official* unemployment rate in the United States in July 1971 was over 6 per cent, the highest in ten years. The actual rate is probably 8 to 9 per cent. Of course the extent to which poverty accompanies unemployment depends on the adequacy of provisions for income maintenance.

of these advantages, but all of them hope to achieve in a few decades gains which took many of the industrialized nations two hundred years to attain.

Remedies: underdeveloped nations

Virtually all authorities agree that the most basic and pressing need of the poor nations is *economic development* through an increase in their productive capacity.[27] The major means through which any substantial increase in production can occur is industrialization, which enables workers to produce goods of greater value than the cost of their subsistence needs[28]. Through industrialization, agricultural workers (the 'primary sector' of the economy) produce sufficient food and other farm products for themselves and for the industrial workers (the 'secondary sector'). At some point in the process the surplus generated by both sectors becomes sufficient to support a set of service occupations (the 'tertiary sector').[29] The incentive to increase productive capacity or to utilize it fully is dependent on the existence of markets for it. That is, there is no reason for agricultural workers to produce a surplus if they cannot sell it, even though there may be a great need for food throughout the country.

Industrialization implies the acquisition of mechanical equipment,[30] and mechanization itself requires sources of power.

27. Successful economic development only makes a rising standard of living possible. It does not assure it. Who benefits from economic growth depends on the system of income distribution. If the index of success is a high rate of economic growth, it is possible to have successful development without any substantial improvement in the standard of living, because the base from which many nations start is so low. For example, a 10 per cent increase in a per capita income of $300 a year is a gain of $2.50 a month.

28. The following account is a gross simplification of the process as it occurred in Western, industrialized nations.

29. A number of authorities have pointed out that today's underdeveloped countries have a high percentage of persons engaged in service occupations which provide a bare hand-to-mouth existence. Development in these nations may be accompanied by a reduction in the number of service workers for at least a time.

30. Mechanization is not the only means of increasing production. In agriculture the 'green revolution' has included development of high-yield, disease-resistant plant varieties, use of chemical fertilizers and insecticides, irrigation, and development of quickly maturing livestock. Though increased production is possible, the green revolution has been a mixed

Transportation facilities for the movement of raw materials and finished products are essential. All of these things are extremely costly, and the underdeveloped nations seriously lack capital. Thus, acquisition of capital becomes a major problem, and the various solutions to that problem bring dilemmas of their own in the form of repayment difficulties and restrictive, if not exploitative, foreign aid, to name only two (see Horowitz, 'The Abolition of Poverty', and 'The Crisis in Aid: Facts and Perspective', in Part Three of this volume). Nor is development as orderly a process as the sketch above would indicate. Frequently one sector (usually the industrial, because of greater investment) has moved ahead of the other, sometimes with catastrophic effects. While other factors were also involved, the most notable example of this is the agricultural and industrial disasters in Soviet Russia during the 1920s.

Thus far we have been speaking of economic development independent of its social requisites. As programme planners in the underdeveloped nations have learned, planning for economic development without taking social factors into consideration will have disappointing results. Along with most socialist and capitalist industrialized countries, most underdeveloped countries have recognized a need for a form of central authority to coordinate economic and social planning. Such an authority represents a fusion of the government and the economy, and it may be a pre-eminent organizational need of all the poor nations. Among the questions 'central planning' must cope with are: Is mechanization of agriculture possible under the present system of land ownership? How much of the nation's limited resources should be invested in health and welfare services, and how much should be reinvested to increase productive capacity? To what extent will investment in heavy industry at the expense of consumer items be self-defeating because it limits the people's incentive to produce? (Answers to questions such as these may depend more on political considerations than on 'rational' economic planning, since they vitally affect who gets what at any given time.)

---

blessing. Large land owners are able to operate profitably without using tenant farmers who are left without a means of support. See 'Pakistani Landless and Jobless Increased by Green Revolution', the *New York Times*, 1 November, 1970.

Numerous other societal needs are created by the effort to achieve increased productive capacity through industrialization. Phenomena such as an increasing complexity in the division of labour with its consequent specialization, formal modes of social organization, and urbanization,[31] all of which are associated with industrialization give some indication of what these needs are. To have literate, technically trained workers presupposes the development of educational facilities which also must be staffed. For workers to work efficiently they must be reasonably healthy, necessitating the provision of health and welfare services, in turn requiring professionally-trained staff for these facilities. Because traditional person-to-person forms of social control are weakened, elaboration of the legal institution is required. Failure to develop these social institutions can seriously retard economic development. The level of social development necessary for economic development will raise the standard of living slightly but even this improvement is costly. If the national goal is to raise the standard of living substantially for a large portion of the population quickly, the problems are even more acute.[32]

The cost of such extensive social change is not the only serious obstacle. Earlier we alluded to the comfortable, even luxurious lives enjoyed by a small minority of the population in the underdeveloped countries. It is also characteristic of these nations that this group is lightly taxed, and, as we noted, it contributes little to the national economy because of its consumption habits. Social and economic policies such as agrarian reform which would break up large land holdings or higher taxation are not in this group's interest, although these policies might facilitate development. On another level, educated workers are a potential threat to their power and privilege. None of these observations would be particularly important if it were not for the fact that these same people occupy or control decision-making positions in the underdeveloped countries. These positions, so often strengthened by the military and economic power of foreign interests,

31. The poverty of rural areas and the pull of the cities has resulted in a problem of urban poverty which was not shared by the cities of the developed countries as they began to industrialize. See Ward (1969). In Part Three of this book W. Arthur Lewis's 'Unemployment in Developing Countries', indicates the relationship between rural and urban poverty.
32. For a vivid description see Castro (1970).

permit them to influence development policy in their own behalf. These are some of the realities that suggest why enlightened self-interest, often cited as a compelling motive for backing the changes needed for successful development, has yet to achieve any notable success in improving the lives or opportunities of the impoverished. This is not to say that the privileged group will always prevent social change, for development can increase the rewards available to it, but change may be resisted until the opportunities to profit become apparent. Even then, social change may not be in the direction of improving the lot of the poor as we have seen in the report of the green revolution in Pakistan.

Thus far our discussion of remedies for poverty in the under-developed countries has focused on economic and social development. Many aspects of this account could also have been the basis of a discussion of the *redistribution of wealth and income*. Among these are agrarian reform, progressive taxation, means of assuring an equitable share of economic growth to the entire population, and the provision of health and welfare services. These sorts of measures were dealt with largely in terms of their indirect relationship to the reduction of poverty through their role in accelerating economic development.[33] Some of them have a direct effect as well by putting money into the hands of the poor or improving their living conditions.

We now turn to the third major proposal for the reduction of poverty in the underdeveloped countries – *population control*. The philosophies underlying proposals for economic development and income redistribution and the techniques for achieving them are the subjects of serious contention. However, almost irrespective of their political and economic values, virtually all observers agree that both general paths are essential. Such is not the case with population control. This may surprise the reader who has been exposed to the arguments of its proponents which dominate the scholarly literature and the mass media. In these presentations, 'the population explosion' is seen as a major (if not *the* major) cause of world poverty and the widening gap between the rich and poor nations. Proposals for population control are commonly

33. Although, as the selections in this book illustrate, there is much to be said about measures for the redistribution of wealth and income, a brief treatment here would only repeat a good deal of the foregoing material.

linked in three ways to economic development plans for the reduction of poverty. First, the observation that population is growing faster than the gross national product in many under-developed countries suggests that even somewhat successful plans for development at best can only maintain an already low standard of living. Second, the necessity of allocating the proceeds of economic growth to support a larger population prevents reinvestment of capital for future development. Third, the increasingly large number of deprived persons represents a potential for unrest and instability which can interfere with orderly development. The ultimate result of failure to control population, it is often implied, is the over-running of the world by uncivilized hordes.

Opponents of population control as a major remedy for poverty in underdeveloped countries challenge the assumption that overpopulation is a problem of equal relevance to *all* of them. For instance, some countries are underpopulated. Greater numbers of people would create demand and stimulate economic activity. In some other countries the problem is not so much too many people, *per se*, but too many people who are too young to fill the many productive and service positions that are available. But their basic criticism of the overpopulation thesis is that it supports a thinly veiled ideology designed largely to maintain present political and economic relations among nations. The inability to support a larger population is due far less to a finite supply of natural resources or limited capital, it is argued, than it is to the unwillingness of the developed nations to abandon the exploitative practices through which they maintain their wealth and power.

This introductory commentary ends as it began with an emphasis on ideology. We have indicated throughout how political and economic values limit the entire range of thinking about poverty: its definition, its causes, and its solutions. Indeed, this volume could well have been titled, 'Ideology and Poverty'.

References

BERGEL, E. (1962), *Social Stratification*, McGraw-Hill.
BLOOMBERG, W. Jr, and SCHMANDT, H. J. (1968), *Power, Poverty and Urban Policy*, Sage Publications.

BURNS, E. (1951), *The American Social Security System*, Houghton Mifflin.

CASTRO, F. (1970), *Speech quoted in New York Review of Books*, September 21.

COLES, R. (1969), Testimony before the Select Committee on Nutrition and Human Needs of the United States Senate. February.

FRANK, A. G. (1970), *Latin America: Underdevelopment and Revolution*, Monthly Review Press.

HARRINGTON, M. (1962), *The Other America*, Macmillan.

HORTON, P. B., and LESLIE, G. R. (1960), *The Sociology of Social Problems*, Appleton-Century-Crofts.

HOROWITZ, I. L. (1966), *Three Worlds of Development*, Oxford University Press.

HEILBRONER, R. (1950), 'Who are the American poor?', *Harper's Magazine*, vol. 200, pp. 27–33.

JALÉE, P. (1970), *The Pillage of the Third World*, Monthly Review Press.

KOLKO, G. (1969), *The Roots of American Foreign Policy*, Beacon.

LENSKI, G. (1966), *Power and Privilege*, McGraw-Hill.

MACDONALD, D. (1963), *Our Invisible Poor*, Sidney Hillman Foundation.

NESS, G. D. (ed.) (1970), *The Sociology of Economic Development*, Harper & Row.

ROACH, J. L. (1965), 'Sociological analysis and poverty', *Amer. J. Sociol.*, vol. 11 (July), pp. 69–77.

ROACH, J. L., and GURSSLIN, O. R. (1967), 'An evaluation of the concept "Culture of poverty"', *Social Forces*, vol. 45, pp. 383–92.

ROWNTREE, B. S., and LAVERS, G. R. (1951), *Poverty and the Welfare State: a Third Social Survey of York*, Longman.

SCUDDER, T. (1969), 'The ecological consequences of making a lake', *Natural History*, vol. 78, no. 2, pp. 68–72.

SIMMONS, J. L. (1965), 'Public stereotypes of deviants', *Social Problems*, vol. 13, Autumn.

WARD, B. (1969), 'The cities that came too soon', *Economist*, December, pp. 56–62.

Part One
The Life of the Poor

What does it mean to live one's entire life under conditions of abject poverty? The following set of brief portrayals of disease-ridden, severely malnourished or starving people eking out their lives in crowded, filthy hovels gives some idea of the miserable existence of hundreds of millions of people in today's world.

Four of these sketches are vignettes of the poor in nations variously described as developing, non-industrialized, or Third World – Tanzania, India, Ecuador, and Brazil. The last two depictions are of life in 'Third World' segments of industrialized societies – Italy and the United States.

These selections are not atypical examples of poverty at its worst. Similar portrayals of equally horrendous poverty could have come from any of the nations of Africa, Southeast Asia, or South America. The range of possibilities is not as large in Western lands. Yet comparable descriptions are available of the poor in the slums of London, in rural Nova Scotia, or in the cities and villages of Greece, Turkey, and Portugal.

There are important dissimilarities in the general contexts of the vignettes in this section. Most obviously, six different lands with diverse cultures and different modes of social organization are represented. Some settings are rural, others urban. Four of the six vignettes are accounts of poverty in nations where the vast majority of the population suffers from severe deprivation, while two portray the life of the poor in countries where poverty afflicts a minority of the population.

The differences in cultural, social, and regional settings understandably lend some diversity to the lifestyle of the poor. But these diversities are overridden by striking commonalities in behaviour, motivation, and thought-life so often noted in studies of the poor: their preoccupation with the present and dread of the future, their apathy and resignation interspersed with episodes of rage and violence. The existence of such common traits in different settings is an almost inevitable consequence of the progressive dehumanization of persons through a never-ending and often fruitless struggle to obtain the bare necessities for day-to-day survival.

1 Arthur Hopcraft

Born to Hunger

Excerpts from A. Hopcraft, *Born to Hunger*, Heinemann, 1968; Houghton Mifflin, 1968, pp. 3–11.

Tanzania

As the medical officer in charge of the government nutrition unit he was concerned with what people ate and with preventing children from resembling the grim photographs on his office walls. These were of children suffering from different forms of severe malnutrition: the most compelling was a case of advanced marasmus, the starvation condition in which the body swells misshapenly and the limbs waste to the bone; another illustrated kwashiorkor, the kind in which open sores spread over the flesh, particularly on the thighs and lower body, so that the child looks as if he has been badly burned.

These were not case history illustrations of purely academic interest, like unusual elbow fractures suffered by anonymous unfortunates and set before a medical students' class. These children, photographed in the extremity of suffering, lived less than an hour's drive from Dr Lema's office. They were the casualties of rural ignorance and poverty and, close to the silky rustling of the Indian Ocean in 1967, not at all unusual.

Dr Lema could match the photographs with some equally grim information, which had been gathered since his unit began systematic work in 1965. In the area within a seventeen-mile arc of Dar a survey in 1966 listed 30 per cent of all the children aged under five as suffering from malnutrition, and it resulted in sixty-five of them undergoing hospital treatment for severe kwashiorkor. Fourteen of those died. Dr Lema was shocked by the situation revealed by that survey. The region is fertile, not like the harsh scrubland to the west, where a death rate of nearly one in two among children under five is distressing but no great surprise. [. . .]

Their mothers lay with them on the stained mattresses, all of them small women with the prematurely old, exhausted characteristic which was to become familiar to me as the mark of mothers who rear hungry children. They lay as silent as their infants, watching us with a distinct uncertainty. Dr Lema tickled the tummy of a little boy sitting up against his mother's breast, and the child stared without response, the round eyes dull and lined with puckering so that they looked older than his mother's. The flesh on his arms and legs was puffed and pulpy.

Many of these children, who arrived at the hospital looking hideously sick, could be put on the mend by nothing more than the proper protein, Dr Lema said. Within three days improvement would be visible to a doctor, and within five days it would be seen by the mother. The first sign of progress was usually some slight movement out of the corpse-like condition in which the child arrived. It might be a tiny smile. Often enough the end of numbness came with tears.

But it is only a qualified satisfaction to a doctor to save the life of a dangerously malnourished child, and then send him home with his sores healed and his limbs and body restored to a reasonable approximation of their proper proportions. Such severe cases of malnutrition as these leave permanent damage. These children suffer delays in growth which can never be compensated for. The child will grow up small, probably puny and almost certainly dull. [. . .]

Most of the children were already back in their classrooms after the meal break, and we went in to talk to a class in the charge of an energetic young teacher who bounced about on his toes between sentences. He had thirty-eight children to teach, most of them aged between twelve and fourteen but some much younger. Dr Lema, trying to get them to show off their English to me, chose instinctively the subject of food. The first question he asked around the class was: 'What did you have for breakfast before you came to school this morning?'

The answers came shyly, with a good deal of wriggling and foot-scraping, while the teacher fussed and his forehead sweated below his black and white hat. When the last child had answered we knew that some of the class had drunk tea for breakfast; at least half of the children had had nothing at all.

'All right,' Dr Lema said to me, 'that was what I expected. That is why we are trying to set up this school meal service all over the country.' Then he began another round of the class, asking each child what he had eaten for lunch. The class knew the English word he was looking for well enough. 'Porridge,' said the first child, deliberating over the two syllables. The second child got the word right too. The third child said: 'Nothing.' So did the fourth.

Dr Lema abandoned the little game with the English language immediately. In Swahili he asked for all the children who had not had the school lunch to put up their hands. Twenty hands went up. He got the same response when he asked how many children never had lunch at school on any day. He was puzzled and angry.

The explanation came from the teacher. Although the food was free, he said, parents had to make a contribution toward the transport costs, and if they didn't their children did not eat. How much were the parents asked to pay? About eighty-five cents a year, the teacher said.

Here was another lesson about the condition of underdevelopment. School had been recognized as the ideal place in which to concentrate part of the nutrition programme. With free food from UNICEF and American voluntary relief agencies children all over the country could be assured of at least one sound meal a day. A levy of eighty-five cents per year for transport seemed a trivial sum. But now it was found that it was beyond many families' reach. Their children still went hungry until evening. The children's dullness in class, which so irritated the young teacher, would not be cured by all his hectoring and hopping about. They were not lazy, but hungry. [. . .]

There is nothing to be gained by comparing the quality of African rural life with that of, say, the poor Italian village and recoiling appalled at the disparity. The people of Mwea Tebere come from the landless, and their condition can usefully be considered only against that most hopeless of all situations in a peasant society. A man who had nothing feels he has advanced enormously when he has four acres and a bicycle, can watch his children eat and can get dancing drunk once in a while.

But it seemed to me, snooping about those mud huts in that

musty-sweet smell of dirty living, that an opportunity was being missed. The settlement had no form of welfare service attached to it, no patient nutritionist drumming home the ingredients of a balanced diet, no one nagging and encouraging the families into cleanliness, no one caring how the money was spent once the dues had been deducted. Yet the people were captive, receptive, conditioned to following instruction and seeing it proved much to their benefit. By 1977 would today's new houses have rotted about their tenant's ears, just as those built in 1957 already had?

2 Mervyn Jones

In Famine's Shadow

Excerpts from M. Jones, *In Famine's Shadow*, Beacon Press, 1965,
pp. 6–10. First published as *Two Ears of Corn: Oxfam in Action*, Hodder
& Stoughton, 1960.

. . . The natural increase in Calcutta's population is quite enough
for any city to cope with. Babies die in shocking numbers, but not
so many as are born. The incidence of disease – cholera, dysentery,
tuberculosis, diphtheria – is on a scale that would have been
scandalous in the London of Dickens's youth; but there is always
a hospital or a dispensary nearby, even if you must sit on the
steps for three days to get attention, and the dead are not numerous
enough to provide extra space for the living.

Calcutta a generation ago was already the poorest, shabbiest,
and least modern of Indian cities. So it has remained. I find it
symbolic that, while Delhi has auto-rickshaws powered by a
Vespa engine, and Bombay has cycle-rickshaws, Calcutta still has
rickshaws moved by trotting feet. However, the old Calcutta did
make provision on the accepted low level for its population of
two million. Today, the city makes provision – for a population of
two million. To be brief, there is not enough of anything. There is
an ample supply only of tiny shops whose trade is minuscule, of
rickshaws, and of prostitutes.

There is not enough work. It is reckoned that a third of the adult
population, at any given moment, are unemployed – naturally,
without a dole. Many more have casual jobs, being often hired by
the day, or part-time jobs that do not pay the barest living wage.

There is not enough electricity, and the back streets are dark.
There is not enough clean water, and the poor fill their drinking
and cooking vessels from filthy gutters. There are not enough
trams even for the people who want to cling on to the outside.
There are not enough schools; to say nothing of truants or
children whose parents make them work, thousands of children
sent to school are turned away because they simply cannot be

crammed into the classrooms. There are not enough hospitals even for the sick to lie on the floors. There is never, even in a year of bumper crops, enough food for the city. And there are not enough homes, taking that word to mean the least that it possibly can. Ever since the great famine, people have lived in the railway stations; children have been born, have grown up, and many of them have died amid the bustle of passengers and luggage. Now the stations have been cleared – this is Calcutta's only recent claim to civic achievement – but nobody can say where the people have gone. Thousands, certainly, sleep on the pavements. During the four months of heavy monsoon rain, they huddle into door-ways or under projecting eaves.

Home, for the poor of Calcutta, is the bustee. That one can only guess at the population of the bustees becomes apparent when one sees what a bustee is. It is a connected series of long, low buildings with walls of dried mud and roofs of tile, intersected by narrow lanes where two people cannot meet without touching, and intricately subdivided within. So long as the owner of the bustee gets his rent, neither he nor the authorities ask how many souls it contains. Births, deaths, and arrivals from the countryside pass unchronicled. 7 Kammadanga Bustee, which I happened to visit, is the address of about 4,000 people. Not that they get any letters.

The home to which I went was one of ten in the building. There was only one door, leading straight through to a corridor along the back, off which the rooms opened without doors of their own. After the sunlight, it was dim inside. The only light came through a single hole in the roof – a small hole, since the tenants could only afford a small square of glass. It was also hot and stuffy, though this was winter. No description of Calcutta is effective unless the reader remembers the climate, among the nastiest and most unhealthy on earth. Only three months of the year are pleasant, an opinion shared by Indians as well as Europeans. The summer heat often goes over 100 degrees, along with a humidity that makes New York seem balmy. This is the season of fevers. The monsoon is very wet – the bustee lanes become rivers, and the foot-high board at the door does not prevent the water coming in to turn the bare earthen floor into mud – but the sticky heat continues. This is the season of rheumatism and pneumonia.

The room measured eight feet by six and was six feet high. It was home for a husband and wife and four children. This is where they were conceived, this is where they were born, and very likely this is where they will die. The family had no possessions of any kind – no furniture, no cooking-stove, no lamp; nothing but their rags of clothes and a single pot from which they all ate. This poverty, abject even for Calcutta, derived from the fact that the father was blind and so permanently unemployed. The mother earned fifteen shillings a month by making and selling patties of mixed dung and coal-dust. The rent of the home, by an odd coincidence, was set at fifteen shillings a month.

What gave the scene a peculiar horror was that the youngest child was blind too. He was a lively child, and in the confined space it was practically impossible for him to move without bumping into another member of the family, or Mr Gardiner, or me. This one could only prevent by standing quite still and talking continuously. I was glad to go. I hope never again to spend five minutes in such a place; the idea of living there, for the fortunate minority among the human race, is almost beyond imagining [...]

I have said that the poverty just described represents the lowest depths. But, in the vast numbers of Calcutta, it is the standard of hundreds of thousands. The worst and most crowded of the bustees are largely populated by the afflicted – naturally, because they are the people who can never expect work. To the question, 'How long have you lived here?' the answer is always, 'Since I fell ill.'

The blind. The crippled and the paralysed. The victims of factory accidents and the amputees, for whom there are no artificial limbs nor even crutches. The victims of galloping consumption, coughing blood as they lie on the floor – and one old man, in a tenement building, ending his days in the corridor where passers-by step over him because there is no space in any room. The faces pitted with smallpox. The feet shrunken from Hanson's disease until they cannot walk. The drooling idiots and the Mongol children. These are the people of the dim and hidden city.

How do the bustee-dwellers live, when they are without work? 'Most of them manage somehow,' said Mr Gardiner, who is without false sentiment. They run errands, fetch taxis, clean cars, guard premises at night, are taken on at busy times to do chores for the servants who rank above them. They make pitiful odds and ends which they sell on the streets. They beg, simulating such diseases and deformities as they happen not to possess. They steal, darting past the little shops while the owners are dozing. They pimp for their real or alleged sisters. They scavenge among the universal rubbish. It is when a man can do nothing, and has no member of his family who can do anything, that he ultimately starves.

3 Rhoda and Earle Brooks

The Barrios of Manta

Excerpt from Rhoda and Earle Brooks, *The Barrios of Manta*, New American Library, 1965, pp. 1–4.

For half an hour we had lain in our borrowed bed, listening to the pitiful crying of a baby next door. In little gasps and whimpers, the crying filtered through the bamboo slats that were the walls of the fishermen's houses. Finally, I sat up and put my hand on Earle's shoulder.

'I'm going over there. That baby sounds as if it's dying.'

María Franco opened the door for me. Her face was sad and drawn, and I could see that she didn't look well herself. She understood my questioning glance.

'I don't think the baby will live another night,' María said. 'He hasn't eaten for weeks.'

I looked at her arm, wrapped in a white rag, the skin swollen and bluish. She explained that she had gone to get an injection for her anemia and that it had become infected, a not uncommon occurrence because in Manta, injections are often given anywhere by anyone; doctors are too expensive.

With a tiny lantern made from an old tin can and a kerosene-soaked rag, I picked my way through the darkness of the bedroom. 'It's the *gringuita*,' whispered little voices from the floor and from the one bed made of boards from a packing box. The five older Franco children were sleeping without any bedding and I knew two reasons why. One was that they couldn't afford bedding; another was that when they urinated, the urine just ran down through the loose boards in the bed or through the cracks in the split-bamboo floor and there wasn't the odor that would come from wet blankets.

In the dim light, my head almost hit the bamboo trough hung by the Franco family several years before during one of Manta's rare rainfalls. Although there hadn't been any rain since then, the trough was still in place, ready to catch any miraculous drop of water that might drip from under the eaves of the thatched roof and channel it through the bedroom to an open storage barrel in the kitchen.

I ducked under the trough, but I didn't stoop low enough to avoid the cobwebs. Coastal Ecuadorians are short people. The Francos had brushed away the webs high enough to allow them to pass, but not high enough for a lanky girl from Minnesota who had come with her husband as a volunteer in the Peace Corps.

On his back, in a cardboard box that María had begged from us, lay three-month-old Doilito Franco. His thin body was naked except for a flimsy shirt. Rags covered the bottom of the box. I was stupefied to see the withered-up little mite of life. The babies I had seen in the States were robust, chubby, active youngsters. This one's sunken cheeks heaved in and out as he gasped for breath. He made a few limp movements with his feeble arms and legs.

'I was sick during pregnancy and I never did have any breast milk. I sent him to my sister-in-law for a while to nurse, but now he won't eat anything,' María said as the lantern light flickered across Doilito's pinched face.

I hardly dared ask, 'What do you feed him?'

'*Maizena*.'

She motioned me into her kitchen, where she kept the cornstarch in a bowl made from a gourd. She dipped into the open barrel in the corner, where flies hovered low over the water, and showed me how she mixed the milky-looking liquid. Even a starving baby knows better than to drink this stuff, I thought.

'Sometimes I try him on *plátano*, too,' María said. Plátano, a kind of banana, makes a cheap flour when powdered.

'But what he needs, María, is milk.'

She shook her head and shrugged her shoulders. 'I don't have money to buy milk. None of my children drink milk.'

'What do they drink?' I knew the answer would be water, just deadly, unboiled, contaminated Manta water.

'Coffee', she said.

That really startled me. But at least, I thought, the water was boiled.

'We'll take Doilito to the doctor in the morning', I announced firmly. I didn't have much money, either, but I had enough to get a baby to a doctor and to buy milk. And this time I had some second thoughts about our usual policy of not giving out money. You can't just lie in bed and listen to a baby die.

As I stooped to go out through the low doorway, two-year-old Koki Franco came across the emptiness of the room and threw his arms around my legs. I ruffled his hair and took him into my arms. He grinned and gave me a hug and a smile. How could this little fellow, whom I had seen and waved to out on the beach among the fishermen's boats, be so bright eyed and energetic on a diet of bananas and rice and coffee? Survival of the fittest.

. . . Earle was asleep when I got back to bed, so I lay awake and alone for a long time, wondering, asking myself questions, listening to little Doilito crying. How was it that I was here, sharing the washed-up lives of a beachful of poverty-drowned fishermen in a blighted seaport town?

4 Carolina Maria de Jesus

Child of the Dark

Excerpts from Carolina Maria de Jesus, *Child of the Dark*,
New American Library, 1963, pp. 17–128.

15 July 1955. The birthday of my daughter Vera Eunice. I wanted
to buy a pair of shoes for her, but the price of food keeps us from
realizing our desires. Actually we are slaves to the cost of living.
I found a pair of shoes in the garbage, washed them, and patched
them for her to wear.

I didn't have one cent to buy bread. So I washed three bottles
and traded them to Arnaldo. He kept the bottles and gave me
bread. Then I went to sell my paper. I received sixty-five cruzeiros.
I spent twenty cruzeiros for meat. I got one kilo of ham and one
kilo of sugar and spent six cruzeiros on cheese. And the money
was gone.

I was ill all day. I thought I had a cold. At night my chest pained
me. I started to cough. I decided not to go out at night to look for
paper. I searched for my son João. He was at Felisberto de
Carvalho Street near the market. A bus had knocked a boy into
the sidewalk and a crowd gathered. João was in the middle of it
all. I poked him a couple of times and within five minutes he was
home.

I washed the children, put them to bed, then washed myself
and went to bed. I waited until eleven o'clock for a certain someone.
He didn't come. I took an aspirin and laid down again. When I
awoke the sun was sliding in space. My daughter Vera Eunice
said: 'Go get some water, Mother!'
16 July. I got up and obeyed Vera Eunice. I went to get the water.
I made coffee. I told the children that I didn't have any bread,
that they would have to drink their coffee plain and eat meat with
farinha.[1] I was feeling ill and decided to cure myself. I stuck my
finger down my throat twice, vomited, and knew I was under the

1. *Farinha:* a coarse wheat flour.

evil eye. The upset feeling left and I went to Senhor Manuel, carrying some cans to sell. Everything that I find in the garbage I sell. He gave me thirteen cruzeiros. I kept thinking that I had to buy bread, soap, and milk for Vera Eunice. The thirteen cruzeiros wouldn't make it. I returned home, or rather to my shack, nervous and exhausted. I thought of the worrisome life that I led. Carrying paper, washing clothes for the children, staying in the street all day long. Yet I'm always lacking things, Vera doesn't have shoes and she doesn't like to go barefoot. For at least two years I've wanted to buy a meat grinder. And a sewing machine.

I came home and made lunch for the two boys. Rice, beans, and meat, and I'm going out to look for paper. I left the children, told them to play in the yard and not go into the street, because the terrible neighbors I have won't leave my children alone. I was feeling ill and wished I could lie down. But the poor don't rest nor are they permitted the pleasure of relaxation. I was nervous inside, cursing my luck. I collected two sacks full of paper. Afterward I went back and gathered up some scrap metal, some cans, and some kindling wood. As I walked I thought – when I return to the favela there is going to be something new . . . João told me that the truck that gives out money was here to give out food. I took a sack and hurried out. It was the leader of the Spiritist Center at 103 Vergueiro Street. I got two kilos of rice, two of beans, and two kilos of macaroni. I was happy. The truck went away. The nervousness that I had inside left me. . . .

7 June. The boys drank some coffee and went to school. They are happy because today there is coffee. Only those who have gone hungry know the value of food.

Vera and I went to look for paper. We passed the slaughterhouse to beg for some sausage. I counted nine women in line. . . .

We are poor, and we live on the banks of the river. The river banks are places for garbage and the marginal people. People of the favelas are considered marginals. No more do you see buzzards flying the river banks near the trash. The unemployed have taken the buzzards' place.

24 July. How horrible it is to get up in the morning and not have anything to eat. I even thought of suicide. But I am killing myself now, by lack of food in the stomach. And unhappily I get up in the morning hungry.

The boys got a few hard rolls but they were covered with cockroach droppings. I threw them away and we just drank coffee. I put the last of the beans on to cook. I picked up my sack and went out taking the children with me. I went to see Dona Guilhermina, on Carlos de Campos Street. I asked her for a little rice. She gave me rice and macaroni. I stayed on to talk with her husband. He gave me some bottles to sell. And I picked up some scrap metal.

After getting a few things for the children to eat, I felt better. It calmed my spirit. I went to Senhor Manuel to sell the bottles. I got 22 cruzeiros. I spent ten on bread and a cup of coffee.

Returning to the favela, I made lunch and went to wash clothes. Three weeks without washing clothes for lack of soap. [. . .]

26 July. I was dizzy with hunger because I got up very early. I made more coffee. Later I went to wash clothes in the lagoon, thinking of the State Health Department who published in the paper that here in the favela of Canindé there are 160 positive cases of snail disease. But they don't give any medicine to the favelados. The woman who ran a film explaining the snail disease told us that the disease is very difficult to cure. I didn't take the examination because I can't buy the medicine to cure it.

I sent João to Senhor Manuel to sell some scrap. And I went looking for paper. In the garbage at the slaughterhouse there were many sausages. I picked out the best ones to make soup. I went up and down the streets looking for scrap metal. [. . .]

2 September. I made a fire and warmed up some food for the children because I don't have any money to buy bread. I changed the boys and they went to school and I took Vera out with me. I almost went crazy. Because there was so little paper in the streets. Now even the garbagemen steal what the paper pickers could take. Those egoists! In Paulino Guimarães Street there is a metal shop. Every day they put their trash in the street and the trash has a lot of metal. I used to pick out the scrap and sell it. Now the garbage truck, before starting its regular collection, comes down Paulino Guimarães Street, picks up the trash, and puts it inside the car. Selfish! They have a good job, hospital, drugstore, doctors. And they are allowed to sell anything they find in the garbage. They could leave the scrap for me.

I spent the afternoon flattening the cans. Then I went to Bela

Vista to get a box. When I went by the slaughterhouse the bone truck was parked there. I asked the driver for some bones. He let me have one that I picked out. It had a lot of fat on it. . . .

1 January 1959. I got out of bed at 4 a.m. and went to carry water, then went to wash clothes. I didn't make lunch. There is no rice. This afternoon I'm going to cook beans with macaroni. The boys didn't eat anything. I'm going to lie down because I'm sleepy. It was nine o'clock. João woke me up to open the door. Today I'm sad.

4 January. In the old days I sang. Now I've stopped singing, because the happiness has given way to sadness that ages the heart. Every day another poor creature shows up here in the favela. Ireno is a poor creature with anemia. He is looking for his wife. His wife doesn't want him. He told me that his mother-in-law provoked his wife against him. Now he is in his brother's house. He spent a few days in his sister's house, but came back. He said they were throwing hints at him because of the food.

Ireno says that he is unhappy with life. Because even with health life is bitter.

5 January. It's raining. I am almost crazy with the dripping on the beds, because the roof is covered with cardboard and the cardboard is rotten. The water is rising and invading the yards of the *favelados.*

6 January. I got out of bed at 4 a.m., turned on the radio, and went for water. What torture it is to walk in water in the morning. And I catch cold so easily! But life is like that. Men are leaving for work. They are carrying their shoes and socks in their hands. Mothers keep the children inside the house. They get restless because they want to go out and play in the water. People with a sense of humor say that the favela is a sailor's city. Others say it is the São Paulo Venice.

5 Danilo Dolci

Report from Palermo

Excerpts from D. Dolci, *Report from Palermo*, Orion Press, 1959, pp. xxi, 73–7, 99–100. First published in Italian in 1956.

The Department of Public Works gives the number of families living in makeshift shacks and shanties as 15,000 (60,000 persons). And, according to the Regional Housing Department, as against 65,984 houses in good condition, 36,131 houses (which provide accommodation for 200,000 persons) are in a dangerous state of disrepair.

The living conditions of this part of the old city are similar to those that exist in the lowest slum quarters of Naples. Most families have only one small room, a few have a second room so small that there is not even space in it for a single bed; none have lavatories or proper kitchens. Hardly any of the rooms have running water or electric light. They are sunless, airless, filled with dust from the courtyard, and the stench that rises from the open drains below is unspeakable. These conditions, together with the appalling overcrowding and the consequent promiscuity, have led to a state of moral and physical degradation which can only be described as terrifying. [. . .]

The section known as Cortile Cascino is barely two hundred yards from the Cathedral; it extends from Via D'Ossuna to Cortile Grotta and is bisected by the railroad tracks. In 1945, forty cases of typhus were confirmed by the health authorities; since then, however, not a single step has been taken to improve conditions. No matter how often one has seen it before, the sight of swarms of naked children playing in the mud and filth, or scrambling about on the tracks, comes as a fresh shock. There are five sordid two- and three-story houses in the last stages of dilapidation, and in the southern part of the section, a few squalid huts and shacks. The walls sweat with damp and the rooms are alive with scorpions, fleas and cockroaches.

Here, the hundred and thirty families, numbering four hundred and ninety-eight persons, live in a hundred and eighteen rooms (plus five cubbyholes). The average number of persons to a room, then, is 4·22. In one room measuring nine by twenty feet, eleven people sleep. In another, measuring sixteen by seventeen feet, ten. Some fifteen families live in dark, windowless cellars. About half of the remaining families have no light except what filters in from other rooms.

Four rooms have floors of packed dirt; seven have floors of packed dirt and broken tile; thirty-seven, of broken tile and cracked cement; fifty-one, of broken tile; and four, of coarse cement. The remaining fifteen rooms have floors of sound tile that are fairly good.

There are no water taps. Only one family has a toilet. The other families work, eat, sleep, and do their business in their own room. ('Decent men relieve themselves on the railroad tracks.')

Among the children from three through six years old, two go to kindergarten, forty-three do not. Among those from six through thirteen, thirty-three go to school; but forty-five do not go and have never gone, although school is compulsory. On the average, the three hundred and eighty-six persons over six years old have finished only four-fifths of the first grade. Only three families can boast of a mother and father who are able to read and write; in the previous generation of these families, two couples alone were literate. Keeping this in mind and allowing twenty years to a generation, we can estimate that twenty-five hundred years will pass before the couples in this section will be literate. [. . .]

The boys usually take up their fathers' callings and become junkmen, ragpickers, etc. Thirty-one of these youngsters have been to prison, most of them for 'nothing much.' [. . .]

There are sixty-seven babies under the age of three, many of them suffer from malnutrition and are frequently ailing; the commonest illnesses are digestive complaints, chest diseases and various forms of blood poisoning. These illnesses are aggravated by the inability of a large number of mothers to breast-feed their babies. Eighty babies have died here within the last ten years. [. . .]

We older men who live in Cortile Cascino – Via D'Ossuna, Cortile Grotta – never get taken on in the building trades. Most of us are ragpickers and junkmen; the women earn a little by doing washing. Some of the young men get a few odd days as laborers, but when they're fired they come back to the rag-and-bone trade – there's one thing to be said for it, it never stops.

About seven years ago, typhus broke out here and ten people died. They sent the *carabinieri*; we weren't allowed to leave the district for fear we'd spread the infection. The whole place stinks; the courtyard is one mass of mud and filthy puddles. Every morning the women empty the toilet pots over the railroad tracks; some of them are sluts, though, and they just dump the stuff in the space by the water tanks. The slush and slop piles up higher and higher in the winter; the firemen come along, pump off a little water, syphon some of it from the cellars, and leave it at that.

'That's the best we can do,' they say, and they go. The lousy typhus is always breaking out here, you know what I mean. Once, two people died, and a number of kids went down with it – it's generally kids who die from typhus.

That time I was telling you about, when the *carabinieri* were sent to see that we kept within limits, our food was cooked for us in great big pots. As soon as it was ready the *carabinieri* blew a blast on their trumpets, and hundreds of us came with our cans, bottles, empty jam jars and so on, and waited in a long line like soldiers. When we had to relieve ourselves, we had to do it in the courtyard; sometimes the *carabinieri* were decent and let us go as far as the railroad tracks. The food they dished out to us had medicine in it to kill the germs; it must have been a laxative because all fifteen hundred of us – men, women and kids – had terrible runs.

It's no wonder we get typhus. Look at the filth, look at the way the houses are all crowded together on top of each other. There's no running water, and eight, ten, twelve people live in a room where there isn't space to swing a cat. Most of the rooms have dirt floors, several are nothing but cellars. We hardly have any furniture; some families haven't even got chairs and have to sit down on empty cans or on broken stones. Fleas and bugs? There are tons of them – when you lay out the dead, you find their bodies are covered with them. The sanitary units come by and sprinkle powder in the streets and houses. Men and women

loosen their clothes so the DDT can be sprinkled on their skin. [. . .]
'You couldn't live in a worse place than this,' say the people of
Cortile lo Cicero, yet, although the layout is different, there is
nothing to choose between Cortile lo Cicero and slums already
described.

From Via Colonna Rotta, a flight of stone steps leads down to
number nineteen. Below is the courtyard, and when it rains
heavily the basements of the houses are invariably flooded. The
passages are dark and without air, and in many of the rooms it is
impossible to see unless the lamp is lit or the electric light switched
on.

Twenty-eight homes were picked at random for consideration.
They house thirty-six families numbering a hundred and forty-four
persons, who live in thirty rooms (plus one cubbyhole). The
average number of persons to a room, then, is 4·8.

None of the homes has a water tap. None has a toilet. All the
families use a hole in the corner of their room above an open
drain. The smell is terrible!

Eleven of the rooms have electric lights; a few of the lights are
unmetered. Four rooms have no windows; eight have a tiny slit
overlooking the stairs. One has a single window looking out on a
heap of human excrement on the railroad tracks. In seventeen
rooms, most of the windows measure sixteen inches square; the
rest of the windows measure twenty inches by thirty-six.

Only two rooms have good floors; the rest have floors of coarse
cement or broken tile.

There are sixty-one sleeping places. The average number of
persons to a place, then, is 4·2.

Among the children from three through six years old, two go to
kindergarten; the remaining thirty-seven are exposed all day long
to the filth and contamination of their surroundings. Among
those from six through thirteen, only seven go to school regularly;
ten have never even seen the school. On the average, the people
over six years old have finished only a fifth of the second grade.
Only three married couples can read and write. [. . .]

6 US Senate Hearings

Nutrition and Human Needs

Excerpts from *Nutrition and Human Needs: Hearings before the Select Committee on Nutrition and Human Needs of the US Senate, 90th Congress.* Testimony by National Council of Negro Women Inc.: *Workshops in Mississippi: A Report on Operation Daily Bread,* October 1968, pp. 202–4.

The poorest of the poor – 'If only we could have an acre'

In general it was mud, ramshackle porches, bare floors, and small rooms crammed with endless beds, bumpy with uncovered mattresses of corn shucks, broken windows, rain-stained ceilings and walls, bare cupboards, bare refrigerators, scrawny or bloated children with listless eyes, and flies and insects – and dirty tubs of water – and more flies. Everywhere the aura of despair and hopelessness. No jobs, no houses fit for habitation, no money, and little chance of getting any and, worst of all, no food.

In many instances the residents themselves were as indignant about their poverty as any outsider would be. 'Look at that hole in the roof,' said one with disgust. 'And the windows are broken. How we supposed to live in a house like this.'

'I haven't even got a sink – just that big hole there – and we have to carry water a half a mile down the road,' said another.

Two cases were typical – their names have been changed for this report:

Mrs Moore, like most Southern Negroes had been raised on the plantation, shopped at the plantation general store where coupons or just 'accounts' are the general tender of exchange. Now a woman of 50, she had worked in the fields, picking and chopping cotton since she could remember – 'I started at five in the fields, I think' – and had enjoyed the 'privilege and protection' of living at the grace of a white man in a plantation shanty. Under the plantation system the laborers are allowed to live in houses on the plantation and their 'rent' is automatically deducted from their earnings, which are pitifully small – about $7 a day. The coming of the giant cotton picking machines and automation in general have all but eliminated the need for cotton field hands on the large, wealthy plantations. But if the Negroes stay in line, even though there is little or no work to do, they are allowed to remain in their homes on the plantation without payment of rent. With no money, no skills, no available jobs, no filing of Social Security records by the boss, subservience to the master becomes the only means of survival, and the system becomes an effective instrument of political oppression. The black man who dares to speak out or even exercise his constitutional rights usually finds himself and his family thrown out onto the road, and often deprived of the few possessions he did have. 'They wouldn't even let me back in my place to get my clothes or a picture of my mother. I just had to leave everything there,' said one woman who was evicted after she registered to vote, following the 1964 civil rights legislation.

Such also was the case of Mrs Moore, who registered to vote in 1963. When word of her action reached the white racist community – who kept close tabs on Negroes' activities – Mrs Moore was visited by the owner of the plantation where she had grown up, and had toiled for more than a quarter of a century. Her family had lived there. Her children had been born there – the first when she was only twelve. There she had carried her babies into the field when they were but a few days old, carefully lifting them up and down the rows as she picked the cotton. There one had died in the hot summer sun at the age of two weeks. There, in that house, Mrs Moore had given birth to twenty children – sixteen of whom are still alive – and four of whom still live with her.

'He (the plantation owner) came with tears in his eyes to the house,' she recalls, 'and said he didn't want to put us out, but he had to. The Klan come to him and told him they would kill us all – me and the four children – if they found us there.' Mrs Moore left, and since then she has literally been running from house to house. 'We live in a place a few months, then they find out, then we move on.' She has moved five times in one year. Now she has found a five room house back off a country road across the railroad tracks where she has lived for a month. A white man, she says, consented to rent it to her – most likely because no one else would want it.

The house sits in a giant mud hole. The water like a cesspool is clearly visible under the house's foundation, and she worries what it will be like when winter comes and the water freezes and sends the cold up through the cracks in the floor. The roof leaks when it rains, sending rivers of water down the wall and across the floors. She has stuffed old quilts in the holes of the broken windows to try and keep out the flies. There is one tiny coal stove in one room – the only protection against the onslaught of the coming cold. 'I've got to find something better,' she mumbles over and over, but you know that she won't.

The rooms are furnished only with beds, except for two wooden chairs in a room that would ordinarily pass for a dining room, if it too did not contain two beds. There was nothing in the refrigerator but a carton of cracked eggs, which had presumably come from the two chickens scratching in the back yard. The four children – ages fourteen, thirteen, twelve and nine and unusually handsome despite their poverty – were sitting as were most of the children we saw, totally absorbed in an old television movie – perhaps their only refuge from their surroundings. What do they eat? 'Oh, sometimes they get free lunches at school,' said Mrs Moore. And at home? 'Grits and corn bread and sometimes pork belly and greens – mostly what we get on food stamps when we can get them.'

Mrs Moore has not been able to find a job since 1963. There simply are none – no industries which hire 'black folks,' no work in the fields with the closing in of automation. Even the whites who hire domestics choose the young black women and 'work them to death for $3 a day.' Mrs Moore's only income is from welfare – $55 a month from which she must pay $20 for rent and $22 for food stamps (worth $66 in merchandise) plus expenses for fuel and lights, and other miscellaneous needs. Often she does not even have the lump sum of $22 for the food stamps, so some months are almost completely barren of food. 'One time me and the kids was so bad off, Mrs — had to buy my stamps for me.' When we all had lunch together at a restaurant during our tour, Mrs Moore collected the scraps from our plates (there were none on hers) and took them home.

Mrs Moore, although she is articulate and vigorous, is typically trapped in that cycle of poverty, fed by racism, which pollutes the air of Mississippi, making even the skies on a sunny day, as we rode from dwelling to dwelling, exude a curious atmosphere of bleakness.

Past the lush fields of beans and cotton on the wealthy plantations. Past the green and red cotton pickers and other machinery which, though lying idle for the moment, are said to pick 17,000 pounds of cotton a day, compared with the average 250 pounds per day picked by the men they have replaced. Past the acres and acres of fertile land that lie vacant – turned to weeds – to keep the prices of cotton and other crops jacked up for the wealthy farmers – while people are starving within a stone's throw for lack of a plot of ground to plant some greens and corn. 'Look at all that land,' said our guide sadly. 'If we could only have an acre – half an acre.' But the plantation owners won't rent it because they receive more money from the government for keeping it barren.

On an adjoining plantation we made another visit, one of the day's most pathetic. Mrs Moore was living in relative comfort compared with Mary Lou Carsten, her nine children, and three grandchildren born of her daughter, not yet sixteen. When we entered the house, the woman, thirty years old but looking easily fifty, was sitting crosslegged on a bed with a faded red chenille bedspread draped over her legs. Although she must have been five feet nine inches tall, her flesh was so shrunken that she couldn't have weighed much more than 100 pounds. Her head, grotesque and large on her emaciated body, hung so heavily that she seemed barely able to hold it upright to say hello. Her voice was barely audible. Life had been drained out of her at thirty. We were told she had been sick, that doctors had been unable to determine the cause – and it seemed obvious that she was dying.

The stench in the house with only three rooms for thirteen people was sickening, especially in the room where the children sat clustered watching the inevitable TV. One little boy, in the fourth grade, sat isolated in a dimly lit corner of one room trying to do his lessons. The legs of the toddlers were bone-thin and bent, presumably from malnutrition. A baby, half-covered by a soiled sheet, was a mass of crawling flies.

This woman obviously could not work, nor were her children we saw old enough to do so even if there was work to be had. How did she live? She had no husband. Are you on welfare? 'No', she said. They wouldn't let her have it because she had had babies by different men. She thought that she was going to get a welfare check of $58 a month starting soon. The family's only income was what her 18-year-old son brought home from working on the plantation – about $15 a week after expenses such as rent, light, medical bills, were deducted.

When we tried to make conversation with the little children, who squatted on the floor and toddled around the porch, they just looked at us with dulled eyes. As we left the woman on the bed raised her over-sized head and managed a half-pleading smile at the neighbor who had taken us there. 'Seems I just can't get enough to eat these days,' she murmured.

Part Two
Measurement, Incidence, and Characteristics of Poverty

Few would deny that the vast majority of the world's population is seriously deprived of the basic necessities for life. Beyond this elementary level of agreement, however, there are controversies over precise estimates of poverty, the feasibility of international comparisons, and the most important indicators of poverty. In large measure, the problems of appraising the extent of poverty and the difficulty of cross-national analysis stem from varying definitions of poverty and lack of consensus on what are relevant data and their use.

Samuel Mencher discusses several of the sources of disagreement in measuring poverty. As he puts it, 'The problems of measuring poverty centers around two basic issues: the establishment of a sound theoretical or conceptual framework and the employment of valid and reliable techniques for the collection and organization of the relevant data.' While Mencher's essay deals mainly with the United States and Britain, his observations, particularly those on the rationale for and consequences of using either 'absolute' or 'relative' standards of identifying the poor, have implications for the study of poverty anywhere.

The selection by Gerald Meier gives an overview, chiefly through statistical descriptions, of the incidence of world poverty. Primarily, he compares developed and lesser developed nations (rich and poor lands), although he also cites a number of differences among the lesser-developed countries (LDCs) themselves. The difficulties encountered in securing data for the LDCs are noted. Meier's data show that the already enormous gap between rich and poor countries is widening. In arriving at his description he has used a number of indicators of poverty: gross national product and per capita income, as well as several non-monetary indicators such as health and life expectancy. The inadequacy of any of the indicators to give a precise estimate of world poverty and why this is the case are discussed. Nonetheless, Meier points out that the overall evidence is sufficient to show a markedly lower standard of living in underdeveloped areas.

Chandler's international comparison analyses poverty in a group of Western European nations and in the United States. While Chandler confines his appraisal to a small set of Western industrialized countries which have much in common with respect to economic and political organization, he too refers to problems in obtaining data permitting adequate comparisons. Nevertheless, his presentation suggests that one is able to turn to elaborate analyses of poverty in modern industrial societies where fuller records are available. Such refined analyses are also more appropriate to nations in which poverty is not a general condition afflicting most of the population.

Poverty Amid Plenty (USA); Poverty in Canada; and the chapter from The Poor and the Poorest (Britain) all contain observations on the problems of establishing an appropriate poverty line in Western, industrialized societies. In addition, they point to the high incidence of poverty in particular categories of the population. Among these are the unemployed and underemployed, the aged, the poorly educated, and in the cases of the United States and Canada, minority groups and residents of particular regions.

It is not surprising that discussions of the incidence of world or national poverty tend to overlap with explanations of the *roots* of poverty in particular nations or groups within nations and discussions of how poverty might best be remedied. Presumably, the estimates are made to assist in answering these questions. This tendency appears in all the articles on incidence which appear in this section, and is particularly evident in the last three.

While much is often made of the differences in the nature and extent of poverty in the developed and underdeveloped countries, most of the causes and solutions proposed in the articles on the United States and Canada are closely related to those presented in Part Three of this book where economic growth and income redistribution are discussed as major remedies for poverty in the non-industrial nations. Area development plans and job training, for instance, are seen as programmes both for improving the lot of the poor directly by increasing their ability to earn a living and indirectly, by promoting general *economic growth* to finance government service and assistance to those who are unable to work. Community organization may be seen as an effort ultimately to enable the poor to achieve sufficient power to effectively demand *redistribution* of wealth and income. Extension of benefits to persons not covered at the present by Social Security as proposed in the article on Britain would also fall into this category.

7 Samuel Mencher

The Problem of Measuring Poverty

Samuel Mencher, 'The problem of measuring poverty', *British Journal of Sociology*, vol. 18, 1967, no. 1, pp. 1–12.

The presence of poverty in what Galbraith termed 'the affluent society' has stimulated more than sentimental concern. For although poverty has always been a source of humanitarian and, at times, revolutionary fervour, its importance has never been as strategic as at present when it is commonly recognized that life is on the whole better for most people. The existence of poverty is considered, on the one hand, inexcusable in the light of the economic potential of the nation, and, on the other, critical in view of the effects of poverty on the continued social and economic welfare of society as a whole. Concentration on the problem of poverty has resulted in greatly increased efforts to appraise scientifically the extent and nature of poverty in the United States as well as in other countries.

Scholarly attention to measuring poverty has had a long, if sketchy, history. Both Arthur Young and Sir Frederick Eden in eighteenth-century England preceded the classical surveys of Charles Booth and Seebohm Rowntree at the end of the nineteenth century, and in the 1930s Rowntree made a second comparative survey of York. However, despite these sound beginnings and numbers of more recent statistical analyses of income distribution generally, relatively limited progress has been made in the development of reliable knowledge. The partisan nature of the subject – one need only recall Malthus, Marx, Henry George, and more recently Galbraith – has not promoted scientific objectivity, but technical progress has been slow for a variety of reasons. The comments on income studies of Dorothy S. Brady, a leading scholar in the field, although made over a decade ago, are still pertinent:

We know little more than that the data are deficient in both quantity and quality, that income is very unequally distributed, and that a high standard of living cannot be attained on average income. This much we knew thirty and more years ago. If the situation in 1950 differs at all from the situation in 1920 it is only in the extent to which the problems of data collection have been brought to light through the experience of a few projects of estimation and analysis. (National Bureau of Economic Research, 1951.)

Dr Brady attributed the slow progress in income studies to the 'gulf between theory and data collection', and the absence of any specialists devoted to the field. 'The centrifugal tendencies away from any unifying core of concepts, methods and principles', she stated, 'are intensified by the numerous and diverse uses of the data, ranging from the propaganda of pressure groups to incorporation in the logical system of a theorist.' (National Bureau of Economic Research, 1951, pp. 4–5.) During the last several years, there has been marked progress, but the fundamental issues, raised by Dr Brady, still plague the study of income and its distribution.

The problem of measuring poverty, or any other level of living, centres around two basic issues: the establishment of a sound theoretical or conceptual framework and the employment of valid and reliable techniques for the collection and organization of the relevant data. The techniques for collection of data on incomes are emphasized here to draw attention to this fundamental problem of all research frequently forgotten when the arrangement of long, neat, and complex tables gives a spurious authenticity to data having little validity or reliability. (For technical aspects see National Bureau of Economic Research, 1951, pp. 2–60; Titmuss, 1962; Miller, 1955.) The use of surveys by government bodies and private researchers has been popular in the United States, and these have, in addition to the general problems of survey research, the unique problems of collecting data on income. For example, noting that wives were the principal respondents in his survey, Rowntree commented on the limitations of the wife's knowledge of her husband's income in English working-class families. He concluded that even if they knew, it was doubtful whether they would have provided reliable information (Rowntree, 1941, p. 25).

Richard M. Titmuss's recent analysis of income tax data in England has indicated the hazards of reliance on income tax reporting as a source for income studies (Titmuss, 1962).

Conceptual problems

Apart from data collection, however, there are fundamental conceptual problems which have affected the value and comparability of studies of poverty. Before discussing several of the most important of these, the trite observation should be made that differences in the definition of concepts in studies of income are not abstract issues, but can only be resolved in view of their practical consequences in clarifying the problem of poverty. Thus, income for purposes of income tax policy differs significantly from a definition of income necessary for an analysis of income distribution. The favourable treatment usually given income related to capital investment, for whatever national goals, results in the absence of the reporting of the proper proportion of such income as compared to other sources of income. For studies of income, however, no source of income may be disregarded. All changes in the income unit's economic potential over the period of time under consideration represent income (Titmuss, 1962, pp. 31–5).

The social units from individuals to household, used as the standard for allocating income are important determinants of the nature of income distribution. The typical taxpayer exercises singular wisdom in deciding how he should define himself and his family for maximizing his allowances or minimizing his income. The student of income, on the other hand, has no clear path in defining income units which give a realistic reflection of the comparative positions of persons in relation to their control of society's resources. In their study of income in the United States, Morgan and his colleagues found that the larger the size of the income unit the smaller the estimate of inequality of distribution of incomes. This results from the reduction of the number of small income units with their amalgamation into larger units. The authors stated:

Adult units tend to live with related adult units when the income of one or both units is low. Combining their incomes thus tends to hide the fact that such low incomes exist, as well as to reduce the difficulty they cause (Morgan, *et al.*, 1962, pp. 314–5).

Most income studies assess income during the current year or the year studied. However, as in other social research, there is no necessary validity to the assumption that the year studied is representative of the economic condition of the unit. Any one year may be atypical of the whole. By way of obtaining a longitudinal dimension without sampling over long periods, current income has sometimes been supplemented by other assets giving some indication of long-term conditions. Morgan, for example, in addition to currently inadequate income, required liquid assets of less than $5000 for those families in the poverty class. Less than five per cent of this group had liquid assets of $5000 or more (Morgan *et al*, 1962, p. 190). David compared the general effects of using current income and current income plus liquid assets, and suggested that current income underestimates the condition of the unit when it is suffering temporary loss, but gross income exaggerates the situation where liquid assets are not actually available for current needs (David, 1959). In England, Dorothy Wedderburn on the basis of a 1954 survey of liquid assets suggested that there was a high correlation between assets and current income, particularly with regard to the low income populations under study (Wedderburn, 1962). Lampman concluded that poverty is a chronic condition, that there are unlikely to be major fluctuations over time, and thus, little advantage in supplementing current status with items providing longer indicators of income. Lampman supported his position by pointing out that roughly the same proportion of low-income families would have been found in the population by using current income of $2000 for families of city workers as by introducing the indicators of longer status suggested by Eleanor Snyder (1958). She had estimated that approximately 19 per cent were of low income based on such criteria as the ratio of home and food purchases to current income and the ownership of a car and home (Snyder, 1958). However, as will be emphasized below, the use of a flat percentage of the population only holds as far as the concern is for total size or proportion, but does not satisfy the need for a description of the specific characteristics of the population under study. Although the size of the total population may be the same, this is no proof that the constituent elements are the same.

When the purpose, or one of the purposes, of income analysis is comparison over time or among areas, further difficulties arise. Are differences in the value of money and changing standards of living or variations in standards among areas at the same time, taken into account? In addition, are such factors as definition of income and recipient unit, held constant over time or between areas? Changing sources or entirely new or different courses of income may invalidate what would appear to be consistency of definition. Even Rowntree concluded his 1936 follow-up survey of York by stating that only limited comparisons could be made with his earlier study (Rowntree, 1941, pp. 460–61).

Among the most authoritative sources of income data in the United States, there are differences about one or more of the characteristics considered. The Current Population Survey of incomes by the Bureau of Census differs from the Office of Business Economics in definition of income, population covered and sources of data. The Office of Business Economics has a higher total national income because of its inclusion of non-money income as well as money income not taken into account in the Current Population Survey. The population surveys of the latter have a lower proportion of income reported than the Office of Business Economics which uses data from business and government. The Survey of Consumer Finances of the Survey Research Center of the University of Michigan, on the other hand, employs its own concept of income units and makes a more exacting survey of types of income than the Current Population Survey. (For a discussion of differences among sources of income data, see US Bureau of Census, 1963; Conference on Economic Progress, 1962.)

The difficulties presented by these conceptual problems are by no means easy to resolve, but they are relatively simple when compared to the selection of cutting points to differentiate levels of living. What income ranges should be identified with poverty, minimal subsistence, destitution, deprivation, and the whole host of terms which have been proliferated to satisfy the nuances or sensitivities of politicians and students of social and economic stratification? In general, two approaches have been used for establishing cutting points, the absolute and the relative. The absolutists seek some definite point on the income scale for distinguishing among income levels; the relativists prefer some percentile or proportion of the total range to differentiate standards of living.

Determination of poverty by absolute standards

A great variety of studies on poverty have selected one standard or another for estimating the numbers or proportion of the population suffering from economic insufficiency. Recently, as Mollie Orshansky has pointed out, there has been a fair amount of consensus on the poverty standard of approximately $3000 for a family of four and $1500 for a single individual (Orshansky, 1965, p. 11). At times, the size of the family is not indicated, and it is assumed that an average family figure may be used since the small and large families will balance out (Conference on Economic Progress, 1962, p. 14). This averaging approach, as Orshansky has shown, is not as useful as the application of specific cutting points for families of different composition. While, as noted above, the overall effect may not be too dissimilar, there are serious differences in distinguishing the kinds of families falling into the poverty class. Thus, for example, an income standard varying according to family size used by the Social Security Administration differs from an average for all families by only 4 per cent in the total number of families in the poverty class, but as much as 18 per cent with respect to families having more than four children under eighteen years (Orshansky, 1965, p. 12).

The use of a single income measure on the assumption that it will represent adequately the averaging out of family units has, of course, the advantage of avoiding estimation of comparable budgets for families of different types and sizes. However, some research has been done in developing scales so that a range of family units may be extrapolated by means of multiples of a basic budget. Should this approach prove empirically sound, it will simplify the problem of budget estimation generally (Monthly Labor Review, 1960).

The crucial issue, however, is the validity of the standard employed. There is a tendency for studies of poverty to use more than one level or cutting point of poverty. The Department of

Agriculture whose figures are the basis of the Social Security Administration budgets has a low-cost and economy food plan. The Conference on Economic Progress uses the levels of deprivation and poverty. Rowntree estimated the proportions living 'below the minimum' and 'in primary poverty'. Rowntree also classified some of his population as living in 'secondary poverty' – 'families whose total earnings would be sufficient for the maintenance of merely physical efficiency (primary level) were it not that some portion of it is absorbed by other expenditure, either useful or wasteful' (Rowntree, 1941, p. 460).

In some cases, the relation between the two standards is obtained by fixing the lower standard at some arbitrary proportion of the higher. Even where a single standard is employed, this may be derived by taking a proportion of some other standard. Thus generally whether explicit or implicit, there are two measures of destitution, and by using the lower the analyst escapes the criticism of being overly liberal. In effect, he is saying, 'If I really wanted to use the proper standard we would have x times the numbers reported, but the number is so great anyway that for practical purposes we can concentrate on the population at the lower level.'

This, however, is a political argument, and may only further confuse the development of objective standards. The legitimacy of the operation depends on the extent to which the generosity of the higher standard permits the interpolation of any other level of living beneath it. The Social Security Administration, for example, in preferring the Department of Agriculture's economy food plan to the low-cost plan set its standard on a budget designed for 'temporary' and 'emergency' uses. In view of the marginal adequacy of the low-cost plan, it was not surprising, as Orshansky reported, that families spending less than the low-cost plan rarely met minimum nutrition standards (Orshansky, 1965, pp. 10–11).

Where two levels or standards are involved, a second difficulty is the ratio established between them. In some cases the lower standard may be developed independently, merely including only the most 'essential' elements of the higher. On the other hand, the lower level may be set by merely taking some percentage of the higher. The Conference on Economic Progress established its poverty line at two-thirds of the 'modest but adequate' level of the Bureau of Labor Statistics budget for city workers' families (Conference on Economic Progress, 1962, p. 14). Morgan and his associates selected the New York Community Council budget as their standard, and then made nine-tenths of this standard, their major cutting-point for poverty (Morgan *et al.*, 1962, p. 188). Thus despite the fact that the New York Community Council budget was chosen because it had proved to be consistently lower than the BLS estimates, the relative proportions of these budgets used resulted in the Morgan study having a higher standard for poverty than the Conference on Economic Progress. It is also possible, as the British have done, to start from a lower standard and increase this to some measure of minimal adequacy. Assistance standards lend themselves to this type of approach. Thus, one study estimates the proportion below National Assistance rates and the proportions less than twenty and forty per cent above these rates (Townsend, 1962).

The logic of the proportion of minimal adequacy used for determining the poverty line is never clearly explained. There appears to be no consideration of the fact that a proportion of an original standard may have no realistic relationship to the original standard. When the budget is cut by a tenth or a third, it cannot be assumed that persons or families are achieving a level of living nine-tenths or two-thirds as adequate as the original, and available evidence would indicate otherwise (Orshansky, 1965, p. 10–11).

The selection of any specific point along the income scale to set off the population suffering from poverty is a hazardous task, and is the more misleading as we become less conscious of the many assumptions underlying the development of the standards. In few instances are the standards empirically validated by field studies of the way low income persons are living. There is a great difference between validating the multiplying by three of the standard food budget through studying the percentages of the total budget spent on food in families of similar income and validating by a study of the actual conditions under which such families live. As Peter Townsend, a most sophisticated British poverty researcher has remarked:

To establish a minimum income standard is meaningless unless we also show that there are some families with that income who do in fact secure a defined level of nutrition. This fundamental criticism could be made of nearly all studies of poverty (Townsend, 1962, p. 220).

The earlier English studies were attempts to describe fully the conditions of the poor, and Rowntree's use of the concept of secondary poverty enriched the notion of poverty by indicating that living in a state of poverty was not entirely a matter of income. Michael Young has again raised the question by suggesting the need to examine the variety of ways by which families administer their income. He has noted, for example, the differing proportions of income earned by husbands which are contributed to family needs even if broadly interpreted (Young, 1952). While income is, no doubt, the best single indicator of poverty, it would be of interest to conduct some studies appraising levels of living using a selected number of other criteria as the independent variables.

Determination of poverty by relative standards

Absolute standards for poverty emphasize economic insufficiency as the frame of reference for poverty. Relative standards, however, stress economic inequality as the primary indicator of poverty. The argument for relative standards rests on the assumption that for practical purposes standards become so fluid that no definition of need, no matter how broad, satisfies the ever-changing expectations of modern life. Thus, poverty, particularly in advanced industrial democratic nations where the basic physical wants have been met, is a matter of deviation from social and economic norms. As Rubinow pointed out in his excellent discussion 'Poverty' (1934), comparative poverty in modern societies 'has led more often to social change than has absolute poverty'.

Luxuries become comforts, comforts become necessaries; and repeated emphasis of the fact that in comparison with civilizations of the past or more backward contemporary cultures the poor in the United States now enjoy what would have constituted unusual luxuries in a thousand or even a hundred years ago may lead to an entirely barren conception of the problem of poverty as an aspect of distribution of wealth. Thus an increase in perceived poverty is a phenomenon particularly characteristic of American life during periods of so-called prosperity.

However, even in underdeveloped countries the term 'needy'

has been used 'to cover persons who through temporary or permanent circumstances peculiar to them have not available, in one form or another, the means of subsistence up to the level prevailing among the majority of people living in the same town or community' (U N Department of Economic and Social Affairs, 1956, p. 12).

The comparative nature of poverty has received support from Herman Miller who has suggested that poor families be defined as 'families at the bottom fifth of the income distribution'. This, he favours, in preference to any absolute income level. Miller does not explain his choice of the lowest one-fifth over the lowest third or any other fraction, and he himself refers to the fact that in earlier eras one-third had accurately estimated the numbers in poverty and that even today a third of city dwellers have inadequate incomes (Miller, 1963).

Miller's approach provides a quick cutting-point emphasizing the significance of relative differences in defining poverty. 'As incomes go up,' writes Miller, '"needs" also go up – evidently in such a way as to leave a large proportion of the population at substandard levels.' He points out that the lowest one-fifth in 1951 had incomes below $2000 as compared to $2900 in 1960. The 1960 income is not the 1951 income adjusted for rising prices; if so, the difference would be almost halved (Miller, 1963).

Emphasis on relative standards obviously conflicts with Galbraith's recent thesis that emulation and consciousness of difference are inconsequential in a society where the general level of material standards is high, as in America today. This appears, however, to be more of a value judgment than a statement of fact. In 1959, the lowest fifth among family incomes received five per cent of all incomes as compared to 44 per cent received by the highest fifth (Miller, 1964, p. 7). In view of these differences and the concentration of the lowest fifth in particular groups in the population, it is difficult to rule out the significance of comparative standards as a measure of poverty.

Morgan and his colleagues employed a 'welfare ratio' which combines some of the advantages of both the absolute and relative approaches. The welfare ratio permits a classification of income based on the ratio of gross disposable income to estimated budget requirements, and provides a distribution of levels of welfare (Morgan, *et al.*, 1962, pp. 189–90; see also David, 1959). Comparative standards have been especially significant in trends in income distribution and of studies of income redistribution. Such studies indicate the extent to which the gap among income groups is being narrowed or the direction and rate of change in income distribution. Trend studies suffer from all the technical difficulties of other income research, and have in addition the problems of comparison over time when the essential variables may have been defined and measured differently. In the opinion of Professor Titmuss (1962), these factors have invalidated many of the British attempts to plot the direction of income distribution.

The United Nations' approach to defining levels of living has combined both relative standards and a variety of measures. By standardizing rates for health, education, clothing, housing, etc., it is possible to make inter- and intra-national comparisons of poverty as, for example, the infant mortality rates serve in the field of public health (United Nations, 1954).

The proof of the declining inequality or the lessening of comparative poverty relies on the demonstration of relatively greater additions to lower incomes at the expense of upper incomes. Possibly the best known of American studies was that of Kuznets who analysed the share of the upper income groups between 1919 and 1948 and concluded that there was a considerable reduction in the shares of the upper one and five per cent of the income range, particularly between 1939 and 1948 (Kuznets, 1953). There has been some questioning of Kuznets's research on technical grounds (Kolko, 1962; Morgan, 1954), but even accepting his data, no assumptions can be made about the way that the share lost by the upper income classes was distributed among the 95 per cent of the population below them.

Other students of distribution have examined both ends of the income scale. Goldsmith analysed changes in personal and family income between 1935 and 1950, and found a shift from upper to lower income groups. Most of this occurred, however, between 1941 and 1944 when the share of the lower two quintiles increased from 13·6 to 15·8 per cent while that of the upper two quintiles decreased from 71·1 to 68 per cent. Over the full fifteen years, however, the total change resulted in only an additional 0·3 per cent for the lowest quintiles (Goldsmith, 1954). Miller also found that major changes in distribution occurred during the war period of 1939 to 1945, and he interpreted this as a special rather than general trend (Miller, 1955, pp. 104–5). Lampman, like Titmuss in England, has been sceptical of all trend analysis. He has suggested that the seeming lessened inequality may merely reflect changing types of wealth and definition of income units rather than real differences (Lampman, 1959a).

Most income distribution analyses stop at the point where redistribution studies begin. The question for the student of income redistribution is what happens to the original distribution of income as a result of taxation and the differential use of public services. Does the governmental system of social services or other benefits result in a net gain to lower income groups and thus effectively increase their income at the expense of the more wealthy and reduce the gap between high and low initial incomes?

Thus far there has been a limited number of ambitious attempts at drawing up a debit and credit ledger for the social services. These, on the whole, suffer from the limitations of income data generally and the theoretical assumptions often made about the relative consumption of social benefits. However, it is clear at this point that the social services cannot be looked upon categorically as acting in the direction of equalizing income. Welfare transfers may benefit all equally, may operate within rather than across income groups, may transfer individual income over different risk periods for the same individual, or may favour the wealthy over the poor under certain circumstances. Thus, for example, while Lampman has been impressed by the radical effect of transfer payments on the incomes of the lower classes, Morgan and his associates have emphasized the extent to which these payments represent transfers over time from earning to retirement years rather than between different income levels (Lampman, 1959b, p. 30; Morgan *et al.* 1962, p. 217). There are sceptics who have seen the chief beneficiaries of poverty programmes as not the poor, but the members of the professions that serve the poor (Arnold, 1964).

A modern definition of poverty

Even before the Social Security Act, Rubinow commented, 'If the form of relief is at all adequate or if, as in the great majority of institutions for child care, the standards of health and comfort are decidedly above those prevailing in the community at large, it is doubtful whether the recipients should be included in the poverty class despite their dependency (Rubinow, 1934, p. 285). Rowntree, in his 1936 study of York, found that the social services contributed on the average in real money over eighteen times as much to working-class families as in 1901 (Rowntree, 1941, p. 214).

Consideration of the effect of public services on income has important implications for the measurement of poverty. Poverty has frequently been associated with economic dependence. The valid income of a person was limited to his earnings from capital and wages in the private sector. However, since the real standard of living of an individual or family comes from many sources, both public and private, it is their total which should define the extent of wealth or poverty. With the variety of measures through which society takes responsibility for maintaining the standard of living of its members, redistributed or social income will play an increasingly important and legitimate role in determining the numbers and kinds of families and individuals who will be defined as belonging to the poverty class in the future.

The concept of poverty must be kept independent of the variety of social and economic problems with which it may be associated. Poverty is but one of the problems of our society, albeit most serious. But there are also, to name but a few, poor education, bad health, and delinquency. These exist related to, but also independent of, poverty. To make poverty synonymous with all forms of social and psychological malaise will neither help in understanding the problem of poverty nor solving the other ills of our age.

Finally, the concept of poverty may be weaned from its dependence on standards of minimal subsistence for the lowest classes, whether relative or absolute, generous or niggardly. For this, there may be substituted a measure of the lowest level which society can tolerate in view of its national objectives. Thus where a minimal income may be argued to be sufficient for its immediate recipients, it may be highly inadequate as it affects the economic and social welfare of the nation as a whole.

References

ARNOLD, R. (1964), 'Mobilization for youth: patchwork or solution?', *Dissent*, vol. 2, no. 3, pp. 347–54.

Conference on Economic Progress (1962), *Poverty and Deprivation in the United States*, Washington, pp. 94–6.

DAVID, M. (1959), 'Welfare, income and budget needs, *Rev. Econ. Stat.*, vol. 41, no. 4, pp. 393–9.

GOLDSMITH, S., *et al* (1954), 'Size distribution of income since the middle thirties', *Rev. Econ. Stat.*, vol. 36, no. 1, pp. 1–32.

KOLKO, G. (1953), *Wealth and Power in America*, Praeger.

KUZNETS, S. (1953), *Shares of Upper Income Groups in Income and Savings*, National Bureau of Economics Research, New York.

LAMPMAN, R. J. (1959a), 'Changes in the share of wealth held by top wealth holders, 1922–56', *Rev. Econ. Stat.*, vol. 41, no. 4, pp. 379–92.

LAMPMAN, R. J. (1959b), 'The low income population and economic growth', US Congress Joint Economic Committee, study paper no. 12, Washington.

MILLER, H. P. (1955), *Income of the American People*, Wiley.

MILLER, H. P. (1963), 'New definition of our "poor"', *New York Times Magazine*, 21 April, p. 11.

MILLER, H. P. (1964), *Rich Man, Poor Man*, Crowell.

MONTHLY LABOR REVIEW (1960), 'Estimating equivalent incomes or budget cuts by family type', *Monthly Lab. Rev.*, vol. 83, no. 11, pp. 1197–1200.

MORGAN, J. (1954), 'Review: Shares of upper income groups in income and savings by Simon Kuznets', *Rev. Econ. Stat.*, vol. 36, no. 2, pp. 237–9.

MORGAN, J. N. *et al* (1962), *Income and Welfare in the United States*, McGraw-Hill.

NATIONAL BUREAU OF ECONOMIC RESEARCH (1951), 'Research on the size distribution of income and wealth', in *Studies in Income and Wealth*, vol. 13, pp. 3–4, New York.

ORSHANSKY, M. (1965), 'Counting the poor: another look at the poverty profile', *Soc. Sec. Bull.*, vol. 28, no. 1, pp. 1–13.

ROWNTREE, B. S. (1941), *Poverty and Progress*, Longman.

RUBINOW, I. M. (1934), 'Poverty' in *Encyclopedia of the Social Sciences*, Macmillan.

SAND, M. (1959), 'Welfare income and budget needs', *Rev. Econ. Stat.*, vol. 41, no. 4, pp. 393–9.

SELIGMAN, E. R. A. (ed) (1934), 'Poverty', in *Encyclopedia of the Social Sciences*, vol. 12, pp. 285, Macmillan.

SNYDER, D. (1958), 'A method of identifying chronic low income groups from cross-section survey data', in G. GARVEY (ed.), *An Appraisal of the 1950 Census Income Data*, Princeton University Press.

TITMUSS, R. M. (1962), *Income Distribution and Social Change*, Allen & Unwin.

TOWNSEND, P. (1962), 'The meaning of poverty', *Brit. J. Soc.*, vol. 13, pp. 210–27.

UNITED NATIONS DEPARTMENT OF ECONOMIC AND SOCIAL AFFAIRS (1956), *Assistance to the Needy in Less Developed Areas*, p. 12, New York.

UNITED NATIONS (1954), *Report on International Definitions and Measurement of Standards and Levels of Living*.

UNITED STATES BUREAU OF CENSUS (1963), *Current Population Reports on Consumer Income*, no. 41, p. 60. Washington.

WEDDERBURN, D. C. (1962), 'Poverty in Britain today, the evidence', *Soc. Rev.*, vol. 10, pp. 257–82.

YOUNG, M. (1952), 'Distribution of income within the family', *Brit. J. Sociol.* vol. 3, pp. 305–21.

8 Gerald M. Meier

Recent Indicators of International Poverty

From *Leading Issues in Economic Development: Studies in International Poverty* Second Edition, by Gerald M. Meier © 1970 by Oxford University Press, Inc., pp. 20–28. Reprinted by permission.

Historical trends have culminated in the extreme degree of inequality that now characterizes international living standards. Not only is the distribution of world income highly unequal; there are also inequalities in other relevant indicators of development such as technology, consumption of energy, education, and health.

Table 1 presents comparative data for developed and less developed areas in several important series. Especially significant are the contrasts in the series of population, gross national product, education, health, and such 'real' indices as passenger motor vehicles, energy consumption per capita, and cement production per capita. This table clearly emphasizes the gap in living standards between the developed and less developed countries (LDC).

It should, however, be noted that there are considerable differences among the LDCs. Latin America is not as poor as Africa or Asia. There are also marked disparities within each region: some countries in Latin America, for example, are poorer than the richer countries in Africa or Asia (see Table 2, below). It remains striking, however, that per capita income would have to grow at a rate of more than 3 per cent a year in most of the African and Asian countries even to reach by the end of this century the average income levels already attained in Latin America. Since the populations of Africa and Asia are likely to continue increasing on average by more than 2 per cent annually, the domestic product would have to grow at an average rate of more than 5 per cent a year over the rest of this century even to reach current Latin American levels.

For a more detailed summary of GNP per capita in a large number of countries as of 1960 and 1967, one should give attention

Table 1a Comparisons Between Developed and Less Developed Countries

Item	Unit	Developed countries		Total	Less developed non-Communist countries				
		Total	United States		Latin America	East and South-East Asia	South Asia	Near East	Africa
Population:									
Total (mid-1966)	millions	636	197	1605	241	284	658	131	253
Annual growth (1960–66)	per cent	1·2	1·5	2·5	2·8	2·7	2·5	2·5	2·3
Persons per square mile	number	50	54	60	30	180	350	50	20
Gross national product:									
Total GNP (1966)	$ billions	1450	748	296	98	40	54	42	33
GNP per capita (1966)	dollars	2280	3797	184	407	140	82	318	131
Education:									
Literacy	per cent	96	98	38	66	55	27	36	17
Daily newspapers circulation (1964–65)	per 1000 population	310	310	27	68	27	14	25	8
Students enrolled at tertiary level (1966)	per cent of all students	6·2	8·9	1·9	2·0	2·0	2·2	2·1	0·8

Table 1b

Item	Unit	Developed countries		Less developed non-Communist countries					
		Total	United States	Total	Latin America	East Asia	South Asia	Near East	Africa
Students enrolled in age group 5–19 (1966)	per cent	79	86	36	46	38	32	35	26
Health:									
Life expectancy	years	70	70	48	57	43	50	50	39
Calories per day (1965)	calories	2920	3090	2250	2560	2160	1910	2145	2350
Real indices:									
Passenger motor vehicles (1965)	per 100 population	21	38	0·5	1·6	0·3	0·1	0·6	0·5
Energy consumption per capita (1965)	kilogrammes of coal equivalent	5050	9200	275	720	185	145	460	95
Cement production per capital (1966)	kilogrammes	390	340	50	100	35	20	125	20

Notes

1. Developed countries – United States, Canada, Japan, S. Africa, Australia, New Zealand, EEC, EFTA, Iceland, Ireland, Finland.

2. Underdeveloped countries – Latin America: 20 republics (excluding Cuba) plus Jamaica and Caribbean islands; South East Asia: Afghanistan, Ceylon, India, Nepal, Pakistan, East Asia: Countries of S. E. Asia plus China (Taiwan), Hong Kong, South Korea; Near East; Cyprus, Greece, Iran, Iraq, Israel, Jordan, Kuwait, Lebanon, Saudi Arabia, Syria, Turkey, UAR, Yemen; Africa: Does not include South Africa nor UAR. The 'total' column for the less developed non-Communist areas is the sum of these five regions plus Spain, Oceania and Puerto Rico.

3. Sources: Population series: UN Demographic Yearbook 1967; GNP series: AID (1968); Education series: UNESCO (1966); Real indices: UN 1965 or 1966.

Table 2 Per Capita Gross National Product (US Dollar Equivalent; Constant 1966 Prices)

Country	GNP per capita 1960	GNP per capita 1967	Country	GNP per capita 1960	GNP per capita 1967
United States	$3071	$3847	China, Republic of	159	249
Sweden	2182	2801	Ecuador	223	241
Canada	2151	2686	Honduras	221	227
Switzerland	2104	2519	Ghana	219	221
Denmark	1824	2340	Algeria	270	220*
Australia	1731	2094	Rhodesia	221	219
New Zealand	1737	2054	Paraguay	209	217
United Kingdom	1679	1938	Tunisia	191	205
Israel	1115	1450	Syria	170	200*
Japan	597	1109	Morocco	190	191
Venezuela	825	892	Philippines	157	175
Spain	506	793	United Arab Republic	130	168*
Greece	497	787	Bolivia	132	161
Argentina	667	718	Ceylon	140	148
Chile	471	563	Thailand	111	144
Uruguay	575	547	Korea (South)	100	139
Jamaica	435	521	Nigeria	n.a.	125*
Mexico	420	507	Kenya	95	118
Portugal	329	456	Pakistan	95	117
Costa Rica	373	420	Sudan	99	109
Nicaragua	285	352	Indonesia	90	100*
Malaysia	266	319	Uganda	83	93
Brazil	288	316	Afghanistan	n.a.	85*
Turkey	252	306	Tanzania	69	82
Peru	243	299	India	71	78
Colombia	272	295	Haiti	80	75*
Guatemala	263	293	Laos	n.a.	70*
El Salvador	238	286	Ethiopia	55	68
Iraq	200	268*	Burma	65	67*
Jordan	179	266	Malawi	40	50*
Iran	205	266			
Zambia	228	266			
Dominican Republic	$282	$264			

* 1966

Source: AID (1968)

to Table 2. Again, the wide differences between rich and poor countries are evident in this table.

There are, however, a number of statistical difficulties involved in using low per capita income as an index of poverty. Prominent among these are the problems of aggregation, especially in a dual economy; the arbitrary valuation of non-market activities; the inadequacy of converting national income statistics at official exchange rates; and the welfare qualifications associated with the changing composition of output and the distribution of income.[1]

In order to avoid these difficulties, several studies have attempted to make international comparisons of standards of living by using 'non-monetary' indicators.[2] A major effort in this direction has been made by Wilfred Beckerman who sought to discover which non-monetary indicators are highly correlated with some meaningful national accounts aggregates, and how, given estimates of the former and the nature of the statistical relationship, to 'predict' real per capita consumption from the non-monetary indicators. The main reason for experimenting with this method is the greater availability of data on non-monetary indicators than on national accounts aggregates and the apparent scope for finding fairly close correlations between certain of such indicators and independent estimates of real per capita consumption (Beckerman, 1966, p. 28). The non-monetary indicators used as 'explanatory' variables in the final computations were: steel consumption, cement production, number of letters sent, stock of radio receivers, stock of telephones, stock of road vehicles, and meat consumption – all on a per capita basis (Beckerman, 1966, p. 29; see also Duggar, 1968, pp. 109–16). The final predictions for 1960 are compared, in Table 3, below, with the results that would be obtained by using official exchange rates to convert national accounts estimates of private consumption. Some major differences between the proposed non-monetary and national accounts series can be noted. The non-monetary indicator

1. For a more thorough consideration of these difficulties, see Barber (1963); Thorn (1968, pp. 206–16), Kuznets (1959, pp. 13–28); Myrdal (1968, chaps. 11, 12, Appendix 13); Usher (1966).
2. These are summarized in Beckerman (1966) chap. 4. A ranking of countries that takes into account not only per capita income but also other indications of social and political development is provided in Adelman and Morris (1967).

Table 3 Predicted Indices of 'Real' Private Consumption
Per Head in 1960 (USA in 1960 = 100)
from Modified Non-Monetary Indicator Method

Rank	Index based on proposed method	Index at official exchange rates	Rank	Index based on proposed method	Index at official exchange rates
1 USA	100·0	100·0	31 Yugoslavia	13·5	6·1
2 Sweden	77·4	54·5	32 Mexico	13·4	16·2
3 Canada	77·0	73·9	33 Greece	12·7	16·4
4 Australia	65·4	57·2	34 Malaya	12·6	..
5 U.K.	61·7	49·9	35 Cuba	12·2	..
6 Denmark	59·2	46·6	36 Brazil	12·1	6·4
7 Switzerland	59·1	55·6	37 Colombia	11·4	10·9
8 New Zealand	58·6	56·0	38 Federation of Rhodesia	11·2	5·4
9 Norway	57·4	34·9	39 Turkey	9·8	27·2
10 Germany	56·1	41·2	40 China (Mainland)	9·4	..
11 France	54·3	47·4	41 Iraq	9·0	..
12 Belgium	53·6	48·3	42 Syria	8·6	..
13 Netherlands	45·0	31·3	43 Peru	8·1	..
14 Finland	41·3	32·5	44 Morocco	8·1	6·7
15 Austria	40·8	29·2	45 Tunisia	7·9	..
16 Italy	30·8	22·3	46 Taiwan	7·4	5·4
17 Japan	28·7	12·6	47 Iran	7·3	..
18 Israel	27·8	45·8	48 Egypt	6·4	..
19 South Africa	26·0	35·8	49 Ceylon	5·3	5·8
20 Roumania	25·2	..	50 Ghana	4·8	7·9
21 Argentina	23·8	18·5	51 Saudi Arabia	4·0	..
22 Lebanon	22·8	..	52 Thailand	3·7	4·0
23 Ireland	22·0	27·5	53 Congo (Leopoldville)	3·2	..
24 Hong Kong	19·6	..	54 India	3·1	..
25 Spain	19·5	13·6	55 Nigeria	2·6	..
26 Venezuela	18·9	31·8	56 Indonesia	2·4	..
27 Portugal	17·0	11·6	57 Pakistan	2·3	..
28 Chile	16·9	20·9			
29 Uruguay	16·2	..			
30 Algeria	13·8	..			

Source: Beckerman (1966)

Table 4 Income Levels and Rates of Growth of Total Output of Selected Developing Countries, 1960–66

| Growth rate of total output per annum, % | GDP per capita in 1965 | | | | |
	Under $100	$100 to under $200	$200 to under $300	$300 to under $500	$500 and more
7 and more	Korea (South)	Thailand	Saudi Arabia China (Taiwan) Jordan Syria	Hong Kong Yugoslavia Nicaragua	Spain Israel Panama Greece
5 to under 7	Pakistan	Philippines Nigeria Vietnam (South)	Iraq Iran El Salvador Turkey	Peru Mexico Guatemala Malaysia Costa Rica	Trinidad and Tobago Chile Venezuela
3 to under 5	Ethiopia Mozambique Uganda Tanzania India	Bolivia UAR (Egypt) Cambodia Sudan Francophone countries	Tunisia Honduras Zambia Brazil Ecuador Paraguay	Colombia Lebanon Guyana	Kuwait Jamaica
Under 3	Angola Indonesia Malawi Burma Haiti Congo (Kinshasa)	Ceylon Kenya Morocco	Ghana Dominican Republic Rhodesia Algeria		Argentina Uruguay

Note: Within each category, countries are listed according to their growth rate of total output.

method of making international income or consumption comparisons has already proved extremely useful when national accounts are not adequately developed in poor countries and when the statistical problems of international comparisons are acute. The non-monetary method deserves more attention, and refinements of Beckerman's study will undoubtedly continue to be forthcoming.

Although the foregoing tables reveal the extremes that exist among rich and poor countries in various indicators of living standards, it is a further cause of concern that the gap between rich and poor countries tends to be widening. Table 4 reveals the considerable differences in the growth records of individual countries. It is a disturbing fact that the majority of countries with Gross Domestic Product per capita of less than $300 had growth rates of total output per annum of less than 5 per cent in the period 1960–66. Table 5 also shows that the rate of growth in per capita GNP has been considerably slower in less developed

Table 5 Trend of Per Capita GNP, 1960–67
(Constant 1966 prices)

Year	Developed	Less developed
1960	100·0	100·0
1961	102·6	102·4
1962	107·0	104·4
1963	110·4	106·9
1964	115·8	110·7
1965	120·6	112·5
1966	125·7	115·1
1967	128·7	118·3

Source: AID (1968)

areas than in the developed areas during the period 1960–67 According to calculations by the UNCTAD secretariat, the average annual growth rate in per capita real product was 3·8 per cent for developed market economies during the period 1960–66, but only 1·8 per cent for less developed countries (UNCTAD, 1968). The absolute gap in per capita income has accordingly widened. Even if the LDCs were to enjoy a much higher rate of growth in per capita income than in the rich countries, the gap in absolute levels of per capita income would still tend to widen – unless the LDCs were to have an incredibly high rate of growth. In actuality, the annual growth of per capita income at the end of the 1960s was less than 2 per cent in Latin America, only about 2 per cent in East Asia, merely 1 per cent in Africa, and only about $\frac{1}{2}$ per cent in South Asia. At these rates, a doubling of per capita income in East Asia would take nearly thirty-five years, in Latin America more than forty years, in Africa almost seventy years, and in South Asia nearly a century and a half.

It is indeed a disheartening fact that between 1960 and 1967, the mere *increase* in the annual per capita income of the major developed countries exceeded the *total* average annual per capita income of LDCs.

At this point, we must also realize that a quick reversal of these trends in international development cannot be expected. Incomes in the rich countries have grown over a long period of time, and it is the power of compound interest over the long run that accounts for their presently high standards of living. The rich countries, however, now have a large base of income, so that even if poor countries were to grow at a much higher rate than the rich countries, the absolute gap in per capita income would nonetheless still widen between the rich and poor countries. (A 10 per cent rate of growth in a per capita income of $200 gives an increment of income of only $20, whereas a rate growth of only 2 per cent of a per capita income of $2000 gives an increment of $40.)

Finally, we should recognize that the problem of international inequalities is further aggravated by the fact that the internal distribution of income within a poor country also tends to be highly unequal. Only limited data are available to determine the size distribution of income in less developed countries, but a careful study has been undertaken by Professor Kuznets. His conclusions may be summarized as follows (Kuznets, 1966, pp. 423–6).

First, for the distributions among families or consuming units of personal income (before taxes and excluding income in kind provided by governments), the shares of the top ordinal groups are much higher in the LDCs than in the developed countries: the share of the top 5 per cent ranges from 30 to 40 per cent of total income for less developed, and between 20 and 25 per cent for developed, countries.

Second, the income shares of the low ordinal groups do not show significant differences between LDCs and developed countries: the share of the lowest 60 per cent of family units is about 30 per cent of total income in both groups of countries.

Third, the intermediate groups (between the lowest 60 per cent and the top 5 or 10 per cent) account for much lower shares of total income in the LDCs than in the developed countries: in the LDCs, the share of the group between the low 60 per cent and the top 10 per cent varies from 20 to 30 per cent; whereas in the developed countries, the share of the similar group ranges somewhat below 40 per cent. This is a reflection of the often-observed absence of 'middle' classes in the less developed countries.

If the foregoing observations were corrected to make allowances for direct taxes and income in kind provided by governments, the distribution of income in LDCs would appear even more unequal as compared to that in developed countries. This is, of course, because taxes are larger relative to personal income and are also more progressive in the developed countries; and the weight of services in kind provided by governments, mainly to lower income groups, is greater in developed than in less developed countries.

Thus, it can be concluded that the size distribution of income is more unequal in the less developed countries than in the developed: the income shares of the very top ordinal groups are higher, even though the shares for the low ordinal groups are not significantly lower. The wide disparity between the low incomes of the lower 90 or 95 per cent and the relatively high incomes of the top 10 or 5 per cent is a problem that is now commanding more attention. A major problem for any country undertaking a development program is to determine whether policy measures designed to correct the extremes of domestic inequality will also facilitate or impede efforts to achieve a higher rate of development. Countries are now deliberately undertaking development programs to mitigate the international inequality in the distribution of income among nations. It has also become apparent, however, that more consideration must be given to the relation between a less developed country's domestic distribution of income and its efforts to maximize its rate of development. Answers to the question of equity may or may not conflict with the objective of maximum development; but they are at least an implicit part of the development problem, and in one way or another they are being answered in reality – even though the answer is perforce more political than economic.

References

AID (1968), *Gross National Product, Growth Rates and Trend Data*, Report RC–W–138.

ADELMAN, I., and MORRIS, C. T. (1967), *Society, Politics and Economic Development: A Quantitative Approach*, Baltimore.

BARBER, W. J. (1963), 'A critique of aggregate accounting concepts in under-developed areas', *Bull. Oxford University, Inst. Econ. Stat.*, November.

BECKERMAN, W. (1966), *International Comparisons of Real Incomes*, Development Center of OECD.

OECD, (1968), *Development Assistance Review*, Paris, p. 124.

DUGGAR, J. W. (1968), 'International comparisons of income levels: an additional measure', *Econ. J.*, March, pp. 109–16.

KUZNETS, S. (1959), *Six lectures on Economic Growth*, Free Press.

KUZNETS, S. (1966), *Modern Economic Growth*, New Haven.

MYRDAL, G. (1968), *Asian Drama*, Pantheon.

THORN, R. S. (1968), 'Per capita income as a measure of economic development', *Zeitschrift für Nationalöeconomie*, vol. 28, pp. 206–16.

UN (1967), *Demographic Yearbook*.

UNCTAD (1968), *Review of Recent Trends in Trade and Development*, TD/B/184, p. 30.

USHER, D. (1966), 'Income as a measure of productivity', *Economica*, November.

9 John H. Chandler

An International Comparison

Excerpts from John H. Chandler, 'Perspectives on poverty, 5: An international comparison', *Monthly Labor Review*, vol. 92, 1969, no. 2, pp. 55–62.

Where does the United States stand, and where do Europeans stand, with regard to poverty?

In making such a comparison, two opposing attitudes or myths can affect our objectivity. One is the myth of European infallibility. Loosely, it may be claimed that Europe has coped with poverty much longer than we have, and the Europeans have more experience with the problems of living together in a compact industrial society.

The opposite myth is that of American superiority. This begins with the fact that we have greater abundance and economic power, and moves to the conclusion that, if we still have social and economic problems, those problems must be much worse in other countries.

The following sections examine a few facts about economic and social conditions on both sides of the Atlantic – conditions that relate in some way to the concept 'poverty'. Because of measurement differences that exist from country to country, many of the comparisons must be regarded as indicative rather than precise findings.

Income

The most elementary measure is to compare per capita income. In 1965, US per capita income was $2893. In Sweden, Switzerland and Canada, income averaged between $1800 and $2000, or about the same as the average for non-whites in the United States. In the major European countries, France, Germany, and the United Kingdom, the average was about $1450, in Italy $900, and in Japan $700.

Such comparisons do not tell very much, however. First, in

another country the purchasing power of a given income may be much higher than in the United States, and indeed this is the case as shown by several studies. Real per capita consumption in Japan is about twice as high as the estimate based on official exchange rates, according to a study by the Organization for Economic Cooperation and Development. Similarly, real consumption in Europe is 15 to 40 per cent higher than indicated by currency conversions at the official exchange rates (Beckerman, 1966).

Then there are the numerous differentials that can be found within countries. Data from a purchasing power map issued by the Chase Manhattan Bank illustrates differences in purchasing power among European provinces and departments:

Table 1

	Per capita income	
	High province	*Low province*
Belgium	$1231	$801
Denmark	1481	972
France	2019	532
Germany	1550	606
Italy	944	272
Netherlands	1143	731
Sweden	1848	987
United Kingdom	1887	539
United States family income, 1959:		
Tunica County, Miss		1260
Owsley County, Ky		1324
Montgomery County, Md	9317	

Similar results can be shown by industry or occupation. Generally, the differentials are narrower in Europe than in the United States, except perhaps for the earnings differential by sex.

Poverty is a relative matter, and the most significant income measure, perhaps, is the dispersion of net income among families, by decile or quintile group. A few years ago we made an attempt to analyse income dispersion and concluded tentatively that the dispersion is greater in the United States than in Germany,

Sweden, or the United Kingdom. In the United States, net annual income in 1960–61 was $2575 for those households at the top of the lowest income quintile, and $8596 for those at the bottom of the highest income quintile. The low income figure was 30 per cent of the high income figure – lower than in Germany (where the low income figure was 35 per cent of the high income), Sweden (57 per cent), or the United Kingdom (48 per cent). The lowest-income fifth in the United States received a 5·0 per cent share of total household income after taxes, compared with 6·4 per cent in Germany, and 8·3 per cent in the United Kingdom. Thus in terms of either comparative dispersion or aggregate income, there was apparently a greater inequality in income distribution in the United States than in the other countries.

Several others have attempted to analyse income dispersion, also with inconclusive results. Irving Kravitz found that in the early 1950s Denmark, the Netherlands and Israel had less income inequality than the United States. Great Britain, Canada and Japan had about the same degree of inequality, and Italy had greater inequality (Kravitz, 1960).

There is also disagreement about the redistribution effects of government programs. On the one hand, it can be demonstrated that the combination of a progressive tax system and a regressive benefit system results in greater equality of net income. On the other, if we examine all types of subsidies provided by government, not just the social programs, the results can turn out differently. The question of income distribution and redistribution obviously needs more study. This has been acknowledged by the United Nations as well as by US statisticians.

Another approach is to measure the per cent of GNP spent on social programs in different countries. An International Labor Organization study in 1960 showed that the United States spent 6·3 per cent of GNP on social security, while leading European countries spent from 11 to 16 per cent (International Labor Office, 1964).

Consumer expenditures

One may recall Engel's Law to the effect that, as income increases, the proportion of income spent on necessities diminishes. Engel's coefficients can be worked out for food alone, or for other groupings of basic expenditures such as food, shelter and clothing. Our consumer expenditure survey shows that, on the average, American households spent 53 per cent of income in 1960–61 on the three basics, slightly less than the percentages reported for other countries.

The US superiority according to Engel's coefficient is, although perceptible, very small. When we examine the three basics separately, we find that US and Canadian consumers spend much less of their income on food and more on shelter than do consumers in Europe.

Low income households

In analysing the lowest income quintiles of four Western European countries compared with the United States, it is found that in 1960–61, the lowest income groups in the United States spent an average of 53 per cent of after-tax income on food and shelter alone, compared with an average for all United States households of 45 per cent. As expected under Engel's Law, the poorest households in all these countries spent a larger proportion of total income on these two 'basic necessities' than the average household. However, the proportion spent was smaller among poor households in the United States than in any of the other countries, with Sweden a close second. The significance of these relationships is that, as a rough generalization under Engel's Law, the lower the proportion of income spent for food and housing, the less 'poor' are the families concerned. From this standpoint, therefore, the poorest group in the United States was not as poor as the comparable group in France, Germany, or the United Kingdom.

Expenditures on shelter, as a proportion of all expenditures, were generally higher at each income level in the United States than in the four European countries, where housing programs for the poor are more extensive. Food expenditures, on the other hand, took up a smaller part of household income in the United States than in Europe.

The proportion of expenditures on prime necessities may be influenced strongly by differences in the average size of households among the five countries, as well as by subsidies or other national programs that do not show up as household income or expenditure.

By way of illustration, the average size of household in the United States was larger than in Sweden or the United Kingdom and smaller than in France. Therefore, the household demands for food and shelter would be greater in France and the United States than in Sweden and the United Kingdom.

Another consideration is that the characteristics of households were quite different from one income quintile to another. The lowest income quintile in each country had the lowest average number of household members (2·14 persons in the United States, 2·40 in France, 1·71 in Sweden, and 1·64 in the United Kingdom). For three countries with income data by composition of household, the lowest income quintile shows a surprisingly low average number of children. In the United States, the average was 0·58 children under 18 per household, in Sweden 0·36 children, and in the United Kingdon 0·22 children.

On the other hand, the number of aged persons in the lowest quintile was disproportionately high. The number of aged persons, 65 or over, exceeded the number of children in low-income households in at least two of the countries. In the United States the number of aged persons was 0·61 per household and in the United Kingdom 0·88 per household, for the lowest income quintiles. The preponderance of elderly people in low-income households is particularly significant in view of budget studies that show lower levels of need for the elderly.

Other measures

The question might be asked, what level of satisfaction is gained by consumers in different countries, regardless of what they may spend on particular necessities? Despite its importance, income is not the only measure of poverty, and maybe not the best measure. There are several measures of physical and social wellbeing that serve as indicators of poverty conditions, for example, mortality rates. We find that mortality is lower in many European countries than in the United States, especially for males. Life expectancy at birth is about 69 years for American men, 71 for Dutch men, and 72 for Swedish men. For women, it is 74 years in the United States, 76 for the Dutch, and 76 for the Swedes.

Infant mortality, another measure of poverty, is higher in the United States than in 16 countries. Here is a matter where the

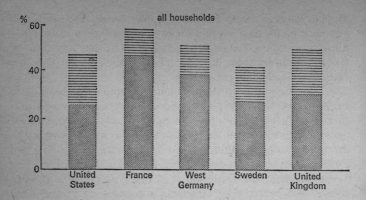

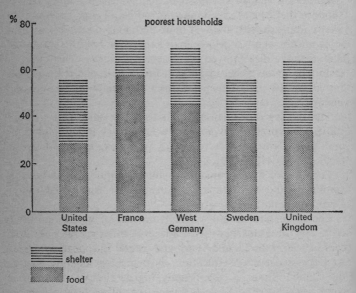

Figure 1 Expenditures for food and shelter as a percentage of total expenditures in the United States and other countries.

1. West German data for 'All households' applies to middle-income households; for 'Poorest households', to low-income households.
2. 'Poorest households' refers to lowest income quintile.

United States is clearly in need of improvement. The belief that our poor performance is due solely to higher infant mortality in our non-white population is not supported by the facts. Nine of the 16 countries show a lower infant mortality rate than the rate for the US white population.

In the field of nutrition, minimum standards have been suggested by the United Nations Food and Agriculture Organization (FAO), but not yet fully accepted. The FAO standard for daily calories per person is 2600, a level that is amply exceeded by the average consumption in the United States and Western Europe. The American diet is generally higher in animal proteins and sugar than the European diet, and lower in grains, fish, cheese, and butter. The American consumes about the same amount of fresh fruits and vegetables as the European. On balance, it is virtually impossible to judge which country has the superior diet, since the amount and variety of food consumption seems ample in both areas. A more pertinent question is whether a significant number of people in either area are missing out on the adequate diet enjoyed by the great majority. This question cannot be answered because of data limitations, but we know from recent reports that segments of the US population are seriously malnourished or underfed.

The quality and quantity of housing, as measured by such standards as presence of piped water, electricity, indoor plumbing, and the extent of overcrowding, may also be considered as measures of well-being. [. . .]

The United States ranks high among nations in its housing conditions, but may be surpassed in some respects by the leading European countries.

Education level is not a direct measure of wellbeing, but it correlates quite closely with income level. Illiteracy rates are 2 per cent or less in the United States and several European countries. At successive levels of education, the percentage of enrollment in the United States is significantly higher than in most other countries. This is particularly true at the college level, where the US enrollment rate is more than double the rate in most other countries. It is in education that the United States most clearly excels in relation to the rest of the world.

The US unemployment rate is still somewhat higher than the

rates in Europe, although the contrast is not as great as it was in the early 1960s. (See table 2.)

Table 2 Unemployment Per Cent Rates in Eight Industrial Countries, Adjusted to US Concepts

Country	1959	1963	1967
United States	5·5	5·7	3·8
White	4·8	5·0	3·4
Nonwhite	10·7	10·8	7·4
Canada	6·0	5·5	4·1
France	2·8	2·4*	3·3*
West Germany	1·6	0·4	0·9*
Great Britain	3·1	3·4	3·1*
Italy	5·7	2·7	3·8
Japan	1·9	1·1	1·1*
Sweden	n.a.	1·7	2·2*

* Preliminary estimates based on incomplete data.

Note: With the exception of Great Britain, all of the adjusted rates are based primarily on data derived from labor force surveys similar to the US monthly labor force survey. The adjusted rates for Great Britain, which has not conducted a labor force survey, are based on a comprehensive 1962 comparative study of British and US unemployment rates.

Although the data are adjusted for all known definitional differences, it should be recognized that it has been possible to achieve only approximate comparability among countries. Nevertheless, the adjusted figures provide a better basis for international comparisons than the usually published figures, which are based on labor force and unemployment definitions that differ from country to country and dissimilar methods of computing unemployment rates.

In summary, US economic averages and education level are generally favorable compared with Europe. Average income is higher, measures of abundance (autos, TV sets, refrigerators, housing) are higher. However, events have shown that US abundance is not reaching all social levels. Social and demographic averages do not show a superiority in the United States. The US performance respecting longevity, infant mortality, literacy, nutrition, illegitimacy and unemployment is less favorable than performance in some other countries. The distribution of benefits, both social and economic, may be more uniform in Europe, although the evidence is not conclusive.

Policies and programs

No European country has a multidimensional program like our 'War on Poverty'. Yet the Northern European countries probably have a greater variety of programs to assist the economically weak than we have in the United States.

The primary means for overcoming poverty in Europe are the numerous programs for maintaining general economic health. These programs range from flexible fiscal policy through area development, including countercyclical spending, investment incentives, economic planning, incomes policies, price restraining measures, and regional cooperation through such bodies as the European Economic Community and the European Free Trade Association. The active efforts to maintain general prosperity and growth are a powerful weapon against poverty and deprivation. During general prosperity the task of providing assistance to those in need becomes more manageable.

The trend in assistance is upward in Europe as well as in the United States. Assistance programs tend to be liberalized over time rather than made more restrictive.

The Europeans seem to emphasize programs to prevent or forestall hardship. Manpower policies are designed to avoid unemployment, maintain income stability, create jobs and facilitate access to jobs. Programs include work projects (public works), standby works plans, public purchasing during slack periods, contraseasonal employment incentives, investment reserve funds, encouragements to labor mobility, investment incentives, development of depressed areas, export stimulation, placement service, and career guidance and counseling. To deal with the traditional immobility of European labor, incentives are given to employers (tax exemption, training allowances, loans, wage subsidies) for locating in labor surplus areas. To encourage employee mobility, incentives such as relocation allowances, housing, transfer allowances, and differential wage payments (for coal miners) are offered.

European countries realize the need for broadening educational opportunities. One step has been to raise the minimum working age in several countries, although it is still quite low in most countries. Financial aid to students is being extended and allowances are furnished to parents in some cases. Vocational education and retraining is nurtured with allowances, and often at no loss of unemployment benefits so that income is maintained. In many countries, vocational training and apprenticeship are considered an extension of general education. Contrary to the American practice favoring increased-general education and free vocational choice at maturity, the entry age into apprenticeship, commonly fourteen or fifteen, is much lower than in the United States. An apprentice in Europe may start at a wage as low as 10 per cent of the journeyman rate; in the United States he earns from 50 to 90 per cent of the journeyman rate. Customarily, a large proportion of school leavers in Europe obtain public vocational guidance and accept apprenticeships.

Other European programs are aimed at promoting independence and self-sufficiency among workers. For example, low-cost loans have been provided for purchase of homes, and savings plans provide bonuses if withdrawals are not made for specified periods.

Then there are social insurance measures to alleviate or forestall the effects of poverty on individuals. These measures are numerous, as they are in the United States. Unemployment benefits are provided and, in recession periods, have been extended beyond usual time limits. Emphasis is placed on value-creating assistance, such as public works, training, furnishing of tools, and rehabilitation. Each European country has pension plans for the elderly, for widows, the handicapped, and disabled veterans. Most also have statutory family or children's allowances, which may add one-third to the average earnings of households.

The Europeans have gone far in relaxing the links between contributions and benefits. Many benefits, such as children's allowances and medical care, are provided from general tax revenues. In the United Kingdom, the 'cradle to grave' security provided under the Beveridge Plan does not include any means test for benefits. Similar schemes operate in Denmark, Sweden, Finland and Iceland.

Finally, for cases not reached by social insurance, there are public assistance programs, as in the United States. In several countries, municipalities are required to organize assistance programs. Special attention is given to children and to rehabilitation. The individual causes of poverty are so varied that social diagnosis can play a major role in providing the right kind of help. Cited causes include old age, sickness, physical handicap, mental retardation, maladjustment, inadequate training or education, irrational consumption habits, wastefulness, divorce, broken homes, alcoholism, drug addiction and others. Often the causes are multiple. The social worker has been used extensively in Europe to identify such problems and to aid in their solution. The aim is to restore the individual or family to constructive life wherever possible.

Possible lessons

The economic and social programs described here illustrate the diversity of activities undertaken in Europe to avoid or mitigate poverty. No single country undertakes every such program, nor are many of the programs universal. Also, many of the programs have their counterparts in the United States. Possibly some lessons can be gained from the Europeans, nevertheless, since many of the countries do not show the symptoms of poverty to any great degree although their economic resources are more limited than ours.

The European countries show a willingness to experiment, to try out novel programs. Some may fail, of course, or may not be applicable to US conditions. Others may provide the type of pilot experience worth studying further.

European programs for youth are conspicuously different and, in some ways, apparently more successful than US programs. The child in Europe receives a measure of protection through the children's allowance that is not available here. Although in most European countries his opportunities for higher education and his chance of upward social and economic mobility are very limited, his chances of leaving school with a skill or vocation are much better. As a youth he is encouraged at an early age to obtain occupational training that will fit him for an adult job. As a result, the transition from school to work occurs much earlier – for better or for worse – and is much smoother than in the United States, judging from comparative unemployment levels.

The role of the employment service is more dominant in Europe. In addition to placement activities, the service may engage in counseling, training, nationwide referral, relocation, initiation of public works, and participation in national economic policy decisions.

Several European schemes are aimed to maintain income when the breadwinner is unable to provide. While income is maintained, major efforts are made to rehabilitate the breadwinner, restore him to productive life, or enable other family members to find work. The principles of prevention and self-help are given top attention in fighting poverty, which is consistent with the historic European attitudes that the community shall accept responsibility for the poor, but that able-bodied persons shall be responsible for themselves.

References

BECKERMAN, W. (1966) *International Comparisons of Real Income*, Organization for Economic Cooperation and Development, Paris.

INTERNATIONAL LABOR OFFICE (1964), *The Cost of Social Security, 1958–60*, pp.243–8, Geneva.

KRAVITZ, I. (1960) 'International Differences in the Distribution of Income', *Rev. Econ. and Stat.*, November, pp. 408–16.

10 The President's Commission on Income Maintenance Programs

Poverty Amid Plenty: The American Paradox

Excerpts from *Poverty Amid Plenty: The American Paradox*, The Report of The President's Commission on Income Maintenance Programs, November 1969, pp. 13–33.

The poor

The postwar period has witnessed a remarkable improvement in the material welfare of most Americans. Even with the effect of inflation taken into account, median family income grew by 76 per cent between 1947 and 1967. The proportion of families enjoying a total income of $10,000 or more increased from 22 to 34 per cent during the same period. And, in recent years, we have taken justifiable satisfaction in the reduction of poverty from 22 per cent of the population in 1959 to 13 per cent in 1968. But the fact remains that 25 million persons are still poor.

Thousands of pages of statistics about the poor have been tabulated and published. The poor have been measured, surveyed and sorted into numerous categories, some of which are summarized in Table 1 for 1966.[1] But in the end, the diversity of the poor overwhelms any simple attempt to describe them with statistics. What may be said simply is that millions of our fellow citizens are living in severe poverty, with few prospects for a better life, and often with little hope for the future.

To the poor, poverty is no statistical or sociological matter. Their condition exists as a daily fight for survival. This Commission has found their deprivation to be real, not a trick of rhetoric or statistics. And for many of the poor, their poverty is not a temporary situation, but an enduring fact of life.

1. Aggregate poverty counts are available for 1968. The latest year for which detailed breakdowns are available is 1966.

Table 1 Selected Characteristics of the Poor and the Non-poor, 1966

Characteristic	Number (millions)		Per cent distribution	
	Poor	Non-poor	Poor	Non-poor
Age				
Total	30·0	163·9	100·0	100·0
Under 18 years	13·0	57·4	43·5	35·0
18–21	1·6	10·4	5·3	6·4
22–54	7·4	68·7	24·7	41·9
55–64	2·5	14·7	8·5	9·0
65 and over	5·4	12·6	18·0	7·7
Race				
Total	30·0	163·9	100·0	100·0
White	20·4	150·2	68·3	91·6
Non-white	9·5	13·7	31·7	8·4
Family status				
Total	30·0	163·9	100·0	100·0
Unrelated individuals	5·1	7·6	17·1	4·6
Family members	24·9	156·3	82·9	95·4
Head	6·1	42·8	20·3	26·1
Spouse	4·1	38·5	13·5	23·5
Other adult	2·1	17·7	7·2	10·8
Child under 18	12·6	57·3	42·0	35·0
Type of residence				
Total	30·0	163·9	100·0	100·0
Farm	2·5	8·5	8·2	5·2
Non-farm	27·5	155·6	91·8	94·8
Rural	11·2	46·7	37·3	28·5
Urban	18·8	117·2	62·7	71·5

Source: Office of Economic Opportunity, unpublished tabulations from the Current Population Survey and draft report, 'Dimensions of Poverty, 1964–1966'.

The poverty living standard

Any discussion of the poor must begin by defining those who are poor and those who are not. But it is obvious that any single standard or definition of poverty is arbitrary, and clearly subject to disagreement. The standard which this Commission has employed is the widely used poverty index, developed by the Social Security Administration. This index is based on the Department of Agriculture's measure of the cost of a temporary low-budget, nutritious diet for households of various sizes. The poverty index is simply this food budget multiplied by three to reflect the fact that food typically represents one-third of the expenses of a low-income family. The resulting figure is the minimum income needed to buy a subsistence level of goods and services; the 25 million people whose incomes fall below the index are poor, while those above it are, officially at least, non-poor. According to this poverty index, in 1968 a non-farm family of four required a minimum income of $3553 per year, or $2·43 per person per day to meet its basic expenses. Table 2 shows the poverty index for families of various sizes in 1968.

Table 2 1968 Poverty Thresholds

Family size	Poverty index	
	Non-farm	Farm
1	$1748	$1487
2	2262	1904
3	2774	2352
4	3553	3034
5	4188	3577
6	4706	4021
7 or more	5789	4916

[...] This food budget requires more than a third of the poor family's income, but still allows only $1·00 a day for food per person. A family can buy a nutritionally adequate diet for this amount, using the Department of Agriculture's food plan, but it must eat considerably more beans, potatoes, flour and cereal products, and considerably less meat, eggs, fruits, and vegetables than the average family. Each member of the poor family may consume less than a quarter of a pound of meat a day.

Unfortunately, the Department's food plan, the basis of the poverty index, is not very realistic. It is estimated that only about one-fourth of the families who spend that much for food actually have a nutritionally adequate diet.[2] The plan calls for skills in meal-planning and buying that are rare at any income level, and it requires extensive efforts by poor families to make the varied and appetizing meals which are ostensibly possible under the plan. Many of the poor lack common kitchen appliances. Moreover, the Department's plan assumes the shopper will buy in economical quantities and take advantage of special bargains, but this is particularly difficult for a poor family with inadequate storage and refrigeration facilities. [. . .]

Technically, an income at the poverty level should enable families to purchase the bare necessities of life. Yet an itemized budget drawn at that level clearly falls short of adequacy. There are many items for which no money is budgeted, although those items may be needed. Funds for them can only come out of sums already allotted to the basic necessities of life. As one witness told the Commission, 'I either eat good and smell bad, or smell good and don't eat.' When another witness was asked how he made ends meet, he simply replied, 'They don't meet.' [. . .]

Medical care

Because the poor often are isolated or without transportation, they have restricted access to proper medical attention. The care they do receive is often too late and of low quality. Yet the relative need for health care is greatest among those groups – infants, expectant mothers, and the elderly – which form a disproportionate share of the population in poverty.

Although the most advanced medical techniques in the world are available in the United States, the poor receive little advantage from them. For example, this country ranks thirteenth in the world in infant mortality and at least that low in maternal mortality. These relatively low rankings are explained in part by the uneven distribution of health services in the United States which results in a greater incidence of poor health among low-income groups.

Poor nutrition during pregnancy can hinder fetal brain development and increase the probability of premature birth. Protein deficiencies in early childhood can retard brain growth.

2. US Department of Agriculture, Consumer and Food Economics Division.

This early damage – perhaps followed by frequent illness, further malnutrition, crowded and unsanitary living conditions – is exacerbated by lack of regular medical attention and may affect the adult's ability to obtain adequate employment. Health limitations are particularly likely to result in unemployment or underemployment among those whose skill levels are low, because jobs open to them are usually physically demanding.

The health problems of the poor are not invisible. The glazed eyes of children, legs that never grew straight, misshapen feet, sallow complexions, lack-luster hair, are easily recognized by even an untrained observer. Other physical limitations, such as low energy levels, are quite real to poor children in school and adults trying to hold down jobs, but these limitations may be misconstrued by teachers and employers.

Most of the poor cannot afford private medical care and are not covered by insurance. And many cannot afford the transportation to free medical facilities, which are often miles and hours away. Or, there may be no medical charity – public or private – available to them. [. . .]

Housing

Millions of the poor live in substandard, squalid housing. The shanties and shacks found in rural areas often look like remnants from an earlier era. [. . .]

The barrenness of housing of the urban poor sometimes is hidden behind the facade of ordinary looking row houses. Yet the interior may reveal serious decay – falling plaster, holes in the wall, gaps in window frames, rats and roaches, and deteriorated plumbing. [. . .]

The physical condition of the homes and neighborhoods in which the poor live and the crowding that often occurs have severe effects on health, as well as on social and behavioral patterns. The struggle to meet basic physical needs under depressing and frustrating living conditions undermines attempts to escape from poverty. [. . .]

Why they remain poor

The paradox of poverty in the midst of plenty causes many to ask why some people remain poor when so many of their fellow

Americans have successfully joined the ranks of the affluent. It is often assumed that anyone who wishes to live well can achieve that objective by seeking and accepting work. It is often argued that the poor are to blame for their own circumstances and should be expected to lift themselves from poverty.

The Commission has concluded that these assertions are incorrect. Our economic and social structure virtually guarantees poverty for millions of Americans. Unemployment and under-employment are basic facts of American life. The risks of poverty are common to millions more who depend on earnings for their income. We all grow old. We all can fall victim to unemployment caused by technological change or industrial relocation. Any of us could become sick or disabled. And becoming unpoor is extra-ordinarily difficult. What does a disabled man, an elderly couple, or a child *do* to escape poverty? How does a woman with six children survive while she is hunting work or being trained? How does an unskilled, middle-aged laborer adjust to the loss of a job?

The simple fact is that most of the poor remain poor because access to income through work is currently beyond their reach.

The aged

Old age is usually a period of nonemployment. Society neither expects nor assists the aged to work. Retirement at age sixty-five is common in both industry and government, and discrimination in hiring against the aged and aging is common among employers.

The aged possess limited earning potential. They generally are expected to live on pensions, savings, and Social Security benefits. Too frequently, savings and pensions deemed adequate at an earlier time become insufficient as inflation raises the cost of living. Millions of hard-working Americans, accustomed all their lives to paying their way, find themselves becoming unalterably and unavoidably poor in old age.

In 1966, 6·4 million aged persons and their dependents were in poverty. Over a million of these persons lived in families where the family head worked for at least part of the year, and almost half a million lived in families where the head worked 50–52 weeks. The average family income was more than $600 below the poverty line; this gap was about equal for low-income aged families whether the head worked or not. Average family income for poor households headed by the aged was below $1200. [. . .]

The poor will remain poor once they retire, and others who retire may become poor in their old age. Opportunities for the aged poor to make any improvement in their own lives are remote and unrealistic. Only public programs can make a difference in their incomes.

The non-aged

While the aged apparently can do little about their poverty, what about the 24·6 million *non-aged* persons who were poor in 1966? Six per cent of these people were in families headed by aged poor persons, so their poverty can be linked to the elderly family heads on whom they depended. What possibilities do the remaining non-aged persons have to escape poverty through their own efforts? The unpleasant truth is that these possibilities are extraordinarily limited.

Work experience

The work experience of the 4·5 million non-aged heads of poor families provides dramatic documentation of their limited ability to change substantially their circumstances on their own. In all, the heads of 1·9 million poor families – 42 per cent of the total – worked fulltime for more than forty weeks of the year. Most of the remaining heads of families did some work. [. . .]

More than 70 per cent of the non-aged heads of poor families worked for some period, yet remained in poverty. The Commission considers the fact that 42 per cent of the non-aged heads of poor families worked full time for most of the year to be as significant in understanding poverty as the fact that 58 per cent worked less than that, or did not work at all.

The different degrees of participation in the labor force among the poor seem due to chance more than to motivation or other factors. Unemployment or underemployment among the poor are often due to forces that cannot be controlled by the poor themselves. There are not two distinct categories of poor – those who can work and those who can not. Nor can the poor be divided into those who will work and those who will not. For many, the desire to work is strong, but the opportunities are not readily available. The opening or closing of a factory, ill health of the breadwinner, inability to find transportation, loss of a babysitter, weather conditions and similar factors greatly affect employment opportunities.

Of the 1·2 million poor non-aged family heads who did not work at all in 1966:

1. Nearly half were women with responsibilities for young children.

2. Another third were unable to perform any work because of illness or disability.

3. Of the remaining 230,000, 40 per cent were unable to work because they were attending school, and about 15 per cent reported that they were simply unable to find any work.

4. A residual group of about 100,000 remains. It includes those who did not work at all during the year for reasons other than those listed.

Thus, less than three per cent of the non-aged heads of poor families might have freely chosen not to work at all. But many in this residual group actually may have had little choice between work and poverty. For example, many poor individuals do not work because of disabilities which ordinarily are not recognized in official statistics, particularly disabilities of a mental, rather than a physical nature.

Factors inhibiting progress

Clearly, the experience of the poor indicates that work alone is no guarantee of escaping poverty. Why is it that employment – the basic source of income for most Americans – fails the poor?

Several factors account for this. Family size is relevant; the costs of supporting a large number of children can result in poverty for workers with even relatively high earnings. Low wages and/or lack of sufficient hours and weeks of work can account for a good deal of poverty. Disabilities prevent many from working. Poor preparation for working careers and discrimination affect many others. And, for large numbers of people, work is simply not available. Let us examine the impact of these factors more closely.

An economy at less than 100 per cent employment

There is some unemployment even in the best of times, and it is not evenly distributed over the economy. A desire to avoid accelerating inflation has led policymakers to accept some unemployment. But it must be recognized that this policy has much to do with explaining poverty for many families. A 4 per cent unemployment rate – considered by many to be the lowest feasible, long-term unemployment rate – means that not everyone can work who wants to work. It also means that wages will be lower than they would be if there were greater competition for workers. It means that young people without work experience, people with low educational attainments, and members of minority groups subject to discrimination will be particularly handicapped in their search for employment. Moreover, official unemployment statistics do not reflect the number of persons who have withdrawn completely from the labor force because of long-term inability to find jobs.

Obviously, the state of the American economy and the consequent structure of opportunities at the local level can enhance or impede employability greatly. A fully employed person, earning good wages one day, can find himself suddenly unemployed and locally unemployable due to a work force reduction or plant closing. In the absence of strong aggregate demand, even well-planned efforts to find jobs can be ineffective. [. . .]

In 1966 at least 160,000 male family heads were forced to work less than they desired because of an inability to find more steady employment. More than a million others were working part-time hours at low-paying marginal tasks. [. . .]

Low earnings

Full-time employment at the current Federal minimum wage of $1·60 an hour will provide a family of four or more with an annual income below the poverty line. In 1966, 3·1 million men working full-time, two-thirds of whom were family heads, earned less than $1·60 an hour. In 1967, almost half of the nation's labor force was employed in occupations or industries not covered by the minimum wage provisions of the Fair Labor Standards Act. Many of the families of such workers are poor.

The sources of low wages can be found on both the demand and the supply sides of the labor market. The spread of complex automated industrial technology continually reduces the relative demand for workers in low-skilled occupations. Emigration from the agricultural sector, the growing number of youth, and increased participation of middle-aged women in the labor force add to the supply of low-wage job candidates.

In certain instances, however, low earnings reflect a breakdown in the market itself, either because of immobility of labor and capital resources or because of discrimination in hiring. There is overwhelming evidence that the employment opportunities of non-white workers and female workers are more limited in number and lower in quality than those open to white male workers. [. . .]

Large families

Large families need substantial incomes just to avoid poverty. According to the Social Security Administration's poverty index for 1968, a non-farm family composed of two parents and five children would need at least $5789 to maintain even the most basic standard of living. If the head worked full-time year-round, he would have to earn nearly $3·00 per hour to achieve this target. In 1966 over 40 per cent of the poor families with children headed by employed men under age sixty-five had more than three children to support. With an average family size of 4·6 persons, many working family heads are financially handicapped even when earning a relatively good annual income.

Poverty and education

The association between education and income is a familiar one. Formal education not only enhances the quality of one's life, it also pays a high dividend in material rewards. Those with little education are at a disadvantage in the labor market. The heads of nearly three-quarters of all poor families in 1966 did not graduate from high school. Indeed, nearly one in five of the poor non-aged male and female family heads had completed less than six years of formal schooling – a level barely above functional illiteracy.

Limited education does not guarantee a life of poverty, but the income distribution is highly skewed in favor of the more educated.

One fourth of those with less than eight years of schooling earned less than $3000 while only 6 per cent of high school graduates had earnings that low. [. . .]

Poverty and location

Two-thirds of the poor lived in urban areas in 1966. However, the risk of being poor was greater for those who resided in rural areas, whether they lived on or off the farm. Almost 20 per cent of the rural population was poor, compared with about 14 per cent for the urban population. Opportunities for earning are fewer in rural than urban areas, and work is more often seasonal.

The poor are somewhat concentrated geographically. Twenty per cent of Southern families were poor in 1966, while only 9 per cent of non-Southern families were poor. Half of all poor families lived in the South. Although nearly two-thirds of all poor non-white families lived in the South in 1966, Southern poverty was by no means confined to non-whites. Close to 2 million white families – 42 per cent of all poor white families – were residents of Southern States. The conditions that are conducive to poverty – low wages, low average education, seasonal employment, and declining opportunities for the unskilled – are especially prevalent in the South. These factors cross racial lines, although non-whites are particularly affected.

Another focal point for poverty is the inner core of major cities, from which it is often difficult, time consuming, and expensive to reach well-paying jobs in outlying areas. [. . .]

In many American cities, the story is the same: there are no jobs where the poor live, the poor cannot afford – or are not allowed – to live where the jobs are opening up, and there is no transportation between these two places.

Poverty and the female-headed family

The employment opportunities for women heading poor families are more limited than those for men. Because of their family responsibilities, women may be severely restricted from holding down even a part-time job. One in every two women heading poor families did not work in 1966.

Getting and keeping a job imposes certain conditions that are especially burdensome for women heading poor families. Working requires either that all children be old enough to care for themselves or that some day care provisions be made for the children. There are few such facilities available, even for those who can afford to pay. Many women heading families with children can work only at the expense of their family responsibilities.

Many of the jobs available do not pay enough to cover the cost of child care and other employment expenses. Jobs for which the majority of female heads of households qualify are at the lower end of the pay scale. In 1966 almost 50 per cent of all employed white women heading poor families and 75 per cent of non-white women heading poor families worked in service occupations, one of the lowest paid groups. [. . .]

Discrimination and poverty

At first glance it seems that poverty is a white problem – two-thirds of the poor are white, while one-third are non-white. However, 12 per cent of the white population is poor while over 40 per cent of the much smaller non-white population is poor.

The greater incidence of poverty among non-whites reflects several factors: larger family size, lower average earnings, a greater proportion of female-headed families, lower educational levels, and the greater proportion of non-whites living in the South. Yet, holding each of these factors constant and comparing across racial lines, non-whites remain at a disadvantage.

Much of this differential is a result of direct or indirect discrimination. Many employers still are unwilling to hire members of minority groups. Others will employ them only in the most menial jobs. Some minority group members find themselves unable to compete for jobs because discrimination in public programs has provided them with inferior education or training. [. . .]

Conclusion

The persistence of poverty and the extensive movements into and out of poverty testify to the fact that problems of income inadequacy and income insecurity are common to large segments of the population. Age and disability, loss of employment for technological or personal reasons, large family size, and poorly paid employment, pose potential risks to all who depend on wages. And, in our society, 80 per cent of the population receive the major portion of their income from wages. The wage earner's income is highly vulnerable to the chance circumstances of life. Few families, for example, could weather long-term illness of the earner without serious financial problems, even if they possessed savings, health insurance, or accumulated sick leave. Few families could afford the retraining of a laid-off primary worker without great difficulty. The living standard of most families would be seriously jeopardized and some would become poor.

For most of those who are currently poor, changes in economic status are largely beyond their control. Generally, they are doing what they can considering their age, health status, social circumstances, location, education and opportunities for employment. Poverty is not a chosen way of life. Both the statistical data and personal observations by members of this Commission have made it clear to us that most of the poor are poor because affluence is beyond their grasp. The aged poor have made their contribution as workers and now many are dependent on inadequate retirement incomes. The disabled are similarly handicapped. The working poor are attempting to be productive and still are poor.

With so many working at jobs that are both unpleasant and financially unrewarding, one wonders how the stereotype of the malingering poor can be sustained. It is wrong that so much attention is focused on the few laggards. Among the poor are a small number who will be very successful in escaping from poverty on their own, and a majority who will work hard but remain poor. Very few of those capable of self-help seem to be doing nothing.

For the bulk of the poor, both young and old, unemployed and working, urban and rural, there are few bootstraps available by which they can pull themselves out of poverty. As individuals, some of our poor fellow citizens can overcome the limitations imposed by chronic significant levels of unemployment and underemployment, various forms of discrimination, and an opportunity system which – while perhaps unparalleled in the world – needs to be improved. But as a group they cannot. Society must aid them or they will remain poor.

11 Albert Rose

Poverty in Canada

Albert Rose, 'Poverty in Canada: an essay review', *Social Service Review*, vol. 43 (March 1969), pp. 74–84.

Canadians, in their enjoyment of the second or third highest standard of living in the world (depending upon where one would place Sweden), have been only dimly aware of the poverty in the midst of their affluent society. Of course, most Canadians have some awareness of the living conditions of their native peoples (the Indians and the Eskimos); some awareness of the under-developed state of the four Atlantic provinces (Newfoundland, Nova Scotia, New Brunswick and Prince Edward Island), by virtue of a very substantial migration of Maritimers to the large urban centers in central Canada; and some awareness of the residents of the deteriorated heart of the central cities of such metropolitan areas as Montreal, Toronto, Winnipeg and Vancouver. Nevertheless, they have followed with some interest the American 'War on Poverty' since its inception five or six years ago with the attitude of spectators at a match between gladiators representing other nations or other parts of this world.

It was a shock, therefore, when the Economic Council of Canada (1968) devoted a considerable portion of its *Fifth Annual Review* to 'The Problem of Poverty'. The Economic Council is a quasi-independent body appointed by the government to analyse public and private economic and social policies, to undertake research, and to point the way toward Canada's future by indicating the most important guidelines, issues, caveats, and policies which must be given serious consideration. It is somewhat akin to the Council of Economic Advisers in the United States, but its chairman is less likely to be a political appointee whose tenure depends upon the complexion of the party in power.

In each of its annual reviews the council has hit hard upon one major theme in Canadian life which it feels deserves the attention of all levels of government and of all citizens responsible for the quality or lack of quality of local and provincial governments and the federal government itself. Two years ago, in its *Third Annual Review*, the Economic Council mustered its battery of technical resources upon the subject of education in Canada's future; a year ago a substantial portion of the *Fourth Annual Review* was devoted to housing. The latest *Review* is entitled 'The Challenge of Growth and Change'. About one-quarter of the document draws strong attention to the existence of poverty in Canada. The impact of the report can be understood by quoting the first paragraph of the chapter entitled 'The Problem of Poverty':

Poverty in Canada is real. Its numbers are not in the thousands, but the millions. There is more of it than our society can tolerate, more than our economy can afford, and far more than existing measures and efforts can cope with. Its persistence, at a time when the bulk of Canadians enjoy one of the highest standards of living in the world, is a disgrace (Economic Council of Canada, 1968, p. 103).

The nature of poverty in Canada

At the beginning, the council's report reads very much like Harrington's first book (1962, pp. 1–38). Many Canadians assume that poverty is identical with the problem of low average incomes in the underdeveloped areas of the country and among the Indian and Eskimo populations. Moreover, in urban areas particularly, the poor tend to be more or less invisible and 'collectively inarticulate'. The council is at pains to argue, however, that although the *incidence* of poverty is higher in the areas and among the groups mentioned, in terms of absolute numbers between a third and a half of the total poverty in Canada is 'to be found among the white population of cities and towns west of Three Rivers'. Three Rivers is a city on the north shore of the St Lawrence, about halfway between Montreal and Quebec City.

The report argues that there are two major problems in defining poverty. First, it is a relative concept and, second, while available data make it necessary that it be discussed largely in terms of low income, poverty means something more than 'simple income deficiency'. Poverty is not quite the same thing as low income, although there is clearly a very strong association between the two:

We believe that serious poverty should be eliminated in Canada, and that this should be designated as a major national goal. We believe this for two reasons. The first is that one of the wealthiest 'societies in world history, if it also aspires to be a just society, cannot avoid setting itself such a goal. Secondly, poverty is costly. Its most grievous costs are those felt directly by the poor themselves, but it also imposes very large costs on the rest of society. These include the costs of crime, disease, and poor education. They include the costs of low productivity and lost output, of controlling the social tensions and unrest associated with gross inequality, and of that part of total welfare expenditure which is essentially a palliative made necessary by the failure to find more fundamental solutions. It has been estimated in the United States that one poor man can cost the public purse as much as $140,000 between the ages of seventeen and fifty-seven (Economic Council of Canada, 1968, p. 105).

It should be noted that Canada did not follow the example of the United States in 1964 in formally declaring a national 'War on Poverty'. At that time Prime Minister Pearson made a strong statement on the subject but carefully avoided the use of the American terminology. He made it clear that a great many existing Canadian programs in the fields of health, welfare, and labor relations were designed in part to alleviate poverty. What seemed to be required in Canada, he argued in 1965, was co-ordination of these programs, and to that end he created a Special Planning Secretariat of the Privy Council of Canada. The Privy Council is not quite identical with the Office of the President of the United States or the Prime Minister's Department in Canada. It is, however, one of the most important bodies in Canada in the sense that it constitutes the inner executive and administrative service available to the Cabinet.

The Special Planning Secretariat was therefore considered to be strategically placed in that it could have access to a variety of ministries and thus achieve the goal of coordination. It had very little budget available; it made no grants to provincial or local governments; it did not dispense funds for research or other investigative procedures. It was thus by no means equivalent to the Office of Economic Opportunity in the United States, nor was a piece of legislation passed in Canada akin to the Economic Opportunity Act of 1964.[1]

1. The Secretariat did, however, issue a series of pamphlets on various

When it came to the analysis of poverty in Canada, the Economic Council was forced to fall back on certain available income data and upon arbitrarily determined criteria which amounted to the drawing of a 'poverty line' for Canadians. The last available census data on incomes were collected in 1961, but the council was able to obtain estimates for 1965. The consequence of its analysis would be anticipated by any American or other student of poverty in Western industrial nations. In 1965 the lowest one-fifth of Canadian families averaged $2263 income per family, which was 6·7 per cent of total Canadian income; the second fifth received 13·4 per cent and averaged $4542 per family. The average income in the same year was $6669, which was in fact greater than the average income of all families in the third fifth as well as the lowest two-fifths. The council admits that the lowest fifth, or the lowest third, or any other fraction of an income distribution, bears no necessary relation to the needs of the poor and is a poor statistical substitute for an appropriate description of poverty. It states that 'the proper object of an attack on poverty should be the careful identification and aiding of those whose circumstances do not permit them to achieve a decent standard of life at any point in time' (Economic Council of Canada, 1968, p. 108).

For purposes of a first estimate, low-income families and individuals were defined as those using 70 per cent or more of their incomes for food, clothing and shelter. On this basis, low-income families and individuals would include single persons with incomes below $1500, families of two with less than $2500, and families of three, four, and five or more persons with incomes of less than $3000, $3500, and $4000, respectively. In 1961 about 916,000 non-farm families plus 416,000 individuals were living below these levels. The total number of persons involved was about 4·2 millions, including 1·7 million children under sixteen years of age. In all they accounted for some 27 per cent of the total non-farm population of Canada. In that year the total Canadian population was about 16·5 millions.

subjects under the overall rubric of 'Meeting Poverty'. Two publications were substantial monographs: Jenness, (1969) and *A Profile of Poverty in Canada* (no author stated) (Ottawa, 1965).

In a second estimate the council raised the cut-off by assuming that expenditures of 60 per cent or more of income on food, clothing, and shelter by an individual or a family indicated poverty or what the council called 'straitened circumstances'. The appropriate figures were thus raised to $2000 for a single person, $3500 for a family of two, $4000 for families of three and four, and $5000 for families of five or more. When these figures were applied to the non-farm population of 1961, the low-income percentage rose from 27 to 41.

The argument that statistics cannot adequately describe poverty leads the council into an examination of the non-income characteristics of Canadians considered to be in poverty. This is very much like Ornati's discussion of the Pi coefficients for Americans in poverty on the basis of 1960 census data (Ornati, 1966, pp. 43–53). Poor Canadians differ statistically from the total Canadian population with respect to age, family size, place of residence, education, relationship to the labor force, and occupation. The council claims that these special characteristics 'are often significant as policy guides to particular kinds of poverty problems' (p. 110). The statistical examination reveals, however, that 62 per cent of low-income non-farm families in 1961 lived in urban areas, and of this group more than half lived in metropolitan areas. In addition, 83 per cent of low-income non-farm families in Canada lived elsewhere than in the Atlantic provinces, 53 per cent in fact lived in Ontario and the Western provinces. Despite the incidence of low income in families headed by females, 87 per cent of low-income non-farm families in 1961 were headed by men.

The Economic Council argues that a set of antipoverty policies directed toward major groups or geographical areas showing a very high incidence of low income would almost certainly fail to deal adequately with poverty. It argues that such policies would neglect those not with an absence of earnings but with an insufficiency of earnings, and would tend to miss many pockets of poverty that are scattered through relatively high-income regions throughout the nation. This argument is termed 'the first warning' with respect to the interpretation of poverty statistics. The second warning is to avoid confusing characteristics with causes and to bear in mind how the total amount of poverty can be affected by such vague forces as the rate of economic growth in relation to potential. Nevertheless, the council examines in considerable depth each of the characteristics (Ornati's Pi coefficients) for low-income families, beginning with the sources of income and concluding with the special problems of Indians, Eskimos, and Métis.[2]

Discussion of the native peoples of Canada and the racially mixed group known as Métis is of particular interest. The report describes a few simple statistics as 'a brutal story'. For example, the average life-expectancy of an Indian woman in Canada is twenty-five years. The infant mortality rate among Eskimos is about 293 deaths per 1,000 live births, more than ten times the rate for the Canadian population as a whole. The problems facing these special groups in Canada are accentuated by a number of special factors. In the first place, these groups are increasing more rapidly in population than any other ethnic group. At the same time, opportunities for making a livelihood by the traditional occupations of hunting and trapping are declining rapidly. Less than a third of Canada's 2200 reservations could possibly provide sufficient resources to support their present Indian population. Finally, Indians, Eskimos, and Métis peoples face continuing difficulties in 'coping with, and adapting to, the problems of the major society, both because of present attitudes within the white community and because of strong cultural differences' (p. 122).

While minimizing its competence to appraise various findings in detail, the council stresses certain common conclusions concerning the native Canadian peoples. The report states that Indians and Eskimos are treated too much as a special group in ways which exclude them from many of the ordinary provisions of public policy. The main reason for this anomaly rests in the fact that Indians and Eskimos fall traditionally under federal jurisdiction, while the social and health services, as well as education, are within provincial jurisdiction. The commission concludes that 'the result has often been that Indians and Eskimos receive either inadequate services or special services that further segregate them from the larger society' (p. 123).

2. The Métis, found primarily in the rural areas of Manitoba, Saskatchewan, and Alberta, are persons of mixed racial ancestry, usually 'half-breeds' of French and Indian parentage.

Particular efforts will be required to help those who are striving to integrate themselves into the larger society. The council believes that the future economic life of most of the Indian, Eskimo, and Métis populations will undoubtedly lie within the larger industrial society. Yet integration does not mean 'the total assimilation and homogenization of these groups, but it does mean the increasing provision of opportunities for these peoples to take part in the main stream of Canadian life' (p. 123).

A third major area of consensus is the need for a 'community development' approach to the problems of education, individual development, adaptation to the larger environment and community organization. The council believes that the New Start program, now being initiated by the federal Department of Manpower and Immigration in certain parts of the Atlantic provinces and the northern areas of the three prairie provinces, constitutes a promising development. It is hoped that techniques in community development will be tested which may be applicable in other communities with substantial Indian and Métis populations. It is worth pointing out, however, that the test areas are not in the least comparable with the urban centers of Winnipeg and Toronto, to which, particularly, large numbers of Canadian Indians have moved during the past ten or fifteen years and in which their social and economic positions, especially their housing characteristics, are abominable. The report states firmly that, no matter how much can be done to develop economic activity on reservations and in other places where significant groups of native peoples live, 'a continuing substantial migration to urban areas must be expected, notably in Western Canada' (p. 123). The council stresses that those who move to the cities must be better prepared, educationally and in other ways, for a very different life; and, at the city end, much more must be done to help these citizens to feel at home in their new environment and to become 'responsible and contributing members of the community'.

Some lessons of the United States war on poverty

The Economic Council of Canada devotes several pages to an analysis of recent efforts in the United States to combat poverty, in the hope that some lessons may be learned by and for Canadians. After a brief outline of the background of the Economic Opportunity Act of 1964 and the major programs of the Office of Economic Opportunity, the Council states:

The primary emphasis in all of these programs has been on self-help, self-development, and maximum participation and involvement of the poor themselves. This emphasis has been most marked in the youth programs with an educational purpose, and in the various Community Action Programs.

The programs of the war on poverty fall into four major categories: 1. manpower development, training and mobility programs; 2. individual improvement and/or educational programs; 3. community action and community change programs; and 4. income maintenance programs (p. 125).

A brief analysis of these four major categories is undertaken, and the report concludes that the community action programs have been evaluated as 'successful in the delivery of services, relatively unsuccessful in the coordination of programs, and fairly successful – though assessment is difficult – in bringing about institutional development and change' (p. 126). A special word of commendation is directed toward the legal-services program. It would be interesting to speculate whether Americans would come to the same conclusion with respect to the community-action programs.

In the Council's view, the community-action agencies have been relatively unsuccessful as coordinating bodies, in part because of the intensely complicated array of federal, state, and local programs that already exist. Nevertheless, these agencies appear to be more successful as instruments of institutional development in bringing together the people of poor communities to plan and implement measures at the community level. They are also experiencing considerable success in influencing the institutional environment – social welfare agencies, courts, police forces – in poor communities.

As far as Canadians are concerned, the lessons to be derived from recent United States experience are the following:

1. High aggregate demand and strong labor markets are a highly necessary condition for achieving substantial reductions in poverty.

2. A full-scale war on poverty should embrace all of the four basic categories of antipoverty programs mentioned previously. These categories are inter-related and mutually supporting.

3. Although the exercise of drawing statistical poverty lines is bound to be somewhat arbitrary, it is necessary for good social planning. Without some definition of the poverty band, the Council believes that there is a great danger that antipoverty policies will be beamed toward the moderately well-off portion of the population.

4. The political popularity of 'trickle-down' approaches to poverty constitutes another danger. The Council argues that the spending of money 'in the general vicinity of poverty groups' by no means guarantees that a substantial proportion of the benefits will, in fact, flow to the poor. The example cited is spending on 'some kinds of economic development'.

5. Individual antipoverty programs should start with realistic expectations and 'the best possible built-in evaluation mechanisms, including notably mechanisms for data collection'.

6. 'Family structure effects' are an important consideration. The likelihood of success in programs for teenagers is increased by success in programs for adults. If one of the parents previously unemployed can be placed in employment this will improve the prospect of lifting the children permanently out of poverty.

7. Education has certain limitations as a specific antipoverty weapon. It is suggested that effects of programs like Head Start have shown a tendency to fade out as children become older. The Council suggests: 'High investment appears to be needed to overcome basic educational deficiencies. At the same time, educational programs have yielded valuable side-effects, such things as bringing children into contact with organized medical care for the first time in their lives.'

8. Substantial benefits have been noted from programs to improve family-planning and nutrition of expectant mothers and of infants up to three years of age.

9. There must be adequate recognition of the social adaptation involved in the absorption of the 'hard-core' poor into employment. Otherwise, states the report, there tends to be a high rate of

drop-out from even good jobs. More needs to be known about the characteristics of the 'hard-core' poor and more done to elicit the co-operation of business in absorbing such persons into productive employment. The report suggests that an examination of growing labor requirements may permit the absorption of trainees from among the hard-core poor if jobs can be subdivided to permit their employment (pp. 127–8).

Antipoverty planning in eastern Quebec

There is one geographical area in Canada in which a considerable amount of progress has been made in a 'community development' approach to the treatment of poverty. The report compares large parts of eastern Quebec and the Atlantic provinces with the Appalachian region in the United States in the sense that these constitute sub-regions where poverty is so widespread that its elimination can be treated in many ways as an area problem.

In 1963 a regional planning agency, le Bureau d'Amenagement de l'Est du Quebec (Eastern Quebec Regional Development Council), was established as a non-profit private corporation. The Bureau was financed under the terms of the federal Agricultural Rehabilitation and Development Act (ARDA) by agreement between the province of Quebec and the federal government, and was given the task of preparing a master development plan for the region within three years. The research program undertaken by the Bureau was extremely broad and interdisciplinary, 'involving the use of agronomists, ecologists, engineers, economists, sociologists, geographers, cartographers, and many other specialists'.

The most unique feature of the past five years in the Gaspé and lower St Lawrence region has been the encouragement of a continuing dialogue between the research workers and the people of the region through the efforts of a specialized team of twenty 'social animators'. The technique of stimulation and motivation, which is known as *animation sociale* in French, was apparently bolstered by the use of all major means of communication, including group discussions, radio, television, films and special publications. The result of these endeavors was the preparation, by 1966, of a development plan looking ahead to 1982. An agreement for the first five-year period, to 31 March 1973, was signed by the two governments in May, 1968. The plan visualizes an expenditure of nearly $260 million, 80 per cent of which will come from federal revenues. The objectives of the plan include the creation of new activities in manufacturing, mining, and tourism; modernization of the 'traditional' economic sectors of agriculture, fishing, and forestry; accelerated urbanization and regrouping of population in a few well-equipped urban centers; and the establishment of a sound institutional structure for the region.

Conclusions

The Economic Council re-emphasizes the need for 'a more concerted and purposeful attack on poverty'. It states: 'The challenge, in the short run, is to alleviate the conditions which today thrust many Canadian families and individuals into involuntary poverty and hold them there. In the long run, the challenge is to prevent the development of these conditions' (p. 130). The report states that the attack envisaged by the council must be well prepared and comprehensive. It warns that false hopes of easy, short-run triumphs should be avoided, as well as sentimentality which takes the form of gestures in the 'general direction of the poor': 'Compassion there must certainly be, but also a very hard-headed and up-to-date preoccupation with the measurement and evaluation of results. Far from being inconsistent, the two are indispensable elements of a sense of commitment that means to get somewhere' (p. 131).

Since the Council is an economic council, it is inevitable that particular attention is paid in the concluding section of the discussion of poverty in Canada to the lack of information and analysis required to mount a truly comprehensive attack. The report calls for extensive research work by experts from all the social sciences and to some extent from the natural sciences. Nevertheless, there are many highly useful actions which cannot wait 'upon the time-consuming programs of data collection and research'. The council states six general principles which should play an important role in both the short-run and longer-run stages of the future Canadian attack on poverty:

1. The maintenance of high employment and strong and stable

economic growth is crucial. Without success in this regard other antipoverty policies are unlikely to be of much use.

2. No effort should be spared to generate a widespread sense of public commitment to and involvement in the elimination of poverty. This is considered especially necessary in Canada, 'where responsibility for social policy is divided among three levels of government and a multitude of private agencies'. The council calls for the breakdown of barriers and the development of a requisite spirit of intelligent cooperation between governments, private agencies, and the general public. It then states, 'It is of course particularly necessary to involve the poor themselves in the development of programs designed to help them' (p. 132). Emphasis is placed again upon the experience in eastern Quebec for indications of how techniques of "action research" and 'social animation" can be used to foster a community-wide sense of involvement'.

3. Antipoverty policies should have an orientation toward specific groups. In particular, where poverty occurs more in the form of pockets rather than on an area-wide basis, antipoverty policies should have 'a more distinct character of their own'. The council argues that the filtering-down effects of national and regional growth through development policies 'do not constitute an adequate solution to the problem of poverty'.

4. Antipoverty policies should also be strongly oriented toward poor people. Once again the council warns that many programs have missed their target and what is required is a careful identification of poverty groups and a careful evaluation of the impact of policies upon them.

5. The report states that the achievement of a correct blend of income-maintenance policies and other antipoverty policies that seek rather to improve people's capacity to participate more effectively in Canadian economic life is extremely important. Nevertheless, for many people, such as the old and the disabled, income-maintenance policies will continue to be required. Where other policies can be effective, however, in enabling people to participate in the mainstream of economic life, these are greatly to be preferred.

6. In fighting poverty great emphasis should be placed on economic use of available funds and skills and on the maximum development and employment of modern techniques of policy evaluation: 'This is not hard heartedness, but compassionate realism. In a society in which there are large, growing and competing claims on scarce resources, the resources available to fight poverty will always be limited, so that it will always be highly important to see that the greatest possible lasting benefit is achieved for each dollar spent' (pp. 131–3).

In Canada an attack on poverty cannot and does not 'start from scratch'. In some areas, states the council, particularly in income maintenance, 'the coverage of Canadian programs is superior to that of their US counterparts'. It is interesting to note, however, that whereas a number of Americans have recently become much more interested in the possibility of introducing a program of family allowances, in Canada very serious questions are now being raised about the perpetuation of family allowances, which have been paid since 1 July 1945. In fact, the original program under which the mother of every child from birth to age sixteen received a monthly stipend of $6·00 or $8·00, depending on the age of the child, was extended as recently as 1965, with the passage of the Youth Allowances Act. The new legislation provided for a payment of $10·00 per month for children aged sixteen and seventeen, provided that they remained in full-time schooling. Despite the familiarity of the program and the political difficulty of modifying or weakening a popular and well-established universal transfer system, family allowances are coming under very careful scrutiny as Canada begins to study the possibility of 'an income policy' for the 1970s and thereafter.

The council argues that the objectives of certain Canadian programs have not been redefined in the light of changing circumstances. More specifically, it cites family allowances as an example and states: 'It is difficult . . . to discover an authoritative statement of the fundamental objectives of the Family Allowances program in the circumstances of 1968. This is not to say that Family Allowances and other long-established programs are not continuing to serve some highly useful purposes but these purposes should surely be re-examined in the light of the many important economic and social changes that have occurred over the last generation' (p. 135).

Despite several references to the council's intention to state specific antipoverty measures, its analysis of poverty closes with a disappointing reaffirmation of clearly acceptable resolutions and proposals. The report states a series of 'near-term measures' and 'a longer-term strategy'. Under the first category, for example, the council proposes that 'all levels of government should immediately review, clarify and update the objectives of their existing social policies' (p. 135). This is hardly likely, since several of the provinces would find it difficult to indicate what their existing social policies are, if indeed, they do exist. Moreover, there is considerable confusion at the federal level about the place of the social services and welfare programs generally in the 'Just Society' propounded as his personal objective by the new Prime Minister. Thus the council comes out strongly for coordination of social policies through the creation of new organizations within intergovernmental relationships and between public and voluntary agencies. It calls for a systematic exchange of information and increased discussion of basic issues.

On a more promising note, the council insists: 'Greater efforts should at once be made to exploit the considerable antipoverty potential of the Canada Assistance Plan. This applies particularly to the preventive and rehabilitative aspects of the Plan, and its capabilities to aid those whose low income is due, not to a virtual absence of earnings, but to an insufficiency of earnings' (p. 136).[3] The provinces have apparently been slow or even reluctant to take full advantage of the Canada Assistance Plan, perhaps because they can scarcely afford their share of the costs involved. The council argues that the provinces are not feeding sufficient information back to the federal government and that such information is vitally needed for effective exploitation of the plan.

As might be expected, the council urges the federal government

3. The Canada Assistance Plan is the name given to major federal legislation passed in 1966, the effect of which is to sweep away federal–provincial programs of categorical public assistance. Moreover, it enables the provinces to sweep away the 'means test' and to replace it with a 'needs test'. The federal government will pay 50 per cent of all financial assistance and the same proportion of the cost of new administrative procedures and personnel required to implement the plan.

to display more initiative in encouraging the 'development of a small number of pilot projects and intensive research into urban poverty' (p. 136). It stresses action research and social animation among the techniques to be employed. The objectives of research would be both to develop effective research techniques for later general use and 'to obtain a first critical assessment of the effectiveness of the various social policies for which the federal government is at present wholly or partly responsible' (p. 136). The council accepts the statement, which has recently been reiterated in the United States, that it is surprising how little we really know about the nature and extent of poverty.

As far as a longer-term strategy is concerned, the Council calls for a series of innocuous and ingenuous measures. A comprehensive re-appraisal of the structure of all policies, both governmental and private, having a major bearing on the problem of poverty is recommended. The negative income tax and other forms of guaranteed annual income are specifically included. Inevitably, the assessment of social policies with respect to poor people requires a more precise identification of this group of people.

The council further recommends that 'very close attention should be given to the hazards of different antipoverty programs working at cross-purposes' (p. 138). This is indeed a very serious problem in Canada, where the welfare system, like that of the United States, discourages increased earnings by individuals and families in receipt of social assistance. The Canada Pension Plan has been tied to the Consumer Price Index since its inauguration on 1 January 1966, but it is already known that the 2 per cent increase payable in 1969 will be deducted by the provincial governments if the family unit is in receipt of assistance. The poor Canadian family, whether dependent or in receipt of a low earned income, faces innumerable hazards in any attempts to better itself. Policies in the field of public housing are also incriminated in that rents geared to income remove a good deal of the tenant family's incentive to add to its income.

Again, the council calls for 'the maximum feasible use of the more up-to-date analytical methods'. Cost-benefit analysis is urged; experimental methods are recommended; and the report notes with interest the fact that experimental approaches to the payment of a guaranteed income through the use of the negative income tax are under way in New Jersey.[4] The impact of taxation policies upon low-income groups is also recommended for intensive study. Finally, the council affirms that it intends to pursue further research into the problem of poverty in Canada and will be reporting in subsequent annual reviews.

This analysis of a major Canadian examination of the problem of poverty makes it clear that Canada is at least five or six years behind the United States in an attack upon this problem. The Economic Council's enunciation of the nature and extent of poverty in Canada is, nevertheless, extremely important by virtue of the council's prestige and because of the widespread additional publicity given to its forthright statement. Canada has experienced a tremendous economic boom, now extending into the sixth year. Canadians have read and heard much about inflation, shortages of investment capital and very high rates of interest,[5] the housing problem from coast to coast, and the difficulties the provinces now face in implementing the federal program of Medicare. In the course of a lengthy period of prosperity it is all too easy to forget that unemployment has been rising and that a substantial proportion of the population is poor, by any set of criteria. The council's report may thus prove to be a timely and sobering warning.

References

ECONOMIC COUNCIL OF CANADA (1968), *Fifth Annual Review: The Challenge of Growth and Change*, The Queen's Printer, Ottawa.
HARRINGTON, M. (1962), *The Other America*, Macmillan.
JENNESS, R. A. (1965), *The Dimensions of Poverty in Canada*, Ottawa.
ORNATI, O. (1966), *Poverty Amid Affluence*, Twentieth Century Fund.

4. See *Wall Street Journal*, 11 October 1968.
5. The NHA mortgage rate for the first quarter of 1969 is $9\frac{3}{8}$ per cent. It is predicted that it may reach 10 per cent during the year.

12 Brian Abel-Smith and Peter Townsend

The Poor and the Poorest

Excerpts from Brian Abel-Smith and Peter Townsend, *The Poor and the Poorest: A New Analysis of the Ministry of Labour's Family Expenditure Surveys of 1953–4 and 1960*, G. Bell and Sons Ltd, 1965, pp. 6 and 57–67.

During the late 1950s a number of developments seemed to justify a survey of poverty and levels of living in Britain. The problems of the aged showed no signs of diminishing; indeed, the proportionate increase in the numbers in the population who were seventy-five years of age and older gave greater emphasis to the difficulties of isolation and lack of resources. The number of homeless families in London, though relatively small, suddenly began increasing. The proportion of men in middle age who were chronically sick or disabled was increasing slightly but steadily. Official and independent reports drew attention to the social problems of immigrants, caravan-dwellers, fatherless families and low wage-earners with large families. The birth-rate trends of the inter-war years had been reversed. The numbers of families with four or more children were increasing.

Very little precise information about general living conditions existed. Income and expenditure surveys had been carried out mainly for the purposes of analysing consumption patterns and producing price indices and other economic data. Yet before embarking on a major survey of living conditions it seemed right to look again at the data collected in at least some of the surveys to find whether fresh interpretations of a general nature could be made. This study therefore arose from the authors' belief that existing income and expenditure survey data could be re-analysed to produce valuable information about poverty and the social aspects of income distribution.

The Ministry of Labour was approached to find out whether the data collected in the 1953–4 survey and, later, in their 1960 and 1962 surveys, could be made available to us. Facilities were granted in the Ministry's offices in London and Watford and we owe much to the generosity and help of many different officials. [. . .]

Conclusions

The limited object of the work upon which this report is based was to find out from data collected in government income and expenditure surveys in two post-war years as much as possible about the levels of living and the social characteristics of the poorest section of the population in the United Kingdom. In the process we have defined and used a national assistance standard of living, have re-applied a subsistence standard adopted in an earlier study of poverty (by Rowntree and Lavers in 1950), and have given some account of the extent to which households range in income and expenditure from the average for their type. In this chapter we will first of all discuss whether the evidence for 1953–4 and 1960 allows us to draw conclusions about changes in living conditions between the two years. We will then discuss briefly some of the implications of this report for future research, for government information services and for government action.

Changes between 1953–4 and 1960

[As previously described] (Abel-Smith and Townsend, 1965, chapters 3 and 4) the proportions of the population found in 1953–4 and 1960 to have low levels of living, defined as less than 140 per cent of the basic national assistance scale plus rent and/or other housing costs. It is a tenable view that the basic assistance scale, with the addition of *actual* housing expenditure and a modest margin for special needs and disregards, represent the officially defined minimum level of living at a particular time. The data for 1953–4 were calculated from expenditure and the data for 1960 from income. We set out below the results for the two years and *discuss in detail how closely they can be compared.* The matter is complex, not only because expenditure is taken into account in the one year and income in the other but also for methodological reasons. (Set forth in Abel-Smith and Townsend, 1965, chapter 2.) It is worth reviewing carefully because the data represent the best available information about the living standards of poor households in the postwar years.

Table 1 shows the percentages and numbers of the total population recorded as having low levels of living in the two years. The crude figures *suggest* a large increase in both the proportion and number of persons with low levels of living. Under 140 per cent of the basic national assistance scale were 10·1 per cent of the survey households in 1953–4 and 17·9 per cent in 1960. The percentage of persons in these households was 7·8 per cent in 1953–4 and 14·2 per cent in 1960. The largest increase took place at the lower levels and it was at these lower levels that the increase in household size was at its greatest. Under the basic assistance rates, the proportion of households increased from 2·1 to 4·7 per cent and the proportion of persons from 1·2 to 3·8 per cent. The estimated total of persons in households with low levels of living increased from nearly 4 million to nearly 7½ million. The estimated total of persons in households living below the basic assistance scale increased from about 600,000 to about 2,000,000.

Table 1 Percentage of Households and Persons and Number of Persons with Low Levels of Living, 1953–4 and 1960

Total expenditure (1953–4) or income (1960) as percentage of basic NA scale plus rent/housing	Percentage of households		Percentage of persons		Estimated persons in United Kingdom (thousands)	
	1953–4	1960	1953–4	1960	1953–4	1960
Under 80	0·5	1·3	0·3	0·9	152	471
80–89	0·6	1·0	0·2	0·9	101	471
90–99	1·0	2·4	0·7	2·0	354	1048
100–109	1·9	4·7	1·4	2·8	709	1467
110–19	1·7	3·1	1·4	2·4	709	1257
120–29	2·0	2·7	1·8	2·5	911	1310
130–39	2·4	2·8	2·0	2·7	1012	1414
140 and over	89·9	82·1	92·2	85·8	46,663	44,945
Total	100·0	100·0	100·0	100·0	50,611	52,383

In considering these increases let us first review the comparability of the samples for the two years. Both under-represented the sick and aged (and therefore national assistance recipients). But, as shown earlier, the under-representation was greater in 1953–4 than in 1960. The crude figures suggest that the proportion of the population living at less than 40 per cent above the basic assistance scale increased from 7·8 to 14·2 per cent. We calculate that a quarter to a third of the difference can be explained by the difference in the extent to which the two samples represented the United Kingdom population of the two years.

Expenditure and income

Second, was any of the recorded increase in the proportion of households with low levels of living due to adopting an expenditure basis for the analysis of the 1953–4 data and an income basis for the 1960 data? In general expenditure tends to be overstated and income understated in inquiries of this kind, particularly among low income households. Thus one would expect to find too few persons recorded as having low levels of living in 1953 and too many in 1960. Moreover, the aged, who were heavily represented among the poorer households, tend to be dissavers. Again, one would expect expenditure figures recorded over a three week period to be less widely dispersed than income figures, even possibly than *normal* income figures. Thus there would be a higher proportion of households recorded as having *temporary* low income in 1960 than a *more permanently* low expenditure in 1953–4.

Ideally we would have wished to examine for 1960 the relationship between expenditure and 'normal' income for each individual household in the sample. In practice we could only examine this relationship for a sub-sample of 152. In addition we were able to take into account a special analysis of the 60 households in the sample of that year with an income of under 60 shillings, which had been produced by the Ministry. On the basis of the results from this sub-sample we were able to make broad estimates for the whole sample. [. . .] Instead of 17·9 per cent of households, and 14·2 per cent of persons, living below or just above the national assistance standard it emerges that there would have been 15·9 per cent and 12·4 per cent respectively if current expenditure instead of normal income had been taken as the criterion. Instead of nearly seven and a half million persons being in poverty or on its margins there would have been about six and a half millions.

Although the 1960 expenditure estimates must be treated with caution since they are based on a small sub-sample of households investigated in the 1960 survey, two broad conclusions can be drawn. First, the expenditure data confirm the income data in showing an increase between 1953–4 and 1960 in the numbers and proportion of the population living below or just above the national assistance 'standard'. Second, the evidence suggests a marked increase in the proportion living *below* the basic national assistance rates. Although the overall percentage living in poverty or on the margins of poverty is lower according to the expenditure than according to the income criterion, the percentage *below* the scale rate is higher. [. . .]

Reasons for more people living at low levels of living

Part of the increase in the proportion of households with low levels of living seems however to be genuine. The most obvious reason for this is that the proportion of the aged (and particularly the proportion of the very aged) in the population increased between the two years. Between 1953 and 1960, the proportion of the population of the United Kingdom who were aged 65 and over increased from 11·1 to 11·7 per cent. We found that over two-thirds of the households with low expenditure in the 1953–4 survey had retired heads. A second reason is the increase in the proportion of large families in the population.

Table 2 Percentage of Households of Different Size with Low Levels of Living, 1953–4 and 1960

Number of persons in household	1953–4 (low expenditure)	1960 (low income)
1	38·6	52·1
2	9·6	18·2
3	4·9	7·5
4	4·6	6·4
5	5·4	10·0
6+	11·5	25·2
All sizes	10·1	17·9

In Table 2 we show the percentage of households of different size recorded as having low levels of living in the two years.

Among households of every size the proportion with low levels of living increased. The proportion of two-person households nearly doubled. The proportional increase was smaller for households of three or four persons and smallest for one-person households where the proportion with low expenditure was already nearly 39 per cent in 1953–4. The largest increase was among the very large households with six or more persons. There were 11½ per cent of such households with low levels of living in 1953–4 and 25 per cent in 1960.

The age distribution of persons in households with low levels of living is shown in Table 3.

Table 3 Age Distribution of Persons with Low Levels of Living 1953–4 and 1960

| Household expenditure (1953–4) or income (1960) as percentage of basic national assistance scale plus rent/housing | Year | Age | | | |
		Over 16	5–15	Under 5	All ages
Under 100	1953–4	83·1	10·5	6·4	100·0
	1960	66·9	21·1	12·0	100·0
100–119	1953–4	68·3	23·2	8·5	100·0
	1960	79·7	14·6	5·7	100·0
120–39	1953–4	69·1	19·6	11·3	100·0
	1960	62·2	25·3	12·5	100·0
All under 140	1953–4	70·9	19·5	9·6	100·0
	1960	69·9	20·2	9·9	100·0

In general there was a modest increase in the proportion of children in the sampled households with low levels of living from 29·1 to 30·1 per cent. This concealed bigger changes at the different levels. There was in fact a fall in the proportion of children at and just above the assistance level from 31·7 to 20·3 per cent. This was more than balanced partly by an increase in the proportion of children at the higher level but also, and perhaps more importantly, by a greater increase in the proportion of children in households under the assistance level – from 16·9 to 33·1 per cent. Too much weight should not however be placed upon these figures in view of the small numbers involved in many of these categories.

Between 1953 and 1960, the proportion of children increased by about 0·5 per cent in both the total population and in the samples. The proportion of children in households with low levels of living increased by 1 per cent. These modest changes conceal much larger changes in family size. While the total population increased by 3·5 per cent between the two years, the number of families with four dependent children increased by about 20 per cent, with five children by about 26 per cent and with six or more children by 45 per cent.[1] Moreover, the economic position of large families was relatively worse in 1960 than in 1953. While we have shown that the general level of incomes of the country increased by just over 50 per cent in money terms, the family allowance for the second child remained at 8 shillings in both years, while the family allowance for a third or subsequent children increased from 8 shillings to 10 shillings – an increase of only 25 per cent. No doubt the failure of family allowances to keep pace with the living standards of the community contributed to the higher proportion of households found to have low levels of living in 1960 than in 1953–4. But in view of the fact that only 14 per cent of low income households were found in 1960 consisting of a man, woman and three or more children, the changing size and economic position of the family can only have accounted for an increase of 3 or 4 per cent in the proportion of households with low levels of living.

A third reason for the recorded increase in the proportion of the population with low levels of living was the increase in the proportion dependent for long periods on sickness benefits. This is partly due to the relative increase in the proportion of the population aged between 55 and 65 and also to the relative increase in the proportions of men in this age-group who are chronically sick.

In addition to the increases in the proportions of the aged, of large families and of the chronic sick, we cannot exclude the possibility that although *average* earnings increased by about 50 per cent, the lowest earnings increased by less than 50 per cent.

1. Calculated from statistics on family allowances given in the Ministry of Pensions and National Insurance Reports for 1953 and 1960.

Definitions of poverty

What implications does this analysis hold for the future? First, much more thought needs to be given to concepts of poverty. The subsistence standards used by earlier writers on poverty seem at first sight to lend themselves to comparisons over time. This approach allows a basket of foodstuffs and other goods to be defined as necessary to provide subsistence. The cost of purchasing these goods can be calculated for different years and the number of households with insufficient income to purchase the goods can be ascertained. Although the principle seems easy to state, there are problems of applying it in practice. For example, the goods on the market at the later period may not be the same as at the earlier period. The cumbrous garments which convention required women to wear at the beginning of this century were unlikely to be found on the market in the 1930s let alone today. Electricity has replaced oil lamps and candles. Even food habits have changed. These are among the problems which face those who attempt to apply the same poverty line at different periods. Again, the choice of goods that are selected initially cannot be defended in narrowly 'physical' or 'nutritional' terms. In laying down what articles of clothing and items of food are necessary for physical efficiency those in charge of the surveys have been unable to prevent judgements about what is conventional or customary from creeping into their lists and definitions.

There are further kinds of difficulties. There is, for example, a difference between defining poverty in any objective or partly objective sense and defining it subjectively – as felt by the individual or by particular social groups. In any objective sense the word has no absolute meaning which can be applied in all societies at all times. Poverty is a relative concept. Saying who is in poverty is to make a relative statement – rather like saying who is short or heavy. But it is also a statement of a much more complex kind than one referring to a unilineal scale of measurement. It refers to a variety of conditions involving differences in home environment, material possessions and educational and occupational resources as well as in financial resources – most of which are measurable, at least in principle. Income or expenditure as defined in this paper should be regarded as only one of the possible indicators.

Brian Abel-Smith and Peter Townsend 145

We need to develop other indicators of the command of individuals and families over resources. Our frame of reference can be local, national or international society, according to our interests. In saying all this we are saying nothing new. The fact that poverty is essentially a relative concept and essentially one which refers to a variety of conditions and not simply a financial condition has been accepted overtly or implicitly by leading writers on the subject almost as long as poverty studies have been undertaken.

Implications of government information and research

Reports on government surveys of the population still contain far too little social information about the poorest sections of the population. This is true not only of the family expenditure surveys, but also of nutrition surveys.[2] Despite searching public criticisms of the analysis of nutritional data the National Food Survey Committee has failed to provide information about families with children, particularly large families, falling short of the standards recommended by the British Medical Association. No government can expect to pursue rational policies in social security and welfare unless information about living conditions, particularly the living conditions of the poor, is regularly collected, analysed and reported.

The first aim should be to develop various standards which indicate need or poverty. Budgets necessary to purchase minimum nutrition, of the kind developed by the United States Department of Agriculture,[3] might be worked out. The environmental, including housing, resources of families might be more carefully assessed, as also the social and other resources, they require to overcome disability.

The second aim should be to collect information regularly and publish annual reports. It would of course be possible to publish a report complementary to that on the Family Expenditure Survey, showing the sources of income, incomes and expenditures of households receiving certain kinds of social benefits, or of

2. See for example, the latest Annual Report of the National Food Survey Committee (1964).

3. Though we hope certain technical criticisms might be overcome. See US Department of Agriculture (1962) and Household Food Consumption Service (1957).

particular kinds of household known to have exceptional social and financial problems – fatherless families, large families or the families of the long-term unemployed. The Central Statistical Office has carried out some useful analyses of redistribution, based on the expenditure surveys, but they give emphasis to overall trends rather than the particular circumstances of poor families as related to middle-income or wealthy families. Government sources in the United States are now publishing very informative analyses of poverty in that country. Perhaps in time the same might be possible in the United Kingdom.

The third aim should be to carry out some immediate inquiries into the information about the relationship between income and expenditure, as collected in family expenditure surveys. In addition, more needs to be known about non-respondents. We believe that such inquiries would help to ensure that future family expenditure surveys can be reliably used to depict the socio-economic conditions of particular groups of the population.

Implications for policy

One conclusion that can be drawn from both surveys is that national assistance is inefficient. While it is impossible to give precise figures it is clear that substantial numbers in the population were not receiving national assistance in 1953–4 and 1960 and yet seemed, *prima facie*, to qualify for it. In the latter year, for example, there were nearly one million persons who had pensions or other state benefits and whose incomes fell below assistance rates plus rent.

This national evidence is extremely important and confirms what has been concluded from independent studies, particularly of the aged, in recent years. It is given greater force by the unambiguous statement in the recent report of a Government committee of inquiry into the impact of rates on households: 'We estimate that about half a million retired householders are apparently eligible for assistance but not getting it.'

This is not the place for a searching discussion of reforms in social security. All that we wish to point out is that there is a twofold implication for social policy of the evidence in this report – not only that a substantial minority of the population in addition to those receiving national assistance live at or below national assistance standards, but also that a substantial minority are not receiving national assistance and yet appear to qualify for it. The legitimacy of the system of national assistance is therefore called into question.

Possibly the most novel finding is the extent of poverty among children. For over a decade it has been generally assumed that such poverty as exists is found overwhelmingly among the aged. Unfortunately it has not been possible to estimate from the data used in this study exactly how many persons over minimum pensionable age were to be found among the $7\frac{1}{2}$ million persons with low income in 1960. However, such data as we have suggest that the number may be around 3 millions. There were thus more people who were not aged than were aged among the poor households of 1960. We have estimated earlier that there were about $2\frac{1}{4}$ million children in low income households in 1960. Thus quantitatively the problem of poverty among children is more than two-thirds of the size of poverty among the aged. This fact has not been given due emphasis in the policies of the political parties. It is also worth observing that there were substantially more children in poverty than adults of working age.

There is a simple if relatively expensive remedy for the problem of poverty among children – to substantially increase family allowances, particularly for the larger family. Alternatively, part of the problem could be dealt with at relatively low cost by allowing national assistance to be drawn despite the fact that the breadwinner is receiving full-time earnings. Such a proposal would mean overriding more than a century of conventional wisdom about incentives. However assistance is paid to families receiving full-time earnings in several States in the United States and this policy enjoys the tacit support of the American trade unions. The acceptance of this principle would make it possible to deal with the problem of poverty among 'wage stopped' families already receiving assistance and among large families with a breadwinner in full-time work. In the case of the latter group, however, there would remain the problem of families who were not prepared to apply to the Board for help.

Summary

... Between 1953 and 1960 the Ministry of Labour surveys suggest that the number of persons living at low levels increased from 7·8 per cent to 14·2 per cent. Of the difference of 6·4 per cent we would estimate that about 1½ per cent was due to a better representation in the sample of aged persons in 1960 than in 1953 and another 0·5 or 1 per cent to a fuller representation in the sample of national assistance recipients other than the aged. Very little of the difference seems to be due to a change, relative to wages, in the definition of 'low levels of living', but part of it (about 2 per cent) seems to be due to the fact that the definition was based on income in 1960 and expenditure in 1953–4. Nonetheless, some part of the apparent increase from 7·8 to 14·2 per cent seems attributable to:

1. The relative increase in the number of old people in the population

2. A slight relative increase in the number of men in late middle age who are chronically sick, and

3. The relative increase in the number of families with four or more children, at a time when family allowances have increased much less than average industrial earnings and when the wages of some low-paid workers may not have increased as much as average industrial earnings.

On the whole the data we have presented contradicts the commonly held view that a trend towards greater equality has accompanied the trend towards greater affluence.

In general, we regard our figures for 1960 to be the more accurate even though we believe that they understate the numbers of the population with low levels of living because of the under-representation of the aged and the sick. We may summarize our findings for that year by saying that about 5–6 per cent of the population were in low income households because wages, even when supplemented by family allowances, were insufficient to raise them above the minimum level. A further 3–4 per cent were in households receiving social insurance benefits (principally pensions) but the latter were insufficient. Many such households would probably be entitled to national assistance but for various reasons had not applied for it. A further 4–5 per cent of the population were in low income households because, under various regulations, they were not entitled to the full scale of national assistance grant or because the minimum we have taken is considerably above the *basic* national assistance scale.

Even if we take a substantially lower base line – the basic assistance scale plus rent – we find that about 2 million people (3·8 per cent of the population) were living in households with exceptionally low incomes. For about a quarter of them the problem was inadequate earnings and family allowances; for nearly half of them the problem was inadequate social insurance benefits coupled with unwillingness to apply for national assistance, and for the remainder the amount of national assistance being received was apparently inadequate.

In terms of national information we conclude from the evidence that steps should be taken by the government to ensure that regular surveys are made of the living conditions of the poorest households in our society and that reports should be published showing their sources of income and how their social characteristics compare with those of other households.

Finally, we conclude that the evidence of substantial numbers of the population living below national assistance level, and also of substantial numbers seeming to be eligible for national assistance but not receiving it, calls for a radical review of the whole social security scheme. Moreover, the fact that nearly a third of the poor were children suggests the need for a readjustment of priorities in plans for extensions and developments.

References

ANNUAL REPORT OF THE NATIONAL FOOD SURVEY COMMITTEE (1964), *Domestic Food Consumption and Expenditure, 1962*, HMSO.

HOUSEHOLD FOOD CONSUMPTION SERVICE (1957), *Food Consumption and Dieting Basis of Households in the US*, Spring 1955, ARS 62 6.

US DEPARTMENT OF AGRICULTURE (1962), *Family Food Plans and Food Costs*, Agricultural Research Service, Home Economics Research Report no. 20.

Part Three
Problems of Roots and Remedies

The selections in this section deal with several broad topics related to the causes of poverty and their solution: underdevelopment–economic growth, overpopulation–population control, and unequal distribution–redistribution of income, wealth, and services.

The excerpt from the *World Economic Survey* (1968), stresses the interdependence of these political, social, and economic factors in achieving a better level of living for the world's people, although it gives prime importance to economic growth. W. Arthur Lewis in 'Unemployment in Developing Countries', discusses some of the problems and disappointments experienced by poor countries as they implement development plans. His interest in urban unemployment leads him to consider the relationship between the urban, industrial sector of the economy and the rural, agricultural sector and the implications of this relationship for development.

David Horowitz points out a common problem of the underdeveloped countries: their lack of capital for investment in enterprises which would improve their productive capacity. Because the methods used for accumulation of capital by the Western industrial nations in the eighteenth and nineteenth centuries are inappropriate to the poor countries, he proposes a scheme for the transfer of capital to them by the developed nations, to their mutual advantage. The essay, *'The crisis in aid: facts and perspective'*, indicates some of the misconceptions about the extent of foreign aid to underdeveloped nations and suggests that the ways in which this aid has been given have made it difficult for its recipients to achieve the hoped-for economic growth.

'Common market' arrangements among poor countries have been seen as a means of efficient use of available capital, assuring markets for goods, and meeting competition from the rich nations. Christopher Eckenstein assesses the feasibility of these proposals in the light of various political, social and economic considerations.

It is commonly believed, based on even the most optimistic projections, that economic growth will not be sufficient to eliminate world poverty if population growth is not severely curtailed. Georg Borgstrom is among those holding this opinion, as he asserts, 'The human race long ago exceeded the limits of what the world can feed.' Although his focus is also on population control, Philip Hauser takes a more moderate view, calling for efforts both to reduce fertility and to increase economic productivity. He argues that rapid population growth contributes to continuing poverty in two ways. In the long run, it impedes economic development which would raise the standard of living. In the short run, it increases the number of persons who must share the world's limited resources. Keith Buchanan doubts that world hunger is 'the result of procreative recklessness on the part of the people of the Third World'. Instead, he sees poverty as the result of the concentration of 75 per cent of the world's wealth in the hands of 30 per cent of the population and views the concern for overpopulation as masking a desire to maintain this unequal balance.

The excerpts from *Social Policy and the Distribution of Income in the Nation* (1969) indicate the general agreement that great inequality of income within nations perpetuates poverty and retards economic growth. The report emphasizes redistributive measures which stimulate economic progress, although it is also concerned with measures whose aims are humanitarian rather than economic. The conclusions of Felix Paukert's comparative study of the redistributive effects of social security programmes in developed and underdeveloped countries illustrate the observation in the United Nations report that government service programmes may not redistribute wealth and income even when they are undertaken with the intention of doing so.

The concluding selection, 'China Story', recounts the means through which China has made extraordinary progress in eliminating poverty. Among the factors in China's development which suggest a model for poor nations to consider are: a unique emphasis on and approach to agricultural development rather than industrialization and preoccupation with the urban sector (which have been the cornerstones of Western capitalistic and Soviet-bloc plans), self-help, and decentralization through communes.

13 United Nations

World Economic Survey

Excerpt from United Nations, *World Economic Survey*, 1968, pp. 3–8.

The synthesis of social and economic policies

If there is any criticism of general validity which can be levelled against postwar discussions of development, it is the compartmentalization of political, social and economic policies. Social thinkers have long recognized the profound importance of political and social changes for economic growth; and they have been no less aware of the converse influence of economic trends on social and political relations within society. In most discussions of development policies, and in many development plans, however, measures to bring about social changes conducive to development have played only a peripheral role. Attention has focused on economic measures directly relating to the level and composition of output, investment and foreign trade, while social and political policies have remained matters for separate consideration. It is being increasingly understood that a strategy for economic development cannot be formulated within these limited confines. As a deliberate objective of national policy, economic development is not a limited aim to be accomplished within an unchanging political and social structure any more than it is a short-term aim to be reached within a few years.

A first condition of development is its acceptance as a political goal. This might seem unnecessary to state since economic growth is universally acclaimed as a proper objective of government. It is part of the present dissatisfaction with much postwar discussion of development, however, that it has not been distinguished from economic growth. Development, as now conceived, is an objective with broad social significance. It is surely true that the power which the concept of development exercises over the imagination of men and women draws much of its strength from the great egalitarian ideals with which most political and social philosophies are imbued. The vision of economic development would be far less imposing were it not for the conviction – born of the immense advances in science and technology – that the opportunity of a better material life can be placed within reach of the great masses of the people. Acceptance of development as a political aim thus puts a broader construction on the purpose of economic policy. Its aim is not only greater output, but changes in the level, composition and distribution of output which lead to improvements in the present and future welfare of the community at large. Thus, the many political problems which have economic origins, such as the social tensions generated by disparities in economic well-being or opportunity among regional or racial groups or classes, are not issues to be regarded as diverting policy from its main purpose of economic growth; on the contrary, they are the very kinds of problems which must be tackled by development policy.

Only one or two decades ago, it might have been possible to accept this broad social purpose of development while concentrating attention on measures of a directly economic nature. It seemed valid to argue that, if an adequate rate of economic growth could be attained – even though its benefits might be immediately confined to narrow segments of the community – social aims could be met through taxation and redistribution of income in the form of social welfare programmes. As understanding of the nature and causes of development has broadened, however, this limited view of social aims and policies has appeared increasingly unsatisfactory. There is now widespread agreement that, if broad-based economic development is to take place, policies to alter and improve social conditions are of fundamental importance. It is the institutions and attitudes conditioning the economic behaviour of the population which, first and foremost, mark the difference between a stagnant and a dynamic economy. Measures to change the distribution of income and wealth, or social programmes for health and education, are not simply desirable in themselves on grounds of social equity or common humanity; they are necessary means of strengthening the incentive, motivation and ability of the population to seek ways of raising output through work, investment and innovation. Thus, social measures can no longer be regarded as separate actions directed toward separate ends; they are also themselves instruments of a strategy for development. The fusion of social and economic measures into a common strategy for development is, however, far from being generally achieved; and a closer synthesis of the two kinds of policy is a major task of development strategy for the coming decade.

Some social policies

Probably the most important social change necessitated by development must take place in the forms of social organization which govern the nature and direction of economic activity. The traditional system of property relations in predominantly agrarian societies has long been recognized to be generally inimical to development. For the introduction of more efficient methods of production, new forms of organization have to be established. This process of institutional change is necessary not only in agriculture but throughout the various branches of economic activity. It is not solely the shortage of financial resources or of skilled manpower which impedes the application of modern science and technology to productive activity; it is also the lack of productive entities with the organizational span and incentives to exploit more modern methods. Thus, a fundamental task of development strategy is to replace the traditional forms of social organization resistant to change with new and more dynamic kinds of productive organization.

A principal means of accomplishing this is by reform of the system of rewards and penalties influencing productive activity. There is room for wide disagreement on what may constitute the appropriate relation between reward and effort, but there is little doubt that in many developing countries the institutional conditions determining the distribution of income and wealth cause major distortions in this relation. Income and effort are not closely related, and the incentive to intensify productive activity is accordingly impaired. This, moreover, is true not only of the incentive to work but also of the incentive to save and invest in productive activity. It has often been assumed than an inequitable distribution of income and wealth should facilitate a rising trend in the level of domestic saving and investment, since higher income groups tend to save a larger proportion of their incomes. But the distribution of income and wealth itself also constitutes the system of rewards for productive activity, and if it offers insufficient incentives to work and innovation, the rising level of saving and investment characteristic of a dynamic economy cannot be expected to materialize. Thus, institutional and fiscal reforms to strengthen the incentives to work, save and invest should be at the forefront of a strategy for development.

This question assumes particular importance in the rural areas where farmers and peasants are deprived of the incentive to raise output through onerous tenurial systems, as in many Asian and Latin American countries, or through the social obligations imposed by the extended family system, as in many African countries. Reform of the systems of land ownership and tenure has long been recognized as a necessary step. The task, however, should also be conceived more broadly as the development of new forms of organization for economic activity in the rural areas. The need is for the provision of adequate incentives for cultivators to work and invest, not only through such means as land redistribution or the provision of security of tenure, but also through the establishment of an infrastructure of services for marketing, credit, extension activities and distribution of input. In fact, there is no necessary presumption that the new systems of farming should take the form of peasant small holdings supported by an infrastructure of services. They can take many different forms, ranging from various types of collective or large-scale farming systems to individual small holdings. An imaginative and flexible approach to new forms of economic organization in the rural areas is clearly desirable if farming systems are to be suited to the technical requirements of the crops to be grown, as well as to provide adequate incentives to cultivators.

Hardly less fundamental than changes in the forms of social organization and the strengthening of incentives is the development of new attitudes and skills among the population. In recent years, the pervasive role of education in the transformation of society has come to be a familiar theme in general discussions of development. The revision of attitudes towards education and their translation into new educational programmes, however, have hardly begun. It is to be hoped that the reappraisal started in the

1960s presages more radical changes in educational policies during the coming decade.

It has to be recognized that, at least at present, empirical knowledge concerning the relation of education to development is quite limited; and it offers only partial guidance to decisions on educational policy. No one doubts that the increasing supply of trained people, at various levels of skills, is necessary to support economic development. Research over the last few decades has yielded convincing evidence that labour productivity and the extension of education are interrelated developments. And it is certainly true that decisions on educational policy can be usefully aided by manpower planning; forward estimates of future requirements of skilled manpower at least indicate the minimum expansion required in educational systems, particularly in training high-level and skilled manpower. Such planning is essential if appropriate action is to be taken to correct the undue orientation towards general education at the expense of technical education frequently observed in educational programmes at the secondary and tertiary levels.

Education, however, should not be considered solely as a means of providing skilled manpower. This does not adequately encompass the broader, if less easily measurable, influence which education may have on development by inducing changes in attitudes, increasing social flexibility, and enhancing the receptivity of the population to social and economic change. To evaluate the significance of education in this regard, reliance can only be placed on broad social judgements. In current thinking, however, the general view is that broad-based programmes of education merit very high priority in development strategy, since they can serve as the principal means of overcoming age-old customs resistant to change, instilling a new spirit of innovation, and encouraging the adoption of more modern techniques and new forms of organization of productive activity.

The expansion of educational programmes – as rapid as resources permit – appears an essential element of long-term development strategy. In most developing countries, expenditure on education is, in fact, one of the fastest growing components of the national budget. However, increased resources are not the sole, or even the main, requisite in most developing countries. It is a widespread criticism of current educational programmes that they display much evidence of waste and that they are poorly adapted to the purposes of general social and economic development. In many countries, if education is to be an instrument of development strategy, the reform of educational programmes to heighten their quality and relevance is at least as important as their expansion.

A major criticism of established educational systems is their comparative neglect of adult education and training. The value of educating the young may be greatly diminished if the society in which they live is not itself undergoing social and economic change; the stream of new economic opportunities, and the receptivity of the community to new ways, must be progressively widening. This brings programmes for adult education and training, such as functional literacy programmes, to the forefront of educational policy. As has been recommended at a ministerial conference of the United Nations Educational, Scientific and Cultural Organization (UNESCO), these programmes merit higher priority than the further extension of primary education if current development appears to be impeded by illiteracy or lack of skills among adults.

Other social policies besides educational programmes or measures for introducing a more efficient distribution of income and wealth are necessary to create a social framework more conducive to development. Despite the progress made in recent decades, mortality rates are still high in many countries of the world and debilitating diseases are prevalent. Reduction of the mortality rates and improvement in general levels of health among the population are elementary objectives of social policy, and a condition of changing attitudes and strengthening motivations in regard to economic activity. The introduction or expansion of family planning programmes similarly offers a major means of improving the welfare of the family. There is evidence that attitudes favourable to the limitation of family size are present among parents in many developing countries. If, along with other social measures, family planning programmes could be successfully expanded over the coming decade to initiate a downward trend in birth-rates, this would decidedly enhance the long-term prospects for improvements in welfare.

Agricultural and industrial development

Policies for agricultural and industrial growth are principal economic issues in a strategy for development. Fortunately, at the inception of the decade of the 1970s, little remains to be said on the long controversy over the relative emphasis to be placed on agriculture and industry. The experience of the last two decades, in which agriculture frequently acted as a brake on general economic growth, has amply demonstrated the complementary nature of these two sectors. However, though this issue has been largely settled between the two activities, the same cannot be said of policies for development within agriculture or industry.

Over the first half of the present decade, food production in developing countries as a whole failed to keep pace with the growth of population. While a new optimism concerning agricultural development has emerged in more recent years, particularly in Asia, following successful innovation of the new high-yielding varieties of grains, aided by favourable monsoons, it would be dangerous to believe that the problem of agricultural development is anywhere near solution. It may be pointed out that, if developing countries were to attain a minimum rate of growth of 6 to 7 per cent by 1980, the annual rate of increase in demand for food might then be expected to be about 4 per cent; and this substantially exceeds any rate of growth in production so far generally achieved. Estimates suggest that even a more modest growth in food output of about 3 per cent per annum would demand very considerable, and continuous, improvements in farming practices.

The development of agriculture has proved to be the most intractable problem confronting Governments of many developing countries. The forces making for a dynamic agriculture are numerous and complex; and the most effective measures are neither easy to identify nor to execute. Over much of the postwar period, discussions of agricultural policy have been characterized by a tendency to single out one or another measure as of strategic importance; land reform, price policy, credit supplies, extension work, and, more recently, technological improvements, have been among the main measures which have been separately stressed. There is an emerging consensus, however, that such partial approaches to the problem of agricultural development are not a sufficient basis for agricultural policy. The transformation of a traditional, and largely subsistence, agriculture into a dynamic, commercial farming system requires a complex of institutional, technical and economic changes; and these changes should be viewed as complementary, being mutually reinforcing in their effects on production.

This comprehensive approach confronts developing countries with a dilemma. The financial, technical and administrative resources are generally far too scarce to permit the adoption of such an approach on a country-wide scale. Comprehensive programmes to implement a full range of institutional, technical and economic measures could only be attempted for selected areas, and even this might require some curtailment of programmes elsewhere. There is no wholly satisfactory solution to this dilemma other than the provision of increased resources. It has been suggested, however, that while the various measures necessary for agricultural development are broadly complementary, they are also, to some extent, substitutable at the margin, at least in the short-run. Thus, by means of a comprehensive analysis, it is possible to identify the more immediate constraints on output and to construct a programme of action in which the whole range of necessary measures have their place in an orderly sequence. Throughout agricultural policies, the keynote clearly must be adaptation and experiment based on the informed analysis of local difficulties and opportunities.

As in agriculture, developing countries will have to accelerate their industrial development in the coming decade if the pace of general economic growth is to be quickened. The attainment of a minimum rate of economic growth of 6 to 7 per cent by 1980 might well necessitate a rate of increase in industrial output amounting to 8 to 9 per cent. Over the first seven years of the 1960s, industrial output in the developing countries as a whole rose by 6·5 per cent per annum.

Policies for industrialization have been undergoing re-evaluation in the recent past. More specifically, concern has been expressed about the efficiency of the emerging structure of industrial production in many countries. The establishment of new industries has often been determined more by the play of circumstances than by the deliberate exercise of policy measures; and there is frequent evidence of industries emerging behind highly protective barriers which have little prospect of operating at reasonable cost. While it was not an uncommon belief in the earlier postwar years that such industrialization could be justified on the grounds that increased domestic production of manufactures would lessen the foreign exchange constraint on overall growth, events have not borne out this view. Industrialization has brought about changes in the composition of imports, but as total income and output have grown, the demand for total imports has risen commensurately, or often, more than commensurately. Thus, the more industrialized of the developing countries have increasingly emphasized the importance of enlarging their export trade in manufactures; and this has turned attention to domestic industrial costs.

If some of the past mistakes of industrialization are to be avoided in the years to come, many countries will need to formulate more deliberate policies for industrial development that take account of the relative efficiency of new industries. It must be stressed, however, that there is no standard pattern of industrialization on which individual countries can model their policies. Not general precepts, but analysis of the specific constraints and opportunities confronting general development in each country should be the foundation of a strategy for industrialization.

The promotion of a more efficient pattern of industrialization implies a measure of specialization within individual countries; and the corollary to such specialization is an expanding volume of imports of manufactures. The ability to implement policies for efficient industrial development thus depends, not only on the individual countries themselves, but also on the possibilities of expanding trade with other countries. The granting by developed countries of non-reciprocal tariff preferences to manufactures from developing countries as recommended by the United Nations Conference on Trade and Development (UNCTAD) would clearly be important in this context. This also emphasizes the significance of the endeavours on the part of groups of developing countries to promote regional economic co-operation among themselves.

This problem of efficient industrial growth presents itself in a particularly acute form among the smaller developing countries. The number of such countries is large; there are, for instance, about sixty member states of the United Nations with populations of less than 10 million each. Once beyond its earliest stages, efficient industrialization in these countries is restricted by the smallness of the domestic market unless specialization through foreign trade can be developed. It is true that the size of the domestic market is not static and could often be appreciably enlarged through a more equitable distribution of income and greater rural development; and it is also true that possibilities for exports of manufactures to world markets could sometimes be exploited through more vigorous export promotion policies. Generally, however, closer regional cooperation offers the most promising solution for most of these countries.

The use of resources for development

The policies for the various social and economic sectors which have been discussed above form the main substance of a strategy for development. It is within the framework set by these policies that decisions can be reached about the allocation of the financial resources available for development programmes. To make the most effective use of these scarce resources is, in the main, a task of strengthening these sectoral policies. Sectoral policies have, of course, to be assessed in combination as well as separately and this is a principal function of national development planning. But no amount of planning in broad aggregates at the national level can compensate for the absence of sound policies and programmes within sectors. In most developing countries, a principal weakness in planning is still the lack of sufficient social, economic and technical information and analysis relating to the specific difficulties and opportunities that confront development programmes within specific sectors. The continued broadening of social and economic research, of technical surveys and of pre-investment studies in general is thus essential for the construction of more effective policies.

The more effective use of productive resources for development is, however, not only a question of the allocation of the resources available for investment. There is the larger, and much more problematic, issue of how to absorb the growing labour force more fully into productive activity. This, of course, is not merely an economic problem; it is also a social issue of major dimensions.

Because of the acceleration of population growth over the last two decades, developing countries are going to be faced in the coming decade with a dramatic increase in the number of young people seeking some form of gainful employment. The population of working age in the developing regions has been increasing at about 2·3 per cent per annum in the present decade, and this rate is likely to accelerate to 2·7 per cent in the 1970s. To absorb such growing numbers of young people into employment would be exceedingly difficult in itself. The problem, however, is compounded by the widespread unemployment and underemployment that now prevails.

It cannot be said that any comprehensive solution to this crucial problem lies readily to hand. Indeed, the issue has not received the attention its social importance demands. It has been suggested, however, that Governments could at least take the question of employment much more systematically into account in the formulation and execution of their policies affecting investment. It has long been maintained by many economists that, in view of the scarcity of capital and the plentiful supply of labour, developing countries should, wherever practicable, give preference to the use of labour-intensive techniques in their investment programmes. This is not to be mistaken for a prescription in favour of exclusive or even primary reliance upon labour-intensive industries. The structure of industrial production should quite properly be based on other considerations besides the supply of labour and capital, and the use of capital-intensive technologies is inescapable in many branches of production. Nonetheless, opportunities to vary the choice of technique do exist in most countries, and the deliberate use of measures to exploit these opportunities has generally not been practised. It appears probable, however, that agriculture provides one of the main areas for a greater enlargement of employment opportunities in most developing countries; and in this sector, the promotion of labour-intensive methods to raise output is not simply a question of the use of alternative techniques, but the reform of institutional conditions to establish or expand labour-intensive systems of farming.

The volume of domestic and external resources

If developing countries are progressively to enlarge the various social and economic programmes necessary for the acceleration of development, they must be able to command an increasing volume of resources to finance current public expenditure, investment and exports. Estimates of the resources which would be needed for an appreciable acceleration of economic growth leave no doubt that their mobilization constitutes a major challenge to policy in the coming decade.

Preliminary estimates suggest that, if developing countries were to attain a minimum rate of growth in output of 6 to 7 per cent by 1980, the share of investment in gross domestic product might have to increase from about 15 per cent in 1965 to about 20 per cent in 1980. If domestic saving in the developing countries were to grow in accordance with historical trends, the share of saving in gross domestic product might increase from about 14 per cent in 1965 to about 18 per cent in 1980. There would thus be a shortfall in the resources required for investment which would have to be met by stronger action to raise the level of domestic saving, by a greater inflow of foreign capital, or by some combination of both.

Many developing countries could undoubtedly do more to raise levels of domestic saving; and in this context, as mentioned above, policies to change the distribution of income and wealth constitute a relevant, though often neglected, line of action. Besides the constraint imposed on economic growth by the supply of savings, however, most developing countries are confronted by the limitation arising from foreign exchange scarcity; and, on the evidence of historical trends, the shortfall in foreign exchange earnings below likely import requirements generally appears to represent the greater barrier to accelerated economic growth. Preliminary estimates suggest that, if developing countries were to attain a minimum rate of growth in output of 6 to 7 per cent by 1980, a small group of these countries might record a foreign exchange surplus. A much larger group, however, could be faced by 1980 with a foreign exchange gap of about $25 billion to $30 billion, which would amount to 6 to 7 per cent of their own gross domestic product.

These estimates indicate the high importance of the policies of developed countries for the acceleration of economic growth in the developing regions. An expanding volume of imports is crucial for their development; and the rate at which imports can be increased is a significant determinant of their pace of overall growth.

The need for more liberal trade policies on the part of developed countries has been a familiar theme of discussion in UNCTAD and other international bodies over recent years. There can be little doubt, however, that until such time as much greater changes in the structure of domestic production and exports have been effected, most developing countries will need an inflow of foreign capital to supplement their earnings from primary commodity exports.

At the outset of the present Development Decade, the economically advanced countries agreed that 1 per cent of their income and output should be devoted to international assistance. Progress towards the fulfilment of this aim on the part of most donor countries has been disappointing. After a sharp increase at the turn of the decade, the flow of official and private capital from the developed market economies rose at an annual average rate of 4·5 per cent between 1961 and 1967; and present indications are that the volume of assistance is now tending to level off. This trend, moreover, has been accompanied by a rising level of debt service payments borne by the developing countries; and debt service payments on official and officially guaranteed funds in 1967 were equivalent to 42 per cent of the outflow of these funds in that year. At the same time, the terms on which new assistance is extended have not, in general, been relaxed but have tended to harden.

In some important respects, however, there has been significant progress in improving the effectiveness of international assistance. Consistent with the greater appreciation of the role of non-investment factors in development, is a better understanding of economic assistance as something more than a means of supplementing domestic resources for investment or of alleviating foreign exchange scarcity; and an increasing proportion of assistance has been taking the form of programme aid. Such assistance is better suited to the financing of the various types of development expenditure now recognized to be as important as fixed investment in promoting growth. Closer coordination of the aid programmes of donor countries through such means as consortia and consultative groups has also helped to improve the effectiveness of this assistance. On the other hand, aid-tying and the inability of most donor countries to make aid commitments extending beyond a fiscal year have continued to restrict the flexibility of aid programmes.

While further improvements in the quality of external assistance programmes are undoubtedly needed, it is the volume of assistance which nonetheless remains the central issue. Developing countries today are better placed to execute the policies and programmes necessary for development than they were at the commencement of the present decade. It would be singularly unfortunate if, at the onset of the Second Development Decade, developed countries failed to support their efforts with a growing volume of external assistance in line with agreed targets.

14 David Horowitz

The Abolition of Poverty

Excerpts from David Horowitz, *The Abolition of Poverty*, Praeger, 1969, pp. 72–109.

Of mobile resources, the most important is capital. It is the key to the solution of the problem of how to expand productive equipment and productive capacity to match a growing population. Only if capital equipment – industrial and agricultural machinery, pipes, water-boring machinery, and the like – expands per capita and not in the aggregate alone and an equilibrium is established between accretion of productive equipment and the demographic increment, can it be assumed that economic growth has been instrumental in raising standards of living and enlarging productivity.

The population explosion postulates higher productive capacity and more equipment; that is a precondition of economic absorption of the demographic increment. So, one of the vital prerequisites of development is capital equipment. It makes for expansion of production, industrialization, and occupational redistribution, for it is a truism that 'lack of capital and of capital equipment is one of the causes of Eastern poverty, and of the greatest obstacles to industrial development' (Butler, 1938, p. 73). Accordingly, a certain relation between accretion of capital, demographic increment, and the average unit per capita of capital will adjust the level of economic activity and the standard of living. The relevance of this calculation is to be seen in the following definitions:

. . . the ability of a country to sustain an increase in population depends not only upon the wealth of its natural resources, but also upon its capital equipment and upon the technical ability of its producers. For this reason, a relatively undeveloped country may give signs of a temporary rural overpopulation in spite of rich natural resources, if the rate of growth of its population is more rapid than the growth of its capital equipment and the development of its industrial and agricultural technique.

A large number of the countries with rapidly increasing population are agricultural and lack capital. Such countries may be faced with serious economic problems as their population growth leads to rural overpopulation. . . . Even if they possess raw materials, lack of capital may prevent them from exploiting these resources and from industrializing; for their own savings will probably be meagre and it will be difficult for them to borrow from abroad (League of Nations, 1938–9, p. 159).

With populations rising so rapidly, capital accumulation could not be swift enough to expand productive factors at a corresponding tempo. It requires the spur of an external source of capital, lent or invested. [. . .]

With more and more emancipation from natural conditions and a greater weight of the knowledge factor, of organizing ability, and so forth, this aspect exerts a stronger influence.

The connection between the greater availability of capital equipment and economic growth is attested by the correlation between economic growth in underdeveloped countries where the pace of it is significant and the injection of capital. A study for the OECD, *Population Control and Economic Development*, confirms this, particularly as regards the integration of modern technology in the economic growth pattern of underdeveloped countries:

To focus on capital seems warranted even if, in a broad view of the obstacles to development, innumerable other factors compete for attention; above all, perhaps, administrative and institutional problems, and foreign exchange difficulties. It is, nevertheless, in terms of capital shortage that development planners most acutely experience the difficulty of 'embodying' modern technology (Ohlin, 1967, p. 56).

Capital supply, therefore, is the crucial problem for the developing parts of the world.

The industrialized, developed economy of the West was built on formation of capital by a ruthless lowering of the standards of living of large sections of the population in the eighteenth and nineteenth centuries. That solution does not offer itself comparably to the underdeveloped nations because their minimum subsistence level, just keeping body and soul together, is already so low tha not much more can be extracted for investment. Moreover, modern technology magnifies the capital requirements for investment. And, even now, some 80 per cent of all capital formation in underdeveloped countries is derived from internal sources of saving and accumulation of capital. In other words, some four-fifths of investment there is resources wrung out of populations living on or below subsistence levels. Even this apparently positive development is not an unmixed blessing, for it implies a reduction in consumption of local products, capital goods as a rule being imported. Paradoxical as it may sound, in the underdeveloped world it is almost as important to finance primary consumption as it is to finance development. The main driving force for any stepping-up of production is a larger market. At the outset of development, higher consumption elicits demand and allows for the establishment of many an enterprise whose feasibility is predicated on economies of scale. The experience of countries that are presented as 'success stories' teaches that their development was based above all else on effective demand, on which are founded their economies of scale in numerous industries. Besides, rising levels of consumption prompt a rise in productivity and efficiency through the medium of higher standards of nutrition and education.

In the eighteenth and nineteenth centuries, there was no alternative in the West to internal formation of capital. Today, an alternative exists – the simple device of transfer. The difficulty of primary accumulation of capital was virtually overcome by transfer of capital from more developed countries – in such new areas as the United States, Canada, and Australia – and the resources are equally available now. The periodic recessions in the developed economies affect, in the main, industries producing capital goods and contract their output to four or five times below that of other industries. A transfer of capital to underdeveloped countries, particularly in such periods, would help to iron out the unevennesses of boom and slump in the industrialized world. [. . .]

Where is the capital to come from to solve this ever acute problem? Internal formation of capital is necessarily limited by the low level of per capita income in underdeveloped countries, and it would be intolerable, in present conditions, to virtually squeeze every ounce of possible savings from their undernourished peoples when the developed world enjoys immense increments of GNP, some \$80 billion every year.

Capital is, of course, raised domestically in developing countries up to four-fifths of the total investment; but it must be supplemented to a much greater degree than it now is by transfer of financial resources from the developed world, particularly with modern technology – demanding investment of large sums – and, be that transfer ever so massive, development is still a long and steep and arduous trek.

However, it is a reassuring fact that, wherever capital was available, the results pleased. To quote a report on research carried out for the Office of Program Coordination of AID:

The possibilities of securing rapid and sustained development by effective use of foreign assistance have been strikingly demonstrated in the past decade by such countries as Greece, Israel, Taiwan, and the Philippines. In each case, a substantial increase in investment financed largely by foreign loans and grants has led to rapid growth of GNP followed by a steady decline in the dependence on external financing. Not only was growth accelerated by foreign assistance, but the ability of each economy to sustain further development from its own resources was very substantially increased.

Most of the countries – Iran, Israel, Korea, Malaysia, Mexico, Pakistan, Taiwan, Thailand, Tunisia, Venezuela, and Yugoslavia among them – that were catalogued at the 1967 meeting of the board of governors of the World Bank by President Woods as exemplifying success in economic growth are incontrovertible demonstrations that investment, although not the only condition, is one of the chief prerequisites of development. [. . .]

One possible way of overcoming the obstacles of access of developing nations to capital markets is the application of the so-called Horowitz proposal, accurately summarized in the report of UNCTAD's Secretariat:

The proposal rests on the generally accepted premise that the flow of aid to developing countries needs to be greatly increased and that the terms of assistance have to be softened considerably so as to permit an adequate net transfer of resources to developing countries and also to prevent explosive debt situations from emerging. It further assumes that, because of budgetary constraints, there are limits to the growth of official aid flows but that requisite resources for aid can be found in the capital markets of the developed countries. Since funds on the capital markets can only be raised on commercial terms, there is need for subsidies to make these funds available on soft terms to developing countries. Thus, the proposal envisages an international institution raising funds on national capital markets of developed countries on normal commercial terms and relending these funds through the IDA to developing countries at low rates of interest for a suggested period of thirty years.[1] The difference between the cost of borrowing to the institution and the lower rates of interest on lending would be covered by an interest equalization fund. The resources for this fund would be obtained through budgetary allocations of the developed countries to the IDA, through the allocation of some portion of net income of the World Bank, or through some combination of both methods. [. . .]

It is decidedly preferable to enable the developing countries to buy money on the market on conditions compatible with their capacity to repay, rather than rely entirely on taxation to provide the necessary capital. It is illusory to suppose that, in a democracy, taxation yielding enough for aid to other nations is a realistic concept; experience of the extent of capital flow to developing countries and of IDA replenishment in particular is the proof. Money is always available at a price, if the proper collateral and interest are forthcoming. The Horowitz proposal is meant to build a bridge of collateral and concessionary terms for the borrower and a reasonable yield for the lender by making it possible to borrow hard and lend soft. Under present conditions, even the exemption from interest equalization tax extended by the US government to developing countries on the US capital markets could not be utilized, and only two such countries were able to make their way in, favored by specially and virtually unique circumstances.

The important point of the Horowitz proposal is not only the alleviation of the terms of aid, but also – possibly even to a greater extent – the promotion of a larger flow of loan capital to the underdeveloped nations. Obviously, with the interest subsidy, the constraint and limitations imposed by the price of money

1. The international institution concerned could be the World Bank or the IDA itself. The funds raised would be additional to those required by the Bank for its normal transactions, and the resulting obligations would be backed by new and independent guarantees.

on the capital markets are reduced, and greater flexibility in meeting the commercial terms of capital is conferred on the international institutions, such as the World Bank and the regional development banks. [. . .]

Thus, the Horowitz proposal can be summarized as an attempt to build a bridge between capital markets and the underdeveloped nations and to make it possible to borrow hard and lend soft and to assure a high priority for the flow of resources to underdeveloped nations. The proposal is not a panacea and could not, by itself, solve the problem of capital supply to the underdeveloped world; it could, however, be one of several promising channels for the provisions of development capital.

In every area of economic endeavor, investment in the widest sense is the 'open sesame' of progress and expansion, and the most vivid example is in agriculture. To expand it and to enhance the supply of food are the most urgent concerns of the under-developed world. Yet, with the measure of land that can still be brought under cultivation constantly diminishing, any such improvement depends overwhelmingly on larger yields per unit, and that can be realized only by irrigation, soil betterment, a sufficiency of fertilizers, and the like – all dependent on input of capital. The development of manufactures in countries that as yet have no industries to speak of is certainly a function of import and formation of capital, of skill, and of availability of technological knowledge. [. . .]

National wealth cannot be expanded magically and speedily in the highly developed countries, where full employment is already the rule and further increment of the GNP depends on further technological advances. But, in the developing countries, there is a gigantic reserve of unemployed and underemployed manpower, with low productivity, and an excessive proportion of agricultural labor yielding a relatively low output. Added capacity there, brought about by adequate import of capital, would make new forces available and mean an economic revolution, with the wealth thus produced seeping into every part of the world's population and, besides, enriching the nations of high development even more.

Such a vision requires a statesmanlike approach, transcending the narrow horizons of a bookkeeper. It could be economically sound. And the choices are unmistakable: on the one hand, famine, political instability, perhaps war; on the other, eradication of poverty and unprecedented affluence and prosperity for all mankind.

What is needed is imagination and a political will to respond to the challenge. What is needed is the spirit that fired civilization after the Second World War, the spirit of the Bretton Woods conference, a spirit the affluence has dimmed.

The Keynesian revolution did more to change the economic conditions of the developed world than any sanguinary clash of agonizing conflict. The integration between the developed and the developing world is a pioneering task and calls for a sense of history if the perilous abyss between promise and performance is to be safely crossed.

References

BUTLER, H. (1938), 'Problems of industry in the east, with special reference to India, French India, Ceylon, Malaya and the Netherlands Indies', International Labour Office, Geneva, p. 73.

LEAGUE OF NATIONS (1938–9), *World Economic Survey.*

OHLIN, G. (1967), *Population Control and Economic Development,* Development Center of the Organization of Economic Cooperation and Development.

15 W. Arthur Lewis

Unemployment in Developing Countries

Excerpts from W. Arthur Lewis, 'Unemployment in developing countries', *The World Today*, vol. 23, 1967, no. 1, pp. 13–22.

My subject is urban unemployment, which is growing rapidly in many underdeveloped countries. Economists have written at length on rural unemployment, but urban unemployment is new to our literature. There have always been unemployed in the towns, but it has been assumed that this was due to lack of development, and would diminish with development. Now we can see that this is not so. The underdeveloped countries have been doing quite well over the past fifteen years. Their growth rate averages more than 4 per cent per annum, whereas a dozen years ago most people expected no more than 3 per cent. Unemployment seems to be growing most rapidly in the countries which are developing most rapidly, and at first glance looks like a by-product of development itself.

Apart from lack of development, it used to be fashionable to attribute unemployment to population pressure, but this also is now clearly untenable. In a well organized social system everybody finds some source of income, however large the population may be. In the countryside agriculture is organized on the basis of family farming. As population grows the family holding gets smaller and smaller, but everyone is attached to some farming unit, from which he derives an income. In the towns the social code demands that all who can afford it keep as many domestic servants as possible, and the relationship involves the so-called masters and mistresses in wide responsibilities for the servants and their families, far beyond anything in the normal capitalist contract of employment. Then there are vast hordes in retail trade, and very large numbers living by casual and part-time employment in various sectors, especially building and transportation. Retail margins are high, and so is the hourly rate for casual work. If retailers or casual workers were kept busy all day every day their incomes would be enormously higher than those of the farmers. But the great excess of people in these trades keeps the average income not much above the rural earnings. So a state of equilibrium is established between town and country such that there is just enough casual unemployment in the towns and disguised unemployment on the farms to keep the percentage of population living in towns constant.

India is still in this condition of balance between town and country. In nearly every other country in the underdeveloped world, the urban proportion grew swiftly between 1950 and 1960, but the Indian census reports no significant change in urbanization during that decade. Relative wage rates and the relative amounts of casual unemployment and disguised unemployment seem to have remained in equilibrium. But in many other countries this state of equilibrium has come to an end. People have been pouring out of the countryside into the towns, and as employment opportunities have not risen so rapidly in the towns, the proportion of unemployment has been rising. What we have to try to understand is both why the exodus from the countryside has stepped up and also why the towns, despite high investment rates, have not been able to provide enough employment for the new-comers. I shall take each of these aspects in turn.

Flow of population to the towns

The supply of people offering themselves for wage employment in the towns has increased for three main reasons. First, the gap between urban wages and rural earnings has widened enormously. Secondly, in many countries, mainly African, rapid acceleration of schooling in the countryside has speeded up the drift of young people to the towns. Thirdly, development and welfare expenditures have been concentrated disproportionately on towns, thus making the towns relatively more attractive. Let me say a word about each of these.

We are used to the idea that unskilled wages are higher in the towns than in the countryside, and usually expect a margin of 50 per cent above the rural income to compensate for the higher cost and inconvenience of urban life. This gap has widened sharply in recent years. Cases are now not uncommon where the minimum wage paid, say to government employees, is two or three times the farmer's income. The biggest anomalies are found in the countries with rich mines. For example, the lowest wage on the bauxite mines in Jamaica is about five times the normal earnings, say of a jobbing gardener. The high wages established by a few firms in profitable new industries, or by politicians newly arrived in office on a wave of civil service unrest, tend to pull up wages throughout the rest of the economy. For one thing, the trade unions in each sector strive to get their wages up to the highest that other industries are paying. And in any case people are unwilling to work for low wages in traditional occupations when their cousins are getting high wages in new industries. The general effect is that urban wages have been rising sharply while the farmers' real earnings have remained constant. The disturbance of the traditional equilibrium sends more people into the towns and mining areas, looking for work and counting that even one or two days' work a week will be worth having. In countries like Jamaica or Nigeria it is now quite common for heavy unemployment in the towns to coexist with a shortage of labour in the countryside.

Most students of development economics are familiar with the model of the dual economy in which a modern capitalist sector expands relatively to a traditional subsistence sector at a real wage which remains constant over a long initial period. There seems to be historical justification for this model in nineteenth-century Europe, though the historians are still arguing about the British standard of living in the first half of the nineteenth century. And the model seems also to fit the case of Japan. It also works not too badly even for contemporary India or Egypt. But clearly in much of the developing world today the wage level of the expanding sector has cut itself loose from the standard of living of the great mass of the people in the traditional sector. Why this has happened cannot be explained by traditional economic theory. Clearly marginal productivity has nothing to do with it. For even if the wage is assumed to be equal to marginal product in the modern sector, it is not marginal product that determines the wage but the wage that determines the level of employment and its marginal product. The real explanation must lie in the emergence of new political and social factors which determine urban wages without reference to demand and supply.

Whatever the cause may be, the effect of the widening gap between urban and rural earnings is an unprecedented outflow of people from the countryside, faster than they can be absorbed by the towns. No doubt, there is some equilibrium level of urban unemployment which corresponds to each ratio of urban to rural incomes, subject to some maximum unemployment level at which the chance of getting even one day's work a week becomes so small that it is better to go back to the countryside. But we do not yet know how far this process can go.

The second reason I have advanced for the outflow from the countryside is accelerated schooling. This phenomenon is confined to Africa. The emphasis is not on the word 'schooling' but on the word 'accelerated'. Some people say that it is schooling that causes the migration, but this is unlikely, since literacy and rural life are not incompatible. Others say that anything which enables country folk to find out what happens in towns will cause migration, since life in the towns is attractive, while life in the villages is dull. This also seems unlikely, since if the average villager is offered the same real income in town or village he stays in the village. People born and bred in the towns dislike village life; but people born and bred in the villages have an equal dislike for urban life.

The rapid acceleration of African school numbers has produced a disequilibrium between expectation and reality. Ten years ago less than 20 per cent of African children were in school. Now the figure probably exceeds a half, and in some parts of West Africa is up to 80 per cent. When only 20 per cent were in school, all who completed school could find well-paid jobs waiting for them in the towns, paying several times a farmer's income. Hence, the rural school was identified in the minds of parents and children as a route to a well-paid urban career. This is no longer possible when more than half the children complete the curriculum. Indeed, the superior jobs available to a primary school leaver are even more restricted now since a further 10 per cent of children are going through the secondary schools and driving the primary school leaver lower down in the hierarchy.

This is a transitional phenomenon. It cannot take more than a decade for rural children to learn that the towns cannot now offer them employment. Then the great majority will remain in the countryside and make the best of the opportunities available there. But in the meantime many African towns are clogged with school leavers, turning into juvenile delinquents because they cannot find the types of job they expect – or any job at all.

The third factor promoting the exodus has been excessive concentration of development expenditures on the towns – whether the investment in productive enterprises such as factories or the investment in infra-structure, including water supplies or medical services. When the first draft of Ghana's second development plan was completed, I pointed out to Nkrumah that he was planning to spend 50 per cent of the money in Accra, which has only 5 per cent of the population. 'Why not?', he asked me. 'When you think of England, you think of London; when you think of France, you think of Paris; when you think of Russia, you think of Moscow.' 'No sir', I said. 'When I think of England, I do not think of London because I live in Manchester, and this is also why I know that capital cities exploit the rest of the country.'

This over-concentration on the cities has many causes. One of these is the kind of identification of national pride with civic monuments, to which Nkrumah was referring. Another cause is political. The most ambitious politicians gravitate to the cities and above all to the capital; city voices, therefore, have most say in deciding where money is to be spent. A third element is a fallacious identification between industrialization and urban size, which leads people to want to concentrate all their factories in one or two very large cities. As a matter of fact, most investigations of the economics of city size show that the economies of scale are exhausted well before one reaches a city size of 300,000. It would be quite economic to develop a large number of small country towns, each with some factories, electric power, secondary schools, a hospital, and such other amenities as attract population. People are more likely to remain on the farms when the nearest town is only thirty miles away on a good road than when everything one wants is concentrated in one or two distant centres.

The welfare expenditures follow the same pattern as the development expenditures. Here the politician faces a difficult problem. As unemployment rises in the cities, the case for relief payments becomes overwhelming. But if one pays to the urban unemployed a subsistence subvention, one will attract even more people from the countryside. Strong-minded politicians have usually done the opposite. It has been quite common in history to pay relief only to persons who were born in the town. It has also been common to restrict entry into the town, and the right to live there, to persons who produce evidence that they have employment there. Five years ago the Nigerian Government rounded up all the 'beggars' in Lagos and sent them back to their native villages, from which, of course, they duly returned. The twentieth century is hostile to such measures because they interfere with individual freedom, but the twentieth century solution of paying outdoor relief must aggravate the problem when it is confined to the urban poor.

I have been enumerating the reasons for the increased outflow from the farms, citing wages, schooling, and unbalanced development and welfare expenditures. Earlier I had rejected population growth, pointing out that, when the social system is in equilibrium, surplus population does not flood into the towns but remains in the countryside. But, of course, when the equilibrium breaks down, and the excessive flow begins, then the greater the population pressure the larger the potential overflow. The rapid rate of population growth since the end of the war has, therefore, compounded all the other causes.

Lack of employment in towns

Now let me turn to the other side of the question. Why do the towns provide additional employment for so few people? As we have seen, output has been growing rapidly, by more than 4 per cent a year; manufacturing by 7 to 8 per cent a year. The ratio of investment in new capital has also been high. Yet net employment has expanded slowly. There are some spectacular cases. In his book on Puerto Rico, Professor Lloyd Reynolds reports that, despite enormous investment and a striking increase in output, the number of persons employed was no greater in 1960 than in 1950. (See Yale Economic Growth Center, 1965.) In nearby Jamaica during the 1950s output grew by 8 per cent a year and net investment averaged 18 per cent; 11 per cent of the labour force migrated, but unemployment was as great in 1960 as in 1950. The extreme case is reported by Messrs Ndegwa and Norbye (1966), who say that in Kenya between 1954 and 1964, while private real output increased by 4 per cent per annum, excluding subsistence, the corresponding employment *declined* by 1 per cent per annum. In the nineteenth century 10 per cent per annum gross investment would increase non-agricultural employment much more than it does in today's developing countries.

Two factors contribute to the small employment generated by current investment. One is that much of this investment is wasteful, in the sense that cost factors are deliberately ignored. Another is that, as a result of price distortions, investment is more capital-intensive than it should be.

The excessive role of the prestige element in public investment is well known; but private investors also are enabled to ignore cost factors insofar as their investments are heavily protected. Waste shows up in the large scale on which things are done, resulting in under-utilization of capital – factories built in anticipation of demand, super-highways carrying only a few cars per hour, vast airports and terminal buildings – all these are common sights. A third aspect of waste is the tendency to build everything lavishly. This is particularly true of government buildings. The countries which had their industrial revolutions in the nineteenth century used capital very sparingly; it therefore went a long way and provided much employment and output. In contrast, underdeveloped countries today waste capital in a big way; thus it is not surprising that at the end of heavy investment programmes the amount of new employment created turns out to be much smaller than had been expected. We are always being told that these countries are short of capital, yet under-utilized capital and wasted capital are among their most obvious characteristics.

This waste of capital for prestige reasons is also a problem which can be solved only at the political level, since it is due to the peculiar value system of the current crop of politicians. There are signs that this situation is altering as the politicians who led the independence movements are displaced by a new set. The leadership of an independence movement requires an aggressive, flamboyant personality, with more than a touch of paranoia. Such men are seldom capable of laying sound political and economic foundations after independence has been achieved, for this requires the conciliatory arts of peace rather than the blustering arts of war. It also calls for government by men who gather facts and think rather than by men who follow mainly their emotions, instincts, and hunches. No wonder then that Africans have done well in every sphere over the past ten years save that of politics. We can think with pride of the achievements of our scholars, farmers, entrepreneurs, novelists, boxers, athletes, or any other group you care to name; only the antics of our politicians have made us hang our heads in shame. The set of politicians who came to power at independence are now discredited in most of their countries from which they are rapidly disappearing. As the new schools and universities pour out their products, we can hope for a better sense of values.

Waste due to the distortions of the price system is analytically more difficult. Three of these distortions all point in the same direction. The rates at which governments borrow are low, relatively to the real shortage of capital. Foreign-exchange rates are too high in those countries (not all) which are experiencing balance-of-payments difficulties. And urban wages exceed the marginal product of labour in agriculture. Each of these promotes a greater substitution of machinery for labour than is justified by real factor scarcities. Investment is too capital-intensive and so employs too little labour.

Many people have remarked on the high capital-intensity of the investments taking place in factories, mines, and construction. But the effect of high wages is also felt in other spheres which normally employ far more people than the factories. One of these is domestic service. The housewife may keep a couple of servants at a pound a week each, but when wages go up to three pounds she installs instead a cooker, refrigerator, vacuum cleaner, and washing machine. Similarly at low wages the average commercial establishment is swimming with clerks and messengers. As wages rise, offices are mechanized and retailing converts to self-service. Since the expansion of services normally absorbs more people than the expansion of manufacturing, the fact that the service industries are now tending to throw out surplus workers instead of taking more in is probably just as important an explanation of growing unemployment as is the high capital-intensity of the new factories. [. . .]

It is not in practice difficult to recognize what kind of innovation is beneficial and what kind merely creates unemployment. The big waste of capital in underdeveloped countries has tended to be not in the mechanical processes for transforming raw materials into manufactured products, since these new processes have usually also improved the product and reduced the wastage of raw materials. The wastage has come mainly in substituting capital for labour in moving things about; in the handling of materials inside the factory; in packaging; in moving earth; in mining; and in building and construction. The bulldozer, the conveyor belt, and the crane usually achieve nothing that labour could not do equally well. They spend scarce foreign exchange solely in order to produce unemployment.

I hope I have made the point that an innovation is not to be condemned merely because it reduces employment. A developing society needs to have both employment-creating and employment-destroying innovations. In a full-employment economy, inventions which create employment, causing some industries to grow, could not be exploited unless in other sectors other innovations were destroying employment, to make a transfer of labour possible. In broad sectoral terms, new inventions in manufacturing industry and in large-scale communications absorb labour, while new inventions in agriculture, retail distribution, small-scale transport, and domestic service release labour. Statisticians then find that while part of the increase in national income is due to an all-round increase in productivity, an important part is due merely to workers transferring out of the less productive contracting sectors into the more productive expanding sectors.

The mechanism for keeping these two sets of innovations – the employment-creating and the employment-destroying – in step with each other is not very good. Fifty years ago economists believed that these things happened automatically. If unemployment emerged, wages were too high; they would fall and, by altering the ratio of labour to other factors, would restore full employment. It is still open to argument whether advanced economies work in this fashion. In any case, in underdeveloped countries, where the subsistence level sets a minimum to real wages, there is no mechanism to ensure full employment.

An earlier economist, Karl Marx, believed that in the capitalist system employment-destroying innovations would always be excessive relatively to employment-creating innovations, and he therefore predicted an ever-growing army of unemployed. He was wrong in Europe. In the second half of the nineteenth century these two types just about balanced each other. There were not enough employment-creating innovations to create a shortage of labour, but there were always enough to prevent a secular growth of unemployment.

Since the second World War the employment-creating innovations have been on top in Europe. European economies have had a persistent shortage of labour, draining workers out of agriculture, retailing, old-fashioned forms of transport, and domestic service rather faster than these sectors have been able to modernize, so that throughout Western Europe the less productive sectors have been kept manned only by immigration. The experience has been notably different in North America, where there is no shortage of unskilled labour, and where for a decade the rate of unemployment has seldom fallen below 5 per cent.

The problem is also very different in underdeveloped countries precisely because they lag so far behind technologically. In every one of their sectors the opportunities for saving labour are immense, and this tends to be done not by building up their own engineering industries but mainly by importing machines from abroad. Their distorted price structures favour undue capital-intensity, and even if they did not, there is no automatic mechanism to ensure them the right mix of employment-creating and employment-destroying innovations. Marx was wrong about developing societies in the nineteenth century, but it does not follow that he will prove wrong about developing societies in the twentieth century. The governments of such societies need positive programmes to keep capital-intensity under control.

Let me sum up. Urban unemployment is increasing both because people are leaving the countryside too fast and also because employment in the towns is too capital-intensive. Each side of this has several causes, so there is no single measure which can restore equilibrium. The various possibilities follow from the analysis – wage control and a wider distribution of development and welfare expenditures to check the yawning gap between urban and rural incomes; and greater respect for costs, both real and money costs, to make capital yield more employment. At present not much progress is possible along such lines because people are only just beginning to recognize that development can create more unemployment than it absorbs, and until this sinks in they will continue to expect the problem to solve itself.

References

NDEGMA, P., and NORBYE. P.D.L. (1966), *Rural Development*, paper before a Conference in Education, Employment and Rural Development, Nairobi.

YALE ECONOMIC GROWTH CENTER (1965), *Wages, Productivity and Industrialization*.

16 FAO

The Crisis in Aid

Food and Agriculture Organization of the United Nations, 'The crisis in aid: facts and perspective', *Ceres*, vol. 3, 1970. no. 1. pp. 18–19.

In 1964 the member nations of D A C – the Development Assistance Committee of the O E C D – pledged themselves to contribute 1 per cent of their gross national product to the development of the third world. This 1 per cent came to be widely misunderstood. It refers to *total resource flow* – private investment and loans at normal terms, *together with aid. It is not synonymous with what is understood as official aid, which consists only of grants and loans at minimal or very favourable terms.* Private investment and official credits are not aid when they go from industrialized countries to developing countries any more than when they flow between industrialized countries.

Ironically, the total resource flow from rich to poor nations actually exceeded 1 per cent of the total GNP of the pledging countries during the five years before this goal was formally adopted. Since then not only has the target not been met but both the total resource flow and that part of it consisting of genuine official aid have fallen progressively. Table 1 gives the picture in 1968, the last year for which full figures are available. The figures for 1969 are expected to be still lower. Thus the decline both for aid and total resource flow from the rich nations to the poor ones continues. This uneven and undependable flow of resources makes economic planning for the developing countries precarious and sometimes impossible.

By 1968 the combined total GNP of the DAC nations was valued at about US $1700 thousand million. The total resource flow to developing countries had by then fallen to $12·8 thousand million, or 0·77 per cent. *Of this $12·8 thousand million only 0·39 per cent was actually foreign aid – grants and soft loans.*

This $12·8 thousand million total resource flow may be compared with the $153·5 thousand million that the whole world is estimated to have spent in 1968 on armaments, according to the Stockholm International Peace Research Institute.

In 1961 grants accounted for 87 per cent of official foreign aid. At this point the trend levelled off and in 1968 it was down to 63 per cent. Moreover, the debt service on past loans was mounting for the developing countries. Subtracting these interest payments from the normal and soft loans made in 1968 the recipients were left with an actual total loan of only about $6·3 thousand million.

As foreign aid declined its terms also became more difficult and restrictive. Most aid today is tied to purchasing in donor countries, which cuts the value of the aid by about 20 per cent. It also sours the relationship between the rich giver and the poor recipient even as it promotes the economy of the former.

Table 1 What Went to the Third World and Which Countries Met their 1 Per Cent of GNP Resource Flow Pledge (1968)

Countries pledged to foreign aid (DAC)	Resources flow as % of GNP	Foreign aid as % of GNP	Foreign aid in millions of US $
Australia	0·67	0·57	160
Austria	0·66	0·20	23
Belgium	1·15	0·42	88
Canada	0·49	0·28	175
Denmark	0·55	0·21	29
France	1·24	0·72	855
Germany, Fed. Rep.	1·24	0·42	554
Italy	0·70	0·23	165
Japan	0·74	0·25	355
Netherlands	1·10	0·54	134
Norway	0·65	0·29	26
Sweden	0·50	0·28	71
Switzerland	1·26	0·10	19
United Kingdom	0·83	0·42	428
United States	0·65	0·38	3347
Total	0·77	0·39	6429

Source: OECD, DAC.
Note: foreign aid is a part of overall resource flow.

From the point of view of its usefulness as a tool of development the aid figure shrinks further when it is considered that much bilateral aid is in the form of armaments or other kinds of military assistance. This results in additional costs out of the recipient's domestic savings.

The crisis in aid comes at a time when the record of performance of the developing countries is clearly promising. Their average growth rate in the past 20 years has been 5 per cent per year which, because of population expansion, amounted to an increase in per capita income of about 2·0 to 2·5 per cent per year. The accomplishment of the developing countries is, then, in itself, spectacular and an indication of great promise for the future. By comparison, in Europe and North America between 1850 and 1950 the average income increase per person was 2 per cent per year.

The Pearson report lists 41 countries that achieved a minimum increase of 2 per cent per capita income since 1955, which because of population increase meant at least a 5 per cent overall economic growth rate. They are:

1. *Africa* Gabon, Guinea, Ivory Coast, Liberia, Libya, Malawi, Mauritania, Nigeria, Sierra Leone, Tunisia, United Arab Republic, Zambia.

2. *America* Barbados, Bolivia, Chile, El Salvador, Guatemala, Jamaica, Mexico, Nicaragua, Panama, Peru, Trinidad and Tobago, Venezuela.

3. *Asia* China (Taiwan), Iran, Iraq, Israel, Jordan, Lebanon, Malaysia, Pakistan, Republic of Korea, Saudi Arabia, Syria, Thailand.

4. *Southern Europe* Cyprus, Greece, Spain, Turkey, Yugoslavia.

The Pearson Commission believes that on the basis of experience and performance a 6 per cent overall economic growth rate is within the reach of most of the developing countries.

'At that rate,' it concludes, 'even assuming rapid population growth, a developing country would multiply its income per person by four in half a century, and many could bring themselves up to or beyond the present living standards of western Europe within a century.'

It has been estimated that over the past two decades the investment growth of the developing countries has been financed about 80 per cent from domestic savings. Aid constitutes the extra push, especially in the form of foreign exchange for major expenditure, which they cannot provide themselves. It is the difference between rapid and slow growth.

The possibility of many developing countries being able to reach western European living standards in several generations means that the present decline in aid and resource flow as a whole would have to be arrested and that the trend would then swing

back in favour of development. It means that the 1 per cent of GNP resource flow must be met by the countries that are pledged to it by no later than 1975. It also means that the share of official aid in this goal should grow from the 0·39 per cent of GNP that it is now and reach 0·70 per cent between 1975 and 1980.

This is what the 'crisis in aid' is about.

[Most of this information comes from Partners in Development, Report to the World Bank of the Commission on International Development headed by Lester B. Pearson.]

17 Christopher Eckenstein

Regional Integration: More Realism Needed

Christopher Eckenstein, 'Regional integration: more realism needed', *Ceres*, vol. 1, 1968, no. 6, pp. 22–5.

In the present unfavourable climate for an increase of outside assistance for the developing countries, one may at least hope for one positive by-product of the situation, namely an increased awareness in the third world not only of the need for national self-reliance, but also for economic cooperation and even integration among the poor countries themselves.

Everybody – including economists of nearly all persuasions in developing and developed countries alike – pays lip service to this goal, and the present issue which *Ceres* very appropriately devotes to this problem gives evidence of what can be done in this field.

Yet what dominates the scene are not the few instances of effective economic cooperation among the poor countries, but the fact that developing countries, generally, continue to build a very large number of completely separate national economies, and that trade barriers between them are going up, in contrast to the developed world where countries have been grouping together and where barriers have steadily been going down over the last twenty years.

Special difficulties of the third world

To continue to preach the manifold virtues of multi-national cooperation and integration among developing countries – as regional and international bodies have now done for years – is quite obviously not enough in this situation. If more progress is to be made in the coming years, greater attention will have to be paid not only to what is economically desirable, but also to what is politically feasible, in the conditions prevailing in developing countries.

It should, in particular, be realized more clearly than hitherto that the difficulties of integration among developing countries are much more acute than in similar efforts among developed countries. Developing countries – which tend to be chronically subject to strains regarding their balance of payments, which draw the major part of their revenue from customs duties and which have chronic underemployment problems – are naturally more reluctant to face the elimination of trade barriers than countries endowed with sufficient foreign exchange reserves, with a fiscal apparatus able to tap alternative sources of revenue, with relatively mature industries and with a shortage of workers rather than of jobs.

Equally, the necessary compensatory measures on the part of industrially more advanced countries in favour of less advanced partners of a particular group, are more difficult to negotiate among countries that are all relatively poor than among generally prosperous ones.

A particular difficulty stems from the need to reconcile trade liberalization commitments with the planning of investments. The more the government of a developing country is actively directing the developing process within its own borders, the less it is likely to want to exclusively depend, within the regional group, on the abolition of trade barriers and on the free play of market forces. Such governments will want to coordinate plans or investments at a multinational level, and the case for a strong and efficient institutional framework appears, therefore, to be particularly convincing in connection with integration efforts among developing countries.

Yet countries whose national consciousness has often just awakened, and who have not had the opportunity of forming habits of intergovernmental cooperation, face the political implications of the setting-up of such institutions at least as reluctantly as nations of the old world, among whom there is already a high degree of economic interdependence.

And if mutual commitments can, nevertheless, be negotiated successfully between governments, trade may still not take place, even in those cases where developing countries may be the cheaper producers. Competitors from developed countries may, indeed, still be able to supply goods on more favourable terms because, for instance, freight is usually less expensive on the traditional trading routes with developed countries, because the latter can offer more generous export credits – or benefits from tied-aid or preferential tariff or quota arrangements – which are not available to suppliers from developing countries.

'Minimalists' versus 'maximalists'

It cannot be said that this background of considerable difficulties has always been duly taken into account when trade expansion and integration schemes among developing countries have been envisaged. One may roughly distinguish two opposite methods of approach that have been advocated.

On the one hand, there are those who, over-impressed by the huge difficulties, plead for extreme caution. Those who tend toward such a 'minimalistic' approach want to make sure that the commitments to be undertaken involve absolutely no risk for the balance of payments, for fiscal resources or for existing jobs; and they favour commitments, tailormade for each country, that would guarantee from the beginning an equalization of the benefits arising from the scheme. Accordingly, they prefer to engage in lengthy studies about the likely effects on the commitments envisaged, with the result that the latter tend to remain minimal so as to be on the safe side. One might say, in paraphrasing a dictum, that the 'minimalists', while admitting that something should be done, want to be sure that nothing happens.

More vocal are the 'maximalists' who are so convinced by the undeniably great potential of integration efforts that they advocate a vast leap forward, i.e. to rapidly establish common markets and economic communities with a view to attracting new investments and significantly accelerating the rate of growth. Admittedly, only such far-reaching commitments may decisively break the many structural obstacles to trade expansion among developing countries; and it is certainly highly appropriate that, whenever conditions are ripe, the target for negotiations should be set so high. However, much more numerous are the areas in the developing world where regional cooperation has barely been started, and before one thinks in terms of ideal solutions for these areas, the real implications of the concepts of 'common market' or 'economic community' should be squarely faced.

Christopher Eckenstein 193

Too often, developing countries have endorsed these concepts without being aware of the far-reaching limitations on national freedom of action which they involve, and which usually can be consciously accepted only in the presence of an over-riding sense of political solidarity, or as a result of a long period of cooperation in economic matters.

To set such overly-ambitious 'maximalistic' objectives for negotiations between those who are unaware of such limitations often leads to inconsiderate, merely verbal, commitments or to the failure of the negotiations because governments or influential sectors suddenly realize implications for which they are not prepared.

Of course, it is necessary to know the general direction in which one goes. But it has often been possible to commit governments of developing countries to an integration target to be reached in, say, fifteen years, while these same governments cannot agree on what to do in the next few years. The more distant the future target, the more meaningless it is likely to be, at least in the changing context of developing countries.

Lessons of European cooperation

It would appear that the experience of Europe provides some relevant lessons in the search for approaches that would avoid the pitfalls of both 'minimalism' and 'maximalism'. Thus, if the Western European countries had aimed in 1948 at arriving immediately at commitments for a European common market, the negotiations would, in all likelihood, have failed. For governments and vested interests to accept, at that time, commitments for a common market would have constituted a leap into the unknown.

What was done, instead, was to settle in OEEC on rather limited intermediate targets, such as the liberalization of a percentage of European intra-trade from its most restrictive barriers. Once this target was achieved – and no unmanageable consequences resulted for governments and business – it became possible to agree to increase the percentage. Simultaneously, sectoral cooperation started among a more limited number of countries through the European Coal and Steel Community.

Only after many years of cooperation aimed at such relatively modest targets, were the western European countries ready to accept more far-reaching commitments leading to two multi-national groups with completely free intra-trade.

Progress was greatly facilitated because each country was able to perceive significant advantages accruing to it at every stage of the process. Elements of national support for European co-operation emerged in each country, in this way, and acted in favour of moving into a further stage of the process not merely on the basis of idealism but because of clearly perceived national interest.

Also in the developing world, integration cannot be sold as some kind of 'love thy neighbour' gospel or because it is in the interest of the region as a whole. Whether international experts or idealists like it or not, regional cooperation, in most areas, can still best be presented as a proper means for satisfying national interest of each of the countries involved.

The actual content of the intermediate targets in developing countries' cooperation efforts cannot be copied from the European experience, of course, just as the model of the European Common Market should not be merely imitated under different conditions.

The developing countries' special difficulties in this field will require the application of somewhat different methods. If equitable, and therefore politically acceptable, results are to be achieved for partners in such schemes, commitments regarding trade barriers will have to be closely linked to action with respect to investments, often also to payments. The benefits will, indeed, be measured by the effects on the investment process which, generally, will have to be oriented and stimulated in various ways, at the very least for those countries within a group which are lagging behind. It would be wrong, on the other hand, to underestimate the importance of adopting certain specific commitments regarding the level of trade barriers. The mere reduction of such barriers among developing countries to a more reasonable level than is presently the case would permit the emergence of certain trade currents and might enable investors to engage in complementary activities.

By fixing a ceiling to the protection admissible in the reciprocal relationships within a group, for instance, national investment decisions would become subject to a certain regional discipline.

Such a commitment, similar to the consolidation of duties under the GATT, would make it more difficult to establish or expand industries manifestly uneconomical from a regional point of view.

Reducing trade barriers, rather than completely eliminating them, would also subject the existing industries to a moderate and, presumably, tolerable degree of competition from other developing countries. It may be worthwhile for developing countries to consider the possibility of establishing such areas of reasonable protection among themselves, while remaining free to maintain toward the developed countries the substantially higher trade barriers deemed indispensable for an effective import substitution process.

International trade law as embodied in the GATT has, in recent years, become sufficiently flexible so that developing countries which envisage such 'half-way houses' – rather than full-fledged customs unions or free trade areas – need no longer fear that the international community will seriously object to their implementation. One increasingly realizes that the perfect is the enemy of the good and that if one wants developing countries to move ahead, one should not insist on the rigorous conditions of the past.

Just what are realistic targets depends, of course, on the prevailing circumstances and economic relationships of the region. Sometimes the only practical way of starting a process of co-operation is really 'minimalism' by setting up some project of infrastructure, for instance, such as river basin development where the resulting advantages can be clearly conceived by all partners.

In the field of trade, the reduction of barriers may first have to be limited to a number of selected items so as to favour the emergence of vested interests in exports toward the markets of partner countries. In the field of industry, it may mean a not completely satisfactory project-by-project approach, rather than the much talked about harmonization of development plans which usually becomes politically feasible only at a much later stage of the integration process.

There is also no use denying that difficult practical problems arise in the construction of temporary half-way houses. There is, for instance, considerable perplexity as to what to do to expand trade in those goods that still form the main production line of developing countries, namely, the produce of agriculture.

Market organizations of the EEC type may often not be a practical way of starting the process because they presuppose a strong political will for cooperation on the part of the participating governments. Other uncertainties relate to the determination, short of establishing a federal structure, of politically and practically feasible fiscal compensation in favour of less advanced partners.

Furthermore, which definition for the origin of goods should be adopted that would take into account the relatively low value added in the beginning of the industrialization process and the government policies designed to increase nationally added value? No wonder that little research has been done on such questions for it is, no doubt, a neater and intellectually more satisfying task to think out the terms of a full common market.

While the adoption of reasonable targets and of suitable methods is essential in overcoming the difficulties in regional cooperation efforts among developing countries, international assistance could do a lot to facilitate such joint efforts, enabling the countries to move more speedily in this field.

This was at least verbally recognized by the international community at the New Delhi Conference in the unanimously-adopted Concerted Declaration on Trade Expansion, Economic Cooperation and Regional Integration Among Developing Countries. One of the few examples of such assistance in the postwar years was the financial backing of the European Payments' Union by the United States; without this outside assistance, it can be safely said that European trade liberalization would never have moved ahead as quickly as it did.

It must be realized that there is a whole list of problems which are likely to arise in any systematic integration process, and which can only be satisfactorily solved if sufficient financial means are available. Regional or subregional integration banks can thus be an important means for building a balanced infrastructure, for elaborating multinational projects that are usually neglected by the national authorities, for helping domestic enterprise to adjust to more competitive conditions, for encouraging investments in the less advanced partner countries and for ensuring a certain regional participation in new enterprises. Yet to fulfil these functions, and to have an adequate influence on the investment process within a particular group, these banks would have to receive more than a very minor share of the total assistance flowing into the group.

At present, bilateral assistance to individual countries not infrequently favours the setting-up of enterprises that duplicate those in neighbouring countries. In contrast aid to regional institutions is more likely to be used in a manner consistent with regional perspectives and, inasmuch as increased aid to regional schemes would reduce elements of wastage, it would be fully in line with the present preoccupation to ensure a more efficient use of available resources.

There may also be some presentational advantages in aid to regional efforts for it would presuppose joint self-help efforts by the developing countries themselves. In the present sceptical climate of opinion, it might, therefore, be a new and more attractive use of aid. Such a presentation could be particularly persuasive whenever the use of the aids fund is directly linked with trade liberalization commitments among the participating developing countries, as is the case with integration banks of the Central American type, or with special funds established under the aegis of continental development banks to specifically favour trade expansion and integration. Such a purpose for aid might be a way to enlist greater support of public opinion for the efforts, for instance, of some smaller European countries to attain the 1 per cent aid target.

Even if proper methods of approach are adopted and even if aid efforts are, hopefully, more clearly geared toward the support of regional or subregional schemes, trade expansion and integration among developing countries will remain, essentially, a long-range endeavour. Patient efforts extending over many years will be necessary to attain results having a real effect on the rate of development.

Therefore, the expansion of trade and the promotion of integration among developing countries cannot be regarded as a substitute for improving the conditions of access and remuneration for the exports of developing countries to the developed world. At the same time, once a greater number of countries are engaged in fully exploiting the potentialities of cooperation and integration among themselves, this may also improve the moral and bargaining position of the poor nations, with respect to their requests for increased cooperation on the part of the rich.

18 Georg Borgstrom

The Hungry Planet

Excerpts from Georg Borgstrom, *The Hungry Planet*, Collier Books, 1967, pp. xii–xiv.

The great issue of our age is not the Iron Curtain or the Bamboo Screen, but the Hunger Rampart – the enormous and constantly widening gap separating the 450 million well-nourished inhabitants of the globe from these one and a half billion who are underfed or malnourished.

In 1960 the world population passed the three billion mark (in 1964 in excess of 3250 million). Few have clearly visualized the consequences of having an addition to the world's population of what amounts to a whole new United Kingdom every tenth month or almost a whole United States each third year and a new Soviet Union every fourth year. In the first sixty years of this century the world's population has doubled, and we can look forward to a second doubling before year 2000.

This rising flood of people threatens to deprive the human race of its future. The increase is not the result of any magical rise in the birth rate. Since the turn of the century most countries show a decline in this respect. A few countries, including the United States, show an increase in the postwar period. A drastic reduction in birth rates is important in order to save mankind, as well as civilization – or on the whole any values, including religion. But even if a strict birth control could be implemented, its long-term effects would not be felt for decades to come. We will be faced with an excessive feeding burden in this very century. Despite all our medical and technical progress, still only 5 per cent of the world's deaths are due to old age. This is the picture that is being unrolled before our eyes, making it obvious to everyone what the experts have known for quite some time and warned about – that the human race long ago exceeded the limits of what the world can feed. Contrary to all facts, we continue to talk about an abundant world, whereas the truth is that the world is desperately short of almost everything: food, shelter, homes, clothing, soil, utilities, forests, water – even the lack of physical space is felt in many places.

If the world's population continues to expand at the present rate, it will double itself every thirty-five to forty years, and this means that within 120 years the present production of foodstuffs will have to be increased eightfold if the present standards are to be maintained – and yet these are inadequate for more than half of the present number of people. If the minimum requirements of the entire present population were to be met, food production would have to be doubled immediately. Does anyone really believe that the magic required to meet such enormous needs is feasible? If we were to ration what the globe totally carries in food in such a way that each individual received an equal share, this would mean universal starvation. It has taken the energetic West five centuries to treble its wheat production. In the latest century, with all the aid of modern science and technology, the increase in this progressive part of the world has been a modest 60 per cent. [. . .]

We are horrified at the Chinese communes, yet we are drifting toward similar living conditions. The frightening visions of Aldous Huxley and George Orwell are beginning to take shape before our eyes. In some respects they look mild and humane compared to what seems to be materializing in reality. Mass collectivization is on its way, not unexpectedly, also in the over-populated parts of Western Europe and the United States. A single vote that once may have been influential in the parochial world swiftly becomes deflated in a world community of immense masses. One vote among a million carries little force. No one listens any longer to an individual, unless he represents a powerful, multiheaded organization. One voice among the 420 millions of India is impotent, yet we go on pretending that traditional democracy is viable under these grim conditions. The inundating wave of humans is rising fast. It is threatening to stifle all that is human, and we of the West seem to think that alms are enough. That is a fallacy of illusion that may destroy us. [. . .]

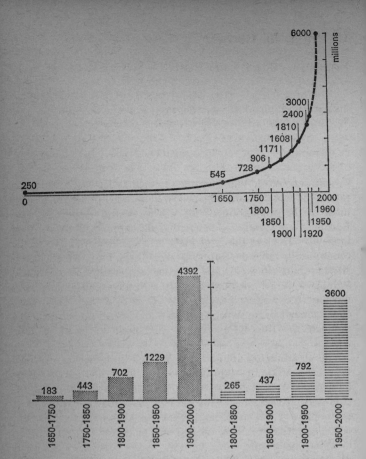

Figure 1 The growth of world population since the days of Christ. Bars in the lower part show the increment per 100-year periods (in the left section) and per 50-year periods (in the right section). Graphs prepared by the author from U N Demographic Yearbook and various estimates in textbooks as to earlier size of total human race.

19 Philip M. Hauser

Population, Poverty and World Politics

Excerpt from Philip M. Hauser, 'Population, Poverty and World
Politics', *University of Illinois Bulletin*, vol. 62, 1965, pp. 1–16.

[...] Prior to World War Two, the spectacular decrease in the death
rate of the economically advanced nations had not been shared by
most of the population of the world. Of the peoples of non-
European stock, only Japan had managed appreciably to increase
longevity. The two-thirds of the world's people who live in the
economically underdeveloped regions – Asia, Latin America, and
Africa – had achieved some decrease in mortality before World
War Two, largely through contact with advanced nations. But
most of the world's people, prior to World War Two, were
characterized by an expectation of life at birth no greater than
that which Western Europeans experienced during the Middle
Ages.

This situation has dramatically changed since the end of World
War Two. A combination of factors including the advent of the
United Nations and the specialized agencies with programs
emphasizing economic development and dissemination of a
chemotherapy and insecticides have resulted in the lower twentieth
century death rates. Since the end of World War Two, declines in
mortality have been more dramatic in the economically underdeveloped areas of the world than in the industrialized areas. For
example, the death rate of the Moslem population in Algeria in
1946–7 was higher than that in Sweden in 1771–80, more than a
century and a half earlier. However, in the eight years between
1947 and 1955 the decrease in the death rate in Algeria was greater
than that Sweden experienced during the century from 1775 to
1875. Between 1940 and 1960, Mexico, Costa Rica, Venezuela,
Ceylon, Malaya, and Singapore decreased their death rates by
more than 50 per cent. Ceylon's death rate was decreased by more
than 50 per cent in less than a decade.

The less developed areas of the world, containing two-thirds of the total population, are now the most rapidly growing regions of the world. They are increasing at rates which would double their population in twenty to forty years.

Should the trends continue, the population of the world as a whole would increase from about three billion in 1960 to approximately seven billion by the year 2000. World population would more than double during the remainder of this century. The effect of declining mortality in the less developed areas may be readily seen by comparing anticipated growth in the second half of this century with actual growth during the first half. Between 1900 and 1950 world population increased by less than one billion persons. Present trends indicate an increase of 4·4 billion persons between 1950 and 2000. That is, the absolute increase in the population of the world during the second half of this century will be almost four and a half times as great as that during the first half of the century. During the second half of this century, there will be a greater increase in world population than was achieved in all the millennia of human existence up to the present time.

Between 1960 and the end of the century, Latin America will have the most rapidly growing population, more than tripling, to reach a total of 650 million from the level of about 200 million. Asia and Africa will each increase by two-and-a-half-fold. Africa's population will rise from 250 million in 1960 to 660 million by 2000. Asia's population will increase to 4·3 billion in 2000 from a level of 1·7 billion in 1960. The slower growing regions of the world between now and the end of this century will be the industrialized areas. Population in Oceania will almost double during the remainder of this century, while North America and Europe will each increase by about 50 per cent. The population of Europe will total about one billion in 2000, compared with 640 million in 1960; that of North America will number 330 million in 2000, as compared with 200 million in 1960. Oceania will have about 30 million persons in 2000 as compared with 17 million in 1960.

Thus, during the second half of this century the developing areas of the world will be increasing five or six times more than the economically advanced nations.

With these perspectives in mind the best way to examine the

interrelations of population, poverty, and world politics is to examine simultaneously the following nine propositions:

1. We live in a world of 'have' and 'have-not' nations.

2. The international differences in levels of living, by reason of the 'revolution of rising expectations,' have become 'felt' differences.

3. The have-not nations are striving to achieve higher living levels, and they have made this goal – apart from independence if they have not yet achieved it – a major national aspiration.

4. There is an inverse correlation between levels of living and present or projected rates of population growth.

5. Rapid population growth is obstructing efforts to raise levels of living in the developing regions of the world.

6. Despite national and international efforts to raise levels of living, disparities between have and have-not nations are increasing rather than decreasing.

7. The accelerating rate of urbanization in the developing areas is exacerbating social unrest, political instability, and threats to world peace.

8. The bi-polar world political alignment – the confrontation between 'capitalist' and 'communist' nations or the 'East – West' cold war – is augmenting the tensions arising from frustrations in efforts to raise levels of living in the developing regions.

9. The bi-polar political world is being fragmented by have and have-not differentiation within the communist bloc; and De Gaullist schism on the Western front. Possible world political realignment is under way on a have, have-not basis rather than on a capitalist-communist basis. This would produce a 'North-South' rather than an 'East-West' confrontation.

Let us proceed to an elaboration of each of these propositions and a consideration of their interrelationships.

1. Have and have-not nations

In 1962 per capita product by continents ranged from $124 per year in Asia and $128 per year in Africa to $2866 per year in northern America (America north of the Rio Grande). Asia, with

56 per cent of the world's population, had but 14 per cent of the world's gross national product. In contrast, Northern America together with Northern and Western Europe and Central Europe excluding the Sino-Soviet countries, with less than 12 per cent of the world's population had 59 per cent of the world's gross national product.

Per capita product in 1962 averaged $489 for the world as a whole. The continental sub-regions with per capita product above the world average – one measure of 'economically advanced areas' – had an average per capita product of $1504. In contrast, the continental regions with per capita products below the world average had a per capita product per year of but $153.

By reason of the world political polarity, as between the capitalist and communist blocs of nations, it should be observed that annual per capita product in 1962 for all the Sino-Soviet countries combined was $269. Within the Sino-Soviet bloc, however, per capita product ranged from $94 in southeast Asia to an estimated $790 in the USSR. The countries of east Asia in the communist bloc, predominantly China, had a per capita product estimated at $95 per annum.

There was a great variation in per capita product, also, within the capitalist or Western bloc. In the Americas, for example, per capita product ranged from $279 for South America to $2866 in Northern America. And in Europe, among the capitalist nations, per capita product varied from $542 in Southern Europe to $1460 in Northern and Western Europe.

Although questions can be raised about the precision of the estimates of per capita product, nonetheless it is clear that, by and large, there are great disparities among the nations in levels of living. Moreover, there are great disparities within as well as between capitalist and communist blocs.

2. The revolution of rising expectations

Throughout human history there have been important differences in levels of living both among and within nations. This fact, however, has gained a new significance in recent times and particularly since the end of World War Two. The world has been swept by the 'revolution of rising expectations', to use the felicitous phrase of our Assistant Secretary of State, Harlan

Cleveland. No longer are there any peoples on the face of the earth who are willing to settle for second place and who are not insisting upon independence if they have not already achieved it.

In consequence, differences between have and have-not nations have in our own time become 'felt' differences, a term used some time ago by Warren Thompson in his discussion of population problems and world tensions.

3. Economic development programs

The have-not nations of the world are striving to achieve higher living levels. They have made economic development a major national aspiration. The economic development of the under-developed areas has indeed become an international goal as set forth in the charter of the United Nations and as manifested in the foreign aid programs of many of the economically advanced nations, both governmental and private. It is probably correct to say that there never was a time in the history of man when the achievement of higher living levels was as universal a goal among all of mankind.

4. Inverse relation between population growth and levels of living

There is an inverse correlation between present and projected rates of population growth and the level of living. For example, of the eight continental sub-regions which had growth rates above the average for the world as projected from 1962 to 2000, the per capita product in seven was below the average of the world. In only one of the continental sub-regions with a below-average per capita product, tropical and southern Africa, was the projected population rate of increase below the world average; and this growth rate, 1·8 per cent per annum, is well above that projected for any of the economically advanced regions. Contrariwise, in every one of the continental regions in which per capita product is above the world average the annual population growth rate projected between 1962 and 2000 is below that of the world average.

In general, it is apparent that for the world as a whole, poverty is associated with relatively high rates of population increase. Among poor European nations, however, relatively low population growth rates are in evidence despite their poverty. But poverty in Europe is a relative matter. It is significant that per capita product in the poor countries of Europe is about four to five times that of poor countries in Asia, and almost twice that of the poor countries in South and Middle America.

5. *Rapid population growth obstructs economic development*

Study of the relationship between population growth and composition in economic development in recent years has disclosed that population factors operate to obstruct efforts to achieve higher levels of living. Per capita product cannot be increased unless aggregate output rises more rapidly than does population. This is evidenced in the over-simplified equation, $L = \dfrac{O}{P}$, where L is level of living, O is output, and P is population.

It is not possible here to elaborate this relationship, but it may be noted that rapid population growth obstructs increases in per capita product in, at least, the following ways:

(a) It imposes requirements for capital investment which strain the underdeveloped economy even to maintain its current per capita product, let alone to achieve an increase.

(b) It produces or threatens to effect population-resource ratios resulting in diminishing returns.

(c) It produces an unfavorable age structure, that is, a population with a relatively high proportion of dependents and a relatively low proportion of producers which, all other things being equal, tends to depress product per capita.

(d) It requires a relatively large allocation of limited savings to the rearing of the young at the expense of using available resources for direct production investment such as investment in fertilizer, tractors, electric power or industrial plants.

(e) It diminishes savings available per capita for investment in human resources, that is, investment in education and training.

Demographic analysis has made it quite clear that decreases in fertility, dampening population increase, can contribute materially to increases in per capita product.

6. Gap between have and have-not nations is increasing

Despite international and unilateral efforts to assist the developing nations to achieve higher levels of living, such evidence as is available indicates that the disparities between have and have-not nations are increasing rather than decreasing. Have-not nations, relative to have nations, are doubly handicapped in efforts to reduce the disparity in levels of living. First, by reason of their small productive and technological base, even relatively large percentage rates of growth produce rather small absolute increments in levels of living. In contrast, the increments attained by the advanced nations are relatively large, even with low rates of economic growth. For example, a 10 per cent increase in product in Asia produces an absolute increment of about $12 per capita; in Northern America a 10 per cent increase produces an increment of $278 per capita.

Second, the rapid rate of population growth in the developing areas requires more rapid rates of economic growth than in the developed areas merely to maintain already existing levels of living. For example, during the remainder of this century Northern America can maintain its present level of living by an economic growth of 1·2 per cent per annum. Asia, in contrast, must achieve an economic growth rate of 2·3 per cent per annum to maintain even her present level of living.

Given their projected rates of population growth, the under-developed regions must achieve the following increases in gross national product to match, by 2000, the levels of living in Northern and Western Europe as they were in 1962: Asia and Africa a twenty-eight-fold increase; South America a fifteen-fold increase; Middle America a fourteen-fold increase.

To achieve such increases in product between 1962 and the year 2000, Asia and Africa must achieve a sustained annual economic growth rate of 9·2 per cent (geometric), South America 7·3 per cent, and Middle America 7·2 per cent.

Similarly, given their projected population increases, the under-developed regions, to match the 1962 Northern American level of living by the year 2000, must increase their product as follows: Asia and Africa a fifty-six-fold increase; South America a twenty-nine-fold increase; Middle America a twenty-eight-fold increase.

To achieve such increases, Asia and Africa must achieve a GNP growth rate in excess of 11 per cent per annum for the remainder of the century, and South America and Middle America a growth rate in excess of 9 per cent per annum.

The magnitude of this task is evident, when we realize that the United States throughout this century has averaged about a 3 per cent per annum rate of growth in gross national product. In fact, for underdeveloped regions to match by the year 2000 either the Northern American or European per capita production in 1962, the necessary growth rates are well above any hitherto achieved even by economically advanced nations. The conclusion follows that unless the underdeveloped areas diminish their rates of population growth through the remainder of this century, they will find it impossible to raise their living levels.

7. *The impact of urbanization*

The rate of world urbanization has been accelerating over the entire period which we are able to measure with reasonable accuracy, that is, since 1800. In the nineteenth century urbanization in Europe and North America gave the major impetus to world urbanization. During the twentieth century, however, the major impetus to world urbanization is given by rapid urbanization in the developing regions of Asia, Latin America, and Africa.

Rapid urbanization in the developing areas has a special significance in any effort to evaluate factors associated with mounting world tensions. For poverty and frustration concentrated in the urban setting have a potential for generating social unrest, political instability, and threats to world peace of a much greater magnitude than poverty and frustration dispersed widely over the countryside.

8. *Bi-polar political world*

Since the end of World War Two the world has been increasingly divided into a capitalist bloc, a communist bloc, and a third neutral or uncommitted bloc. Interestingly enough, one-third of the world's population is to be found in each of these blocs. Never before in the history of man have such gigantic antagonists as those represented by the capitalist and communist, or 'Western' and 'Eastern', blocs been manifest. They confront one another or ideological, economic, social, political, and, from time to time, military fronts. The East and West have each been trying to win the allegiance of the neutral or uncommitted blocs of nations. This is manifest in the prolonged struggle for the minds and the allegiance of the peoples of south and southeast Asia. More recently, it has given rise to increasingly intense competition in Africa; and it continues to constitute a threat to Latin America's identification with the West, especially since the advent of Castro's Cuba. The weapons employed in this tug of war are varied and include propaganda, economic aid, subversion, and military confrontation.

Perhaps the greatest race in the world today is the race between China and India to advance their respective levels of living, the one by a totalitarian communistic method, the other by a partly socialistic but, essentially, free world method. Should either be demonstratively more successful than the other, the story will be writ large for all underdeveloped areas of the world to read.

The outcome of the cold war may depend in large measure on the ability of the developing nations to control their rates of population growth and thereby to effect higher levels of living as measured by per capita product. It is almost certain that failure to advance their levels of living would leave the have-not nations of the world more open to the blandishments of the communist world. The communist bloc is in the advantageous position of appealing to anti-imperialist sentiment as it blames Western imperialism for the present poverty of the underdeveloped nations; and of being able, thus far, more successfully to exploit the inequities and iniquities characterizing economic and social organization in many of the underdeveloped regions. Moreover, the communist appeal is apparently more alluring and appealing to many peoples than that yet developed by the West. The communist appeal in terms of agrarian reform, racial equality, and fuller stomachs seems on the whole to be more effective than the more abstract Western appeal for freedom and democracy.

To the extent, then, that population is a major factor in obstructing economic development, it is a factor which, in the contemporary world, is contributing to mounting social unrest, political instability, and threats to world peace which are being exacerbated by the Cold War.

9. North-south alignment

Over recent years, schisms have become manifest in the East and in the West producing tensions within as well as between these blocs. Within the East at least, the split between the USSR and China may well have occurred not only from publicized ideological differences but also from their disparity in economic development – from the 'have' and 'have-not' positions of the USSR and China, respectively. The present reluctance of the USSR to use war as an instrument of policy for the expansion of world communism, in contrast with the willingness of China to do so, may well be attributed in some part to the have position which Russia has achieved in contrast with China's relatively desperate have-not situation. China, with a population approximating 700 million and a growth rate approximating perhaps 2 per cent per year, may be growing increasingly conscious of the disparities in the man–land ratios in China and in Russian Siberia. In China, inability to control population growth, even though there is much evidence that she is attempting such control, could well constitute a severe threat not only to her neighbors to the south, but also to her communist neighbors to the north.

This split within the communist bloc may conceivably contribute to increased tensions between the have and have-not nations throughout the world. Certainly China, in attempting to form her own bloc, is finding allies primarily among the poorest nations. It is not impossible that the USSR will find she has more in common with the have than with the have-not nations, especially if she is successful in her efforts to advance consumption levels. This possibility may be enhanced and accelerated by her fear of China's acquiring atomic weapons.

Thus, it may be that in the coming decades world tensions may revolve around a 'North–South' rather than an 'East–West' axis. The chief threat to peace may be in the level of living disparities between have and have-not nations rather than in differences between free-world and communist ideologies and systems. And the need for population control may become ever more vital to the alleviation of world tensions and potential conflict.

Concluding observations

High and accelerating rates of population growth in the contemporary world situation are contributing to social unrest, political instability, and threats to world peace. In retarding and preventing economic development, rapid population growth, together with its correlates including an unfavorable age structure and accelerating urbanization, frustrate efforts to raise levels of living in the developing areas and contribute to social unrest and tensions.

Poverty among the underdeveloped regions of the world cannot be regarded as a consequence of the maldistribution of the world's product. This is evidenced by the relatively low world average product per capita in 1962 which, at $489, was only 17 per cent of the income enjoyed in Northern America at $2866. The problem of world poverty, together with the social unrest and tensions it propagates can be resolved only through an increase in world product. The contrast in income between Northern America and Asia, for example, can be explained largely by the fact that non-human energy consumption in the former is at a level twenty times above that of the latter (8029 kilograms per capita v. 398 kilograms per capita based on energy consumption in million metric tons of coal equivalent). To eliminate world poverty, and more specifically, poverty in the underdeveloped regions, it is necessary greatly to increase aggregate product and to effect increases in product more rapidly than population grows.

Never before in the history of man has the relationship between population growth and levels of living been so crucial a factor in world affairs. This is why more nations today than ever before are attempting to dampen their rates of population increase. Such nations include Communist China, India, Pakistan, Egypt, Tunisia, Korea.

Unfortunately, there is no evidence as yet that large decreases in rates of population growth will or can be effected quickly. On the contrary, efforts to decrease birth rates among the mass populations of the world characterized by illiteracy and poverty have thus far had little success. The few success stories in efforts to control fertility, to which reference is increasingly made, have thus far little, if any, extensibility to the mass peasant population in the underdeveloped areas. There is room for encouragement, however, in the fact that increasingly greater resources are being allocated to biomedical research and social research designed to improve efforts to control fertility.

There is a tendency in some quarters to view as alternate solutions either the reduction of fertility or the increase in productivity. In the present world situation this is a misleading if not a dangerous posture. The problem of world poverty and the increasing frustration of peoples in the underdeveloped regions in their efforts to achieve higher living levels constitute a sufficiently grave threat to world peace to call for maximum efforts on both fronts.

20 Keith Buchanan

Hunger: Causes, Extent and Implications

Excerpt from Keith Buchanan, 'Hunger: causes, extent and implications', *Outlook*, October 1967, pp. 14–17.

'No child need starve when the world plans its family.' Thus a poster on the University notice board in support of a world policy of birth control, a poster which reinforces in the minds of many the idea that hunger in the world today is the result of procreative recklessness on the part of the peoples of the Third World [. . .] I find it hard to subscribe to this view. I find it strange that the peoples of the affluent nations, after having themselves multiplied so exceedingly in the nineteenth century that they were able to overflow from Europe and swamp vast areas in the Americas, in Southern Africa and Australasia, should suddenly appear as the peddlers of population planning to all those peoples who are themselves entering on a comparable period of surging numbers. Indeed, were I coloured I would be more than suspicious of the motives behind this sudden enthusiasm for population control on the part of the white man, and as a geographer, as one whose work is concerned with man and resources (with the adequacy of global larder for human needs, if you like), I would echo René Dumont's comments on population planning – that it must be seen as but one component of a many-fronted attack on poverty and hunger and not as 'a convenient alibi for those who want to maintain the status quo' (1966, p. 84). But let us attempt to put this population explosion into perspective.

The 'explosion' is real enough. In the words of Michel Bosquet:

The world did not reach its first billion inhabitants until 1850; but it needed only seventy-five years to reach the second billion and thirty-five years to reach the third. The fourth billion will be reached fifteen years later (1975) and the fifth by the end of the next decade (1985) (Dumont and Rosier, 1966, p. 15).

This accelerating growth mesmerizes some writers on the food problem; they are unable to see beyond the multiplication of mouths indicated by these scaring statistics. They concern themselves little with the causes of this growth; how far, for example, has it psychological roots in that 'love, in its spiritual form and in its physical form is a more intense need for those who suffer than for those who are satisfied'? (Tunc, 1962, p.16); to what extent is hunger a cause rather than a consequence of population growth as Josué de Castro claims? (de Castro, 1961); how far do social structures, and especially the need for the labour of a numerous family, contribute to high growth rates in some countries?[1]; can it be that the people of some cultures value two or three children more than a fridge or a car? (the average New Zealander is fortunate in being able to have both). These basic questions are rarely posed; instead, present trends are projected forward and upward to confront us, or rather our descendants, with a world whose land surface is, by the twenty-first or twenty-second century, hidden by a wall-to-wall (or rather, sea-to-sea) carpet of close packed humanity [. . .]

Let us attempt to get this whole question of population into perspective in a different fashion. First, we must underline that humanity is still a fair way removed from any real congestion; indeed, the whole of humanity, if packed like passengers on our New Zealand rail services at peak hours (say nine persons to the square metre), could be accommodated in a twenty kilometre square (Tunc, 1962, p. 17) – so there's still plenty of elbow room. The main problem is, therefore, not space but the capacity of the earth to feed man and this poses the question: Are the limitations to expanding food production environmental (in the shape of inadequate cropland, inadequate moisture and the like) or are they in fact man-made? De Castro inclines strongly to the view that nature is not niggardly, that 'what is niggardly is the human condition, or rather the inhuman condition, of our civilization' (de Castro, 1961, p. 26) – and this is a view which is not easy to refute. The earth, even more the sea, is only very partially used by man. In tropical Africa and tropical America 400 million hectare

1. As was the case in the Netherlands Indies where the 'culture system' (enforced cropping) instituted by the Dutch played a role in the sevenfold expansion of Java's population in the nineteenth century.

might be added to the cultivated area, in Australia 50 million hectares; over much of Monsoon Asia improved irrigation would make possible two or three crops a year instead of the single crop at present obtained; improved seed varieties and the heavier use of fertilizers, could, given adequate water, double or treble crop output in many areas. These developments are possible with existing techniques; what can be achieved with massive inputs of capital and scientific skills is illustrated by Israel (see de Castro, 1961, pp. 27–31), a country whose carrying capacity, according to British official estimates, was some 600,000 people but which today supports five times that number. It is just not possible to estimate the effect of the diversion into peace-time uses of the scientific manpower being prostituted by each great power in the perfecting of weapons of destruction or of the $133 billion being spent by the world on military hardware and personnel.[2] And just what 'the inhuman condition of our civilization' implies in terms of agricultural productivity is seen more clearly if we take a specific example; the speaker is Miguel Arraes, governor of the state of Pernambuco until the recent Brazilian counter-revolution:

The enormous strip of *massapé* in the Brazilian Northeast is one of the most fertile areas in the world: it is nine times larger than the cultivable land of Japan which feeds 100 million people. But from our land we get only sugar cane and some subsistence products in quantities well below the needs of the 23 million inhabitants of the region. The reason for this is that the exploitation of these soils, when it takes place, is not designed to provide for the needs of the population but to enrich half-a-dozen large land owners.[3]

The quotation focuses attention on one of the most widespread causes of hunger – an unjust and wasteful landholding system – and at the same time underlines the difficulties of correcting this for Arraes, like many who have attempted to get beyond the

2. Benoit, E. (1967). Of this total, the USA was spending $51 billion a year, the USSR $42 billion, China less than $5 billion (about the same as the UK). The USA is planning to spend $35 million on crop destruction and defoliation in Vietnam in 1967. *The Nation* (New York), 1 May 1967, p. 551.

3. Quoted by Michel Bosquet (1966). The *massapé* is a rich heavy black soil. For a fuller dissection of hunger in the Brazilian Northeast see Josué de Castro (1966) and René Dumont (1965, pp. 30–50).

double-talk of those to whom hunger means profit and power, was effectively silenced; he was arrested by the military junta when it came to power in Brazil and now lives in exile. But before looking more closely at this it is appropriate to comment further on the key question of population restriction.

Shades of Malthus

What is the morality, what the logic of the view that hunger must be tackled primarily by population restriction? Let us, when looking at this issue, bear in mind that such a policy, to be successful, must be directed towards those peoples who are increasing most rapidly and that these are the peoples of the former colonial and semi-colonial territories, the coloured peoples of the Third World, the dwellers in those 'enormous peacetime concentration camps which are the underdeveloped regions of the globe.'[4] Let us also bear in mind that to these peoples – and they make up two-thirds of mankind – these policies of restriction must appear largely as a device to maintain the *status quo*, a status quo in which the 'White North', with three-tenths of the world's population, enjoys three-quarters of the world's wealth:

Table 1 Distribution of World Wealth in the 1960s[5]

	% of population	% of world income
Developed countries	30·2	75·5
Western bloc	19·7	58·7
European communist bloc	10·5	16·8
Third World*	69·8	24·5

* including Asian communist countries.

These statistics are conservative; according to an Italian source (quoted in Bosquet, 1966), (*L'Unita*, 15 February 1966) 85 per cent of the world's wealth is controlled by 15 per cent of the population and, failing any revolutionary change in the situation, the proportions twenty years from now are likely to be 90 per cent and ten per cent respectively.

4. The phrase, emotive yet difficult to refute, is de Castro's.
5. Condensed from table in J.-M. Albertini (1967, p. 11).

And so it is not surprising that, even where there are no religious or cultural oppositions to birth control, the whole question of population planning has evoked no great enthusiasm. The poor of the earth have no interest in the stabilization of a situation 'in which their share of the earth's banquet has always been limited to the occasional crumbs from the well-stocked table of the rich'; they see no justice in the attempts to re-establish some sort of global equilibrium at their expense, at the expense of those who to date have most bitterly suffered from the consequences of the disequilibrium; above all, since the gross inequalities highlighted in Table 1 are the result of an economic system imposed by those Western countries who until recently dominated the globe, the correction of these inequalities is the responsibility of those countries and cannot be laid as a further burden on those who were dominated.[6]

It is against the background of these conditions that we should see de Castro's bitter denunciation of the neo-Malthusianism of the affluent nations, his condemnation of:

the pseudo-scientific attitude of those who attribute hunger to the malignity of nature and who, to appease it, demand the sacrifice of human lives in the form of genocide, of successive abortions, of control of births (de Castro, 1961, p. 19).

It is against this background that we should see his denunciation of the affluent nations, of a civilization:

which, after having looted the world in a manner so shameless, so inhuman and so shortsighted that it today realizes that the wealth of our planet is being exhausted, now admits its bankruptcy and advises the

6. As a somewhat unsophisticated example of the attitudes of some Western 'experts' the following extract from a New Zealand daily paper is typical: 'As the aspirations of the agrarian peoples rise while their economic burden falters, the burden of unusually large families tends to force persons to reduce their reproduction.' This trend, the writer adds, should be encouraged, 'by educational measures, by the availability of birth control devices measure (sic) and by a system that holds parents responsible for their children . . .' The *Dominion* (Wellington), 10 June 1967. The slow economic development of the underdeveloped regions is attributed solely to population growth and the effect of Western exploitation in siphoning off wealth from the poorer countries, in impeding an attack on the problem of prices for primary products and in maintaining unbalanced and dominantly agrarian economics is ignored.

marginal peoples to curb their birthrates so as to save the scraps that remain and leave the exclusive benefit of these to the privileged groups of the moment (de Castro, 1961, p. 52).

There is indeed little morality in the neo-Malthusian views which are becoming so fashionable among the intellectuals and politicians of the wealthy nations. These are views which are basically anti-human and this aspect has been driven home, from the Catholic viewpoint, by André Tunc:

The multiplication of men is, to the faithful, the multiplication of beings destined to love and serve God . . . : To the unbeliever, it is at least the increase of life in its highest visible form, the multiplication of hearts which bear love and of minds destined to add to man's genius, to pursue creation, to help fellow-men. Each birth might be that of a Francis of Assisi, a Gandhi, a Plato, a Mozart, a Pasteur, an Einstein, a Teilhard de Chardin, a Charles de Foucauld (Tunc, 1962, p. 18).

And if there is little morality, there is, in a world only partially exploited, in a world which can spend astronomical sums and much of its best brains in space travel or preparation for war, in a world which uses its protein concentrates to fatten the chickens of the rich rather than to feed the children of the poor,[7] precious little logic in advancing the view that population expansion in the poorer countries is creating an unbearable pressure on resources or on capital [. . .]

Let us try and see the realities which lie behind the hypocrisies and the pseudo-science which give the wealthy nations some sort of alibi, and let us focus our attention on each of the great hunger-zones in turn.

The face of hunger in Latin America
'The Industry of Hunger . . .'

Latin America is a poverty-stricken continent. It contains seven per cent of the world's population but these folk share between them only 4½ per cent of the world's income; Anglo-America has, for comparison, about the same share of the world population

7. René Dumont dedicates his book *Nous allons à la famine* thus: 'To the children who died of kwashiorkor because the fish meal which could have saved them went to feed the chickens destined for the tables of the over-fed rich.' There is assuredly something monstrous and distorted in an economic system and a society characterized by such economic irresponsibility.

but enjoys 43 per cent of the world's income. Agricultural productivity is declining (in 1964 it was eight per cent below the level of 1954) (Dumont and Rosier, 1966, pp. 188, 26); population is expanding at the rate of 2·7 per cent per annum (Venezuela 4 per cent, Mexico 3·8 per cent) (Gerassi, 1965, pp. 34, 38); three-fourths of the population are constantly hungry (Gerassi, 1965, pp. 34, 38); impoverishment and disease are on the increase and the expectation of life ranges from 32 years (Paraguay) to 51 years (Argentine) . . . These are the conditions behind the anger[8] and the desperation which show themselves in the mounting tide of violence as the have-nots confront the power and arrogance of the haves . . .

And yet Latin America is by no means lacking in resources; indeed, as Paul Johnson puts it:

Latin America might have been the kingdoms of the world the Devil showed Christ on the mountain. It has more cultivable, high yield tropical soil than any other continent, at least three times as much agricultural land, per capita, as Asia, the biggest reserves of timber in the world. Buried in it are uncalculated but vast reserves of oil, iron, tin, gold, silver, lead, zinc . . . With its oil and hydro-electric power it constitutes one of the greatest untapped reservoirs of energy; its annual population increase . . . provides an inexhaustible supply of future manpower (Johnson, 1963).

Why then, we may ask, the poverty? Why, in a continent with a more favourable man/land ratio than most, a continent which contains 16 per cent of the habitable surface of the globe but only seven per cent of the population, a continent of which little more than six per cent is cultivated, why should there be such grinding poverty and hunger? Even the most conservative of estimates suggests that the cultivated area could be doubled, maybe tripled and, in truth, it is not nature that is miserly – rather is it man, or, more correctly, a limited number of landed proprietors, exploiting the continent in their own selfish interests, ignorant of or caring little for the social function of property.[9]

8. I. F. Stone (1965, p. 91) speaking of Latin America, says: 'There's anger there. There's a terrible anger. They're prepared to pull down the pillars of civilization if they can't get justice.'

9. For the Catholic view of this see John XXIII's Encyclical Letter *Mater et Magistra* (1961) and especially the reiteration that 'the right of

Hunger in Latin America, contends Josué de Castro, 'is indissolubly tied up with the social structures of underdevelopment, with the very principles of social organization in the underdeveloped areas of Latin America (de Castro, 1961, p. 29). The 'get-rich-quick industry' of the few, he observes, is at the same time the 'industry of hunger for the many' (de Castro, 1962, pp. 318–9). Hunger, in his interpretation, is both a cause and an effect of underdevelopment and of the general impoverishment which it causes. We have an almost classic example of the process of 'circular causation' described by the economist Gunnar Myrdal (1963, chs. 2 and 3): low productivity leads to famine, famine leads to low productivity and a continuing degradation of living levels; the result is 'a vicious circle of generalized misery'.

Hunger is 'the inhuman by-product of the system of economic exploitation practised in this region' and its social and historical roots are to be found in the colonial system of land exploitation. This was not, as is often assumed, a feudal system; it was, as André Gunder Frank has demonstrated, fully capitalist from the earliest stages of European colonization and through it the land and the peoples of Latin America became appendages of West European and, later, American capitalism.[10] The development of single-crop economics, often on plantation lines and designed to ensure a constant supply of low-priced primary products for the economies of the metropolitan countries, has been a major cause of hunger. The emphasis of such economies was on the extensive cultivation of export crops rather than the intensive cultivation of foodstuffs for local consumption; these 'robber economies'

every man to use (material goods) for his own sustenance is prior to every other right of economic import and so is prior to the right of property' (page 9 of the English translation). Saint Thomas Aquinas held that: 'If the need be so manifest and urgent, that it is evident that the present need must be remedied by whatever means be at hand [. . .], then it is lawful for a man to succour his own needs by means of another's property [. . .]' *Summa Theologica: Part II* (Second part: 10), p. 233 (London, 1929).

10. See Frank (1966, pp. 17–31). In his scheme the Latin American countrysides are exploited by a parasitic capital city and a parasitic ruling group and these in turn are satellites of the 'world metropolis' i.e. the industrial nations of the Atlantic lands. For a full treatment of his thesis, with supporting historical and regional examples, see Frank (1967).

warped and dislocated the merging societies of Latin America as effectively as they destroyed the ecological balance. Cuba is thus still dominated by its sugar economy, Brazil and Colombia by coffee, Central America by bananas. And elsewhere single-commodity economies based on mining caused the same social and economic distortions: Bolivia is dominated by tin, Venezuela by petroleum ... This cycle of single-crop, export-oriented economies, begun in colonial times, has been continued and strengthened by the great financial groups which control overseas investments and which use the local ruling groups as cogs in the machinery of exploitation. These are the groups referred to by President Getulio Vargas of Brazil in his suicide note:

Once more the forces and interests against the people are newly coordinated and raised against me. . . . After years of domination and looting by international economic and financial groups, I made myself chief of an unconquerable revolution ... A subterranean campaign of international groups joined with national groups revolting against the regime of workers' guarantees ... They do not wish the workers to be free. They do not wish the people to be independent (quoted in Gerassi, 1965, Appendix A, p. 425).

And in Latin America the outstanding example of such an outside group is the United Fruit Company, which dominates the economy (and political life) of Central America, owning 680,000 hectares of land (excluding land 'controlled' by the Company), and controlling 85 per cent of the potential banana land in the American tropics, excluding Ecuador. The group is linked to a certain number of trusts (Chrysler, RKO, etc.) and to the Rockefeller and Morgan banking interests; it is moreover, as the overthrow of the Guatemalan government in 1954 demonstrated, an important political force (Albertini, 1967).

This 'connivance between governments and monopolies' is to be explained largely by the fact that Latin American governments have rarely been 'popular' governments in the Western sense. Rather have they been composed of members of a dominant oligarchy which has profited from the exploitation of the hungry masses; the policy of outside groups has been to collaborate with and, when necessary, support this oligarchy and the latter in turn can be depended on to defend foreign interests within the country [. . .]

It is against this background of collusion and interlocking interests that we should see the maintenance in the continent of an archaic social structure, a system which is an obstacle to all social progress, a system which is the major factor making for hunger. It has been estimated that 'one per cent of Latin Americans own 71·6 per cent of the farmlands' (Gerassi, 1965, p. 33); some of these are miniature kingdoms,[11] of the size of a quarter of a million acres. The other side of the coin is the great number of tiny holdings or *minifundios*; three-quarters of the holdings together contain less than three per cent of the total farm area. The over-big holding and the over-small holding both make for low levels of productivity, for wastefulness of effort and eventually for hunger. And with this archaic system of holdings go archaic systems of tenure, with share-cropping and the like. 80 per cent of the farmers, according to Gerassi, do not receive wages, being paid in kind, with land or with chits redeemable at the landlord's store; he goes on: 'Since the agricultural peonage system means so little cash outlay (almost no wages) or investments (80 per cent free labour is cheaper than tractors) the latifundistas have no intention of changing it' (Gerassi, 1965). It is this vested interest of the landlords in the structures that perpetuate hunger, together with their political power, that explains the survival of the system: as the Government of Chile noted in reply to a United Nations questionnaire:

Owing to the economic and political structure of the country, land reform in Chile is difficult to carry out. Landholders who would be affected . . . vigorously oppose its implementation and their political and economic influence is very powerful (quoted by King, 1962).

It is obviously unlikely that governments dominated by landlords would vote away, by measures of agrarian reform, the economic basis on which the ruling classes' power has rested. And it is noteworthy that the programme of the Alliance for Progress specifically prohibits the use of the monies in the Social Progress Trust Fund for the purchase of agricultural land; since most Latin American governments cannot afford to buy the land for

11. For a picture of the absolute power of the latifundistas see the Latin American novels of Alegria (1962) and Icaza (1962); also Dumont (1965, chapter 3) and Andreski (1966, pp. 56–8).

redistribution,[12] this further strengthens the forces aligned against land reform and leaves a Castro-type revolution as the only alternative to increasing rural pauperization and increasing hunger.

If we look at the situation in the light of the Western European model of development it might be assumed that, in those countries where the beginnings of industrialization are under way, the new industrial and commercial class might emerge as a counterpoise to the landed groups. To some extent this may be discerned in Brazil but both here and elsewhere there has been a significant merging of the landed and industrial-commercial groups. As Huberman and Sweezy (1963, pp. 594–6) observe:

The traditional landowning aristocracies are now mixed up with the financial, commercial and manufacturing bourgeoisies. Landowners have invested in towns and cities; merchants and bankers have bought land; families have intermarried. By now it is probably safe to say that in every country the bourgeoisie owns the land as well as the capital.

Given these conditions, they suggest that the type of agrarian reform which is essential for real economic development (see, for example, Frank, 1963, pp. 656–62) – and the elimination of hunger – can come only with a revolution which will replace these groups by a new ruling class, either the peasantry or the proletariat. But, in the meantime, while important conflicts of interest between local and foreign capitalists certainly exist, they are subordinate to the common interests both groups have in exploiting the continent's human and natural resources. And both are united by a common fear of a revolution, Cuban-style, from below. If this analysis is correct, there will be little change in the continent's dependent status, no real attack on the problem of underdevelopment and thus no real attack upon the problems of hunger as long as the present political structures persist and these are strongly supported by, indeed being reinforced by, the United States. Viewed thus, the problem of hunger in Latin America and American foreign policy are closely intertwined . . .

12. Gerassi (1965, p. 265); the specific reference is to be found in Section .04a of the conditions governing the working of the Fund. See also Aguilar (1963) and, for a case study, Shapiro (1962) pp. 5–13.

References

AGUILAR, A. (1963), *Latin America and the Alliance for Progress*, New York.

ALBERTINI, J. M. (1967), *Les Mécanismes du Sous Développement*, Paris.

ALEGRIA, A. (1962), *Broad and Alien is the World*, London.

ANDRESKI, S. (1966), *Parasitism and Subversion: The Case of Latin America*, London.

BENOIT, E. (1967), 'Disarmament and world economic interdependence', The *Nation*, 17 April.

BOSQUET, M. (1966), 'Cent mille morts par jour', *Le Nouvelle Observateur*, 21 December.

DE CASTRO, J. (1961a), *Le Livre Noir de la Faim*, Paris.

DE CASTRO, J. (1961b), 'La faim et le développement en Amerique Latine', *Developpement et Civilizations*, July–September, Paris.

DE CASTRO, J. (1962), 'Le Brésil en révolution', *Esprit*, September, Paris.

DE CASTRO, J. (1966), *Death in the Northeast*.

DUMONT, R. (1965), *Lands Alive*, London.

DUMONT, R., and ROSIER, B. (1966), *Nous Allons a la Famine*, Paris.

FRANK, A. G. (1963), 'The varieties of land reform', *Monthly Review*, April.

FRANK, A. G. (1966), 'The development of underdevelopment', *Monthly Review*, September.

FRANK, A. G. (1967), *Capitalism and Underdevelopment in Latin America*, New York, Penguin, 1972.

GERASSI, J. (1965), *The Great Fear in Latin America*, New York.

HUBERMAN, L., and SWEEZY, P. (1963), 'Notes on Latin America', *Monthly Review*, March.

ICAZA, J. (1962), *Huasipungo*, London.

JOHNSON, P. (1965), 'The Plundered Continent', in P. Sweezy and L. Huberman (eds.), *Whither Latin America?*, New York.

KING, M. (1962), 'A "theory" of power and political instability', in J. H. Kautsky (ed.) *Political Change in Underdeveloped Countries*, New York.

MYRDAL, G. (1963), *Economic Theory and Underdeveloped Regions*, Verry.

SHAPIRO, S. (1962), 'Peru and the Alianza', in *Studies on the Left*, vol. 3, no. 2, New York.

STONE, I. F. (1965), in Vietnam Day Committee (eds.) *We Accuse*, Berkeley and San Francisco.

TUNC, A. (1962), *Dans un Monde qui Souffré*, Paris.

21 United Nations Department of Economic and Social Affairs

Social Policy and the Distribution of Income

Excerpts from United Nations Department of Economic and Social Affairs, *Social policy and the distribution of income in the nation*, 1969, pp. iii, 2, 14–15, 41–51, 88, 116–27.

It has often been considered that disparities in income are greater within countries than between countries. Statistics to establish this simply do not exist and even if much more were known about income distribution, the difficulty of making intercountry and interpersonal comparisons of welfare would soon present itself. However, the fact that there is a wide gap between the rich and the poor in most developing countries is a common observation, and increasingly in recent years, it has been a matter of concern.

This concern is in part a matter of simple morality: such disparities offend our sense of justice and humanity. But its growth also reflects a spreading realization that gross inequality makes for political instability. Perhaps above all is a new awareness of the inhibiting effects that an excessively skewed distribution of income can have on economic growth. Not only does such skewness stem from undue social and economic rigidity and stratification, but it also tends to hold back the very processes by which manpower becomes more productive and the total income available for distribution is expanded more rapidly. Poverty depresses productivity in one section of the population; the effect of this on the economy is not necessarily offset, however, by the benefit to saving and investment that might be hoped for from the high incomes accruing to those – a much smaller group – at the other end of the scale. For the state of underdevelopment that characterizes such circumstances limits the growth of a capital market and of opportunities for investment. All too often a larger proportion of higher incomes are spent either on conspicuous consumption or outside the country.

While the disadvantages of a very skewed income distribution are becoming more widely appreciated, the means of improving the situation are far from agreed. Developing countries cannot afford elaborate welfare schemes, and where relief systems have been organized, they have often proved to be unsatisfactory palliatives. The premature enlargement of the social security aspects of wage and employment regulations has often proved self-defeating: given the urgent need in most developing countries to expand employment opportunities and increase the mobility of labour, policies that make it more attractive to use machinery than hire workers run counter to the logic of the economy's factor endowments. Efforts to hold down the prices of the goods and services which bulk large in poorer peoples' budgets have often resulted in distortions inimical to production and hence are also self-defeating.

One remedy clearly lies in reform of the tax system. Another lies in more effective control of the inflationary tendencies which bear so heavily on wage earners and low-income groups. Fiscal and investment policies, however, cannot be determined outside the context of the development process as a whole, and in the long run it is to this – and the associated loosening of labour rigidities and opening up of opportunities for training and employment – that the developing countries must look for a more equitable distribution of incomes.

Different kinds of social policies involving redistribution of the income of a country will be appropriate at different stages of development. At the earliest stages emphasis should be on policies that eliminate structural obstacles and build up necessary human resources to promote economic development. Any given policy measure or scheme (for example, high minimum wage levels and social security and welfare benefits) may not be appropriate until and unless consistent with the level of economic development. As development proceeds, social policy may be broadened to encompass a wider range of measures involving redistribution from purely humanitarian and social justice considerations and from considerations of the social consequences of development

Social policy relating to distribution and redistribution of incomes directed to the improvement of the level of living of the population and especially of the minimum level of living should give particular attention to ways and means of attaining full employment, minimum money income, agrarian reform, etc. [. . .

From the point of view of economic development it is necessary to distinguish between different causes and types of inequality of incomes and levels of living. There are inequalities due to excessive concentration of wealth which may create an undesirable social and economic structure and impede development. There are also inequalities due to differences in wages between skilled and unskilled labour, or between high and low productivity labour, which may act as stimuli to development. There may be inequalities where redistributions are not economically feasible. [. . .]

Redistribution, social policy and minimum resources for living

Little is known about optimal redistribution at a given level of development in relation to given social objectives. It is clear that at the one extreme (minimum redistribution) there is the danger of stagnation because of bottle-necks in mobility, skills, capacity, and motivation, and at the other extreme (substantial redistribution) there are problems deriving from outlays of resources that cannot be efficiently absorbed and used. In a search for balance, it is useful to know about pace, selection of measures, their most useful interrelation, and effective strategies. Since systematic knowledge is quite limited, several specific proposals are offered in the final section.

Several major types of intervention (tax policies, redistribution of land and wealth, labour and business policies, social services) are redistributive and may – depending on how they are carried out – affect the number and identity of those who are below the minimum level of resources in a given country, region or group. Each of these approaches may be motivated by concerns other than redistribution and equity. Thus tax policy may be shaped by a Government's need to pay its bills, or to encourage investment. Land policy or labour policy may grow out of political concerns. Social service and social assistance programmes may reflect the organization and professional dynamics of the bureaucracies concerned. None the less, when consciously used to achieve redistribution and to raise specific groups above the minimum, each of these categories contains a series of potentially important possibilities.

There is hardly a government policy which does not, in some

way, affect the distribution of income or level of living. Bearing this in mind, one may also elaborate some of the possibilities in the above categories and list the following as examples involving redistribution: general governmental budgetary decisions; wage and employment policy; laws relating to conditions of life and work; social security; vocational training; general economic and policy decisions; family planning; agricultural policy; measures to encourage social mobility or redistribution; international measures (balance of payments, commodity prices etc.) and the spread of science. These are obviously overlapping categories but they do serve to call attention to the range of the repertoire depending on the context of decision-making. [. . .]

Given the specific social policy focus of the present group, special attention is directed to the following high-priority social service and social assistance programmes, namely: health, nutrition, education, social security, public assistance and social welfare. With specific reference to the underprivileged and excluded groups in all societies and to the bulk of the population in developing countries, these are strategic and potent redistributional devices, directly aimed at redressing the lack of minimum resources. They have the potential for direct and immediate opening and expansion of opportunity through creation of skills and capacity to participate in the economy and through assurance of the necessary vitality and health.

The general list of possible redistributional measures and the specific social service–social assistance measures are interrelated in another sense: many of the measures appear to be mutually dependent. Land reform is not successful unless supported by agricultural extension services, credit, reform of middleman practices and related measures. Educational measures must be rendered effective on the one hand by the creation of home conditions to support a child's education and, on the other, by labour market developments which assure utilization of skills and acquired knowledge. Social services may create the prerequisites of social mobility, but there must also be support from labour policy and concomitant economic growth. [. . .]

While it is true that most government policies tend, in some way, to affect level of living distribution, it is also true that, with little or no loss in efficiency to the policy in reaching its particular goal, it may be made to do a better job in redistributing levels of living in a community or nation. Thus, the redistributional policy of Government may not be found in one department or within the outlines of one discipline. A comprehensive redistributional policy is a multidisciplinary affair. Furthermore, the choice of tools to be used or emphasized in such a policy depends partly on considerations of social and economic philosophy of the Government.

One of the major redistributional tools which may be used by Government is taxation. Limits to this type of policy are set by the complicated question of incentives to capital accumulation and work effort. In developing countries where incomes are low and where investment risk (particularly for foreign capital) and, hence, need for incentives are high, redistributional limits of taxation policy may be quickly reached. Questions of tax incidence and ease of collection are also important in this regard. But within these limits taxation policy may be adapted to redistributional needs. With regard to taxes on consumer groups, this may be obtained by the proper choice of types of taxes and consumer goods made subject to taxation policy (poverty budgets may be important in this latter regard). With regard to the Latin American region it was stated:

The tax instruments appropriate to the high group would be income tax, tax on assets in whatever form, and a tax on expenditure on luxury goods and services. The middle group would be subjected to taxes on expenditures on 'non-wage goods' ('nearly all consumption goods and services except the most essential') and to low rates of taxes on incomes based on payrolls and deducted. The low group would not make a net contribution to public finance in view of the redistributive effect of public expenditure, but would be taxed to the extent that its consumption crossed the borderline between 'wage goods' and 'non-wage goods' (ECLA, 1966, p. 49).

Subsidies and tax concessions, it may be added, may be used in relation to industries producing 'essentials' or industries locating in low level of living areas.

Other, but more radical, government measures which may be used for level of living redistribution relate to redistribution of means of production. Redistribution of private property in agriculture is one example; nationalization and concentration of all means of production in the hands of the State is another. Advocates of these measures maintain that, ideally at least, they should be accompanied by a number of institutional and structural reforms to ensure their success and permanency – reforms varying from the establishment of cooperatives and constitutions for government regulation of industry to measures which would ensure the permanent abolition of the old 'exploiting' classes. The choice of policies dealing with redistribution of wealth depends generally on government's particular view as to their effect on incentives, on the particular situation in the country and on questions of social and economic philosophy.

Considered generally less radical today are policies aimed at improving the relative bargaining power of labour *vis-à-vis* employers. On the labour side these policies include minimum wages, social insurance and the promotion of labour unions. On the employer side these policies include anti-trust and anti-monopoly laws and direct control of Government of natural monopolies. Here again there are greater limitations to these policies in developing than in developed countries because of difficulties relating to incentives and coverage.

Government subsidies and services, finally, may be very important tools of level of living redistribution and elimination of poverty. From this point of view their proper formulation requires knowledge of the characteristics of low level of living families (size, age composition, location etc.) and relative deficiencies in the different goods and services which they require for a minimum level of living (nutrition, health, education, housing etc.). Such knowledge may be gained from a study (using poverty and, if need be, other standard budgets), of the 'characteristics of the poor' and the 'characteristics of poverty'. This study would point out, among other things, groups in need which are not directly affected by market forces, for example, the old and the handicapped, and which, therefore, need to be assisted mostly through cash payments or special welfare services. For other groups, alternative methods of assistance may be devised including such government services as health, education, training etc.

In order to be effective, government policies need to reach particular level of living and social groups. There is evidence however, that social services of Government may not be used adequately by certain level of living or social groups. With regard to such services as public education, health, housing and the like, evidence exists that certain groups such as low level of living, peasants and workers, tend to use these services to much lesser extent than other groups. A number of reasons seem to account for this situation but a major reason seems to be that, as formulated, these services still present costs to these groups which are often higher than the benefits, at least as determined by these groups. . .

These generalizations do not necessarily describe the usual situation. Nevertheless the data suggest that they reveal a state of affairs which is not uncommon. For this reason it may be useful to add to the list of redistributional strategies a category along a somewhat different line: devices to ensure access to services and facilities. It is suggested, in other words, that apart from creating new programmes and policies one also achieves redistribution and aids groups in the population to achieve the socially defined minima by arrangements to facilitate access to the established rights, benefits, services, and entitlements and to assure the actual delivery and use of the intended service. [. . .]

Social security, public assistance and social welfare

In most industrialized countries, social security schemes have become so comprehensive in contingency and population coverage as to constitute a major element of the national system of transfers. Public service schemes of a non-contributory nature and those contributory schemes that are publicly subsidized achieve their redistributional effects in close correlation with the national fiscal policy, whether or not such correlation is formally established in relevant legislation. Non-subsidized schemes combining employers' and employees' contributions and those financed by the employers only (employees' 'fringe benefits', for instance) or by the beneficiaries only (voluntary social insurance schemes are an example) are often less comprehensive in scope and their impact on the 'vertical' redistribution of income is more limited, however much they redistribute income within the workers' lifetime.

Achieving such vertical redistribution is a primary purpose of public assistance programmes, providing publicly financed benefits on the basis of a 'means test'. That public assistance and fiscal policies are, potentially at least, of a complementary character is demonstrated by the current discussion in the United States of a proposed 'negative income tax' – an integrated system under which individual incomes would be subject to a tax or open entitlement to a benefit according to whether they are above or below the poverty line.

Family allowances and children's benefits have been established with widely differing purposes in different countries, where they may be distributed irrespective of income as are other social security benefits or, on the contrary, constitute a part of public assistance. Vertical redistribution of income may be a prominent objective of some family allowance schemes, whereas others tend primarily to some equalization of the level of living among families of different sizes at the same general income level. Considerations of social justice may be combined with demographic objectives, although the impact of family allowances on the birth rate is a matter of continuing and still inconclusive scrutiny.

The intervention of social welfare services such as family and child welfare programmes and community services is usually more heavily concentrated on the low-income groups than is the case for other social programmes such as those in the fields of health or education. Flexibility in determining *clientele* and the types of individual help is a positive aspect of most such social welfare programmes, from an income distribution point of view, but it has also been observed that such flexibility is sometimes practised by the agencies concerned at the expense of the most disadvantaged and neediest population groups. Social welfare services may also be employed in the two-way process of interpreting people's needs to the administrations or agencies responsible for other social programmes and of bringing the benefit of such programmes within the reach of those who most need them.

Social programmes that have a substantial and positive influence on income distribution in highly industrialized countries may not have the same impact at all when transferred to developing countries where the economic and social situation is quite different. The impact of social security and social welfare programmes in the developing countries may be radically different because the coverage of the programmes under consideration is of necessity extremely limited at their initial stages, owing to the scarcity of resources available for social measures and for other, more specific reasons. Social security schemes of the existing types are more easily implemented for the numerically small groups of public employees and industrial wage-earners than for the mass of agricultural workers, casual unskilled day workers and the low-income self-employed (street vendors and the like). With regard to public assistance, the basic concept of a means test cannot be applied in any meaningful way in a situation of widespread low subsistence levels. The prevailing concepts of social welfare have developed alongside industrialization and urbanization, with a view to compensating for the gradual disappearance of the traditional institutions of mutual aid; this helps to explain why their access tends to be limited in a number of developing countries to a minority of urban dwellers.

The positive effects to be expected from social security and social welfare programmes in countries at an early stage of industrialization would best be achieved through the development of these programmes within the framework of comprehensive national planning. The priority to be given to such programmes as a group must be determined in relation to that for general health, education and other social programmes. Furthermore, the relative importance of social security schemes, public assistance and social welfare programmes in industrialized countries is hardly relevant to the conditions of the developing world, the requirements of which need to be considered afresh. [. . .]

Many economists, chiefly followers of Keynes, claim that grave maldistribution of income may hinder economic growth. Navarrete, for example, maintains that such a maldistribution is generally accompanied by a structure of demand which promotes labour-intensive methods of production thus resulting in low productivity of labour. This low productivity is again intensified by the fact that, partly because of maldistribution, a large proportion of the population lives in conditions of poverty. The idea of 'defending inequality on the ground that the aggregate output of wealth is low', states Tawney, '. . . argues in a circle, since the hostility and suspicion resulting from inequality are themselves one cause of a low output of wealth' (Tawney, 1961, p. 129).

But if grave income maldistribution may not promote, or may actually hinder, the process of economic growth, it does not necessarily follow that equalization of income could proceed indefinitely (that is, until all incomes are equal or nearly equal) without eventually having a negative effect on the rate of economic growth. Nor does it necessarily follow that the mere narrowing of the income gap between groups would, in itself, contribute to economic development. The actual policy measures which are used to achieve this goal are themselves of major significance; if, for example, substantial redistribution is effected from groups who tend to invest their savings to underprivileged older people or the handicapped, it could hardly be said that such a redistribution would promote economic growth or that it would not hinder it. In fact Rao (1964), for example, seems to maintain that redistribution should not necessarily be from rich to poor but rather from those who spend on conspicuous consumption to those who invest. Thus, Rao considers that:

... the normal pattern of income distribution in an underdeveloped country encourages neither saving nor enterprise and does not, therefore, promote economic growth. Obviously, therefore, a change in the pattern of income distribution, with incomes diverted into the hands of those who will save or invest or undertake entrepreneurial activity, will be a positive factor for the promotion of economic growth (Rao, 1964, p. 309).

Whether redistribution promotes or hinders economic growth depends also on the extent of maldistribution. Admittedly, where extremes of maldistribution exist, that is where a large segment of the population lives in abject poverty while another segment lives in affluence, there is reason to believe that a more equal distribution of income, given the types of policy measures through which it is effected, may well promote economic growth. There is a point or range, however, beyond which conflicts between a more equal distribution of income and economic growth begin to appear. Such conflicts are serious and real and should not be clouded by the 'natural tendency . . . to believe', as Isaiah Berlin once noted, 'that all the things that hold good must be intimately connected or at least compatible with one another' (Berlin, 1958, p. 13).

What could rightfully be argued, in this regard, is that economic growth should not be the sole criterion of government redistributional policies; social justice and welfare, however, defined should also be considered. Where these aims are compatible, problems of choice do not arise. (Some writers argue that these aims become increasingly compatible with affluence – see Myrdal, 1963.) But where they conflict a decision must be made which is not necessarily always in favour of economic growth and depends on political and social as well as economic considerations. More important, economic growth, measured by the rate of growth of income, need not necessarily be maximized at any cost. The ultimate purpose of economic development, it must be recalled, is the improvement of the level of living and satisfaction of the people and must ideally proceed according to certain rules set by society, which do not negate this fact. Technically, the simplest way to raise *per capita* income in an overpopulated economy, to take an exaggerated example, is to dispose of the surplus population, but such a measure could hardly be recommended as a solution even if it were possible. Nor in fact could one recommend that, in such a situation, Government would do well not to reduce mortality rates when it is in its power to do so. Furthermore, the process of growth of income may, in itself, create additional need for income if only because it increasingly transforms the economy into a monetary one and results in social costs which require income for their satisfaction.

It may finally be noted that many policy-makers in developing countries are attempting, with varying degrees of success, to devise an income policy for a largely market economy which would result in a more equal distribution of income without affecting significantly incentives of capitalists, entrepreneurs, managers and labour. It is stated in the development plan of Jamaica, for example, that 'The Government's policy is to provide as equitable a distribution of income and resources among all sections of the population as is compatible with the maintenance of incentives for the achievement of adequate level of production'.[1] International assistance in this regard has, so far, been relatively scarce and would, probably, be widely welcomed.

In addition to the issue of incentives, contemporary writers disagree on the degree of efficiency of income redistribution in

1. Jamaica, *Five-Year Independence Plan, 1963–8*, (Kingston, 1963), p. 57.

solving problems of mass poverty. Particularly in developing countries, the complete equalization of incomes would generally raise the income of the most needy by a trifle. That argument, however,

makes no allowance for the fact that the effect of a transference of wealth is to be judged, not only by the nominal value of the amounts transferred, but also by the nature of the uses from which they are diverted and to which they are applied. ... Collective expenditure makes possible results which would be unattainable were an identical sum distributed, without further adjustments, in factional addition to individual incomes' (Tawney, 1961, pp. 129–30, 248).

The fundamental issue, therefore, is not whether complete income equality through cash transfers would be sufficient to eliminate poverty, but whether the expenditure of the rich which is curtailed by taxes is more useful socially than the expenditure of the Government made possible by the proceeds of these taxes. Tawney maintains, for example, that at least in the United Kingdom, the expenditure curtailed by taxes on high incomes is mostly on luxury while the additional expenditure of Government made possible by these taxes is on worth-while social causes such as education, health, welfare – in brief, on social and economic progress (Tawney, 1961, pp. 130–32; see also Galbraith, 1958, p. 71; and Iyer, 1969, p. 1236). The truth and generality of this position depend, of course, on the definition and extent of luxury expenditure of the rich and on the nature and efficiency of the alternative expenditure by Government – factors which vary greatly from one situation to another. No one for example can, in truth, claim that the rich always squander all their riches on luxury, nor that government expenditure always benefits the poor. [. . .]

There are still, of course, major disagreements on how incomes should be distributed but these are less intense than in the past; and since issues arising from different criteria have been intensively discussed, areas of agreement have become increasingly common. A great deal of the present controversy between egalitarian and non-egalitarian writers has now shifted from ideals and aims to the kind of policies which would best achieve these aims.

There is a good deal of agreement, for example (with the possible exception of some advocates of guaranteed income), that remuneration for work may not, in present conditions at least, be made completely equal and should be related, in some fashion, to productivity and availability of labour of different skills. The need for this is admittedly due to the effect of material incentives on the acquisition of skills and the productive effort of labour. There is also agreement, on the other hand, that in conditions of *laissez-faire* intolerable extremes of inequality may exist because of 'market imperfections' or other causes such as illiteracy. Disagreements which still persist on these points relate more to degree than principle.

A major area of general agreement is that, irrespective of what the ultimate aims of income distribution policies are, the immediate aim should be the elimination of poverty. The extent to which inequalities of incomes beyond the line of poverty should be tolerated is another question. Even Tawney who claims that 'extremes both of riches and poverty are degrading and anti-social' and that we should strive 'not merely to make the poor richer but to make the rich poorer' (Tawney, 1961, p. 27), nevertheless submits that if abject poverty is eliminated and personal achievement through hard work is permitted, 'the most shocking of existing inequalities would be on the way to disappear' (Tawney, 1961, p. 163).

Non-egalitarian writers have generally accepted the proposition that poverty should be eliminated and that public policy – including progressive taxation – should be used for that end. They emphasize, however, the problems of incentives and economic growth that would arise from carrying these policies too far and that, beyond that point, 'only profound intellectual and moral changes in "human nature" could do much about income inequalities' (Knight, 1956, p. 209).

In other words, what egalitarian writers chiefly deplore as an immediate problem, are grave income inequalities resulting in situations of poverty and in situations where no true equality of opportunity could exist; what non-egalitarian writers have chiefly rejected – on the basis of economic and, often, moral and social grounds – is literal equality of incomes. The common ground in these two positions is found mainly in the desirability of eliminating poverty through a more equal distribution of income. The Babouvist idea that incomes must be completely equal or, on the other hand, the idea that poverty is necessary for economic progress,[2] have become untenable, the former as an immediate goal at least, and the latter generally.

Recent national and international declarations have also reflected this general consensus. Of the thirty articles of the Universal Declaration of Human Rights of the United Nations adopted in 1948, by the General Assembly of the United Nations, twenty-four deal with political and legal equality and the rest – articles 22 through 27 – mainly with economic equality. The articles dealing with economic equality do not emphasize the necessity of closing the income gap among people and nations but rather the rights of every individual to economic security and freedom from want.

Article 22. Everyone . . . has the right to social security and is entitled to the realization . . . of the economic, social and cultural rights indispensable for his dignity and the free development of his personality.

Article 25. (1) Everyone has the right to a standard of living adequate for the health and well-being of himself and of his family, including food, clothing, housing and medical care and necessary social services, and the right to security in the event of unemployment, sickness, disability, widowhood, old age or other lack of livelihood in circumstances beyond his control.

Article 26. Everyone has the right to education (Universal Declaration of Human Rights, 1963, p. 37).

The immediate aim of a number of developing countries, furthermore, as stated in their development plans or declared social policy, is again the elimination of poverty and its causes. In a recent reply to a United Nations questionnaire on social targets the Government of Israel stated with relation to its income distribution policies, that the 'Government aims at the

2. It is now generally recognized that extremes of income inequality and poverty may, as R. H. Tawney maintains, hamper economic development mainly because of resulting lack of participation in development by the poor. This was discussed in the meeting, sponsored by the Economic Commission for Asia and the Far East, of the Preparatory Working Group of Experts on Methods of Inducing Social Changes for Overall Development.

improvement of conditions for families in the lower income groups and families with many children' mainly through improvements in their 'social condition' (education and training), through health and social welfare services and through transfer payments; the Government of Iraq declared in this regard that 'in an economy where the majority of the people are in the low-income groups the demand for social justice, the right to productive work and equal opportunity and to the guarantee of a minimum standard of living is a necessity; and the Government of Nepal announced:

All citizens may have equal opportunity and facility to develop their personality and to make economic progress; citizens may have reasonable and adequate means of livelihood; and the ownership and control of the material resources of the community are so regulated as may bring about equitable distribution of wealth and encouragement to private enterprise . . .

The agreement on the idea that poverty should be eliminated is largely based on moral considerations. It is not altogether surprising, therefore, that after centuries of controversy and debate, the major area of agreement with relation to aims of income distribution policy is that commanded by religious teachings centuries before the controversy even began.

References

BERLIN, I. (1958), *Two Concepts of Liberty*, Clarendon Press.
ECLA (1966), 'Social development and social planning', *Econ. Bull. Latin America*, vol. 11, no. 1.
GALBRAITH, J. K. (1958), *The Affluent Society*, New American Library; Penguin.
IYER, S. K. (1965), 'What is holding up rural housing?', *Econ. Weekly*, September.
KNIGHT, F. (1956), 'The determination of just wages', in William D. Grampp (ed.), *Economic Policy; Readings in Political Economy*, R. D. Irwin Inc.
MYRDAL, G. (1963), *Challenge to Affluence*, Pantheon.
RAO, V. K. R. V. (1964), 'Redistribution of income and economic growth in underdeveloped countries', *Income and Wealth*, series 10.
TAWNEY, R. H. (1961), *Equality*, Capricorn.
UNIVERSAL DECLARATION OF HUMAN RIGHTS (1963), *A Standard of Achievement*, United Nations Publications, Sales no. 63.I.13.1.

22 Felix Paukert

Social Security and Income Redistribution

Excerpt from Felix Paukert, 'Social security and income redistribution: a comparative study', *International Labor Review*, vol. 98, 1968, no. 5, pp. 448–50.

Summarizing the various findings made in this paper, we notice that social security systems in developing countries function in environments where there is much more scope for income redistribution than in developed countries, in view of the more unequal distribution of factor incomes. In the developing countries, however, the social security systems operate on a much smaller scale, not only absolutely but also relatively, because the percentage of national income devoted to social security is much smaller than in the developed countries. For this reason, one can expect social security to have a smaller redistribution effect in the developing countries.

But a more important aspect of income redistribution is the different character of social security systems in the developing and developed countries. Unlike developed countries, developing countries spend a large proportion of social security expenditure on government employees, while other schemes are rather fragmentary. Typically, the poorest sections of society are outside the impact of the various social security schemes.

A similar picture emerges when social security revenue is examined. In the developed countries the lower income groups contribute directly (through insured persons' and employers' contributions) and indirectly (through general taxation). In the developing countries the lower income groups, which are not covered by social security, contribute indirectly through general taxation. Two general conclusions follow. The first is the key importance, even for redistribution through social security, of the character of general taxation. This is found to be much more regressive in developing countries than in developed countries. The second general conclusion is that lower income groups in developed countries contribute both directly and indirectly, but the benefits they obtain much more than outweigh the contributions. In developing countries the situation of a large part of the lower income groups is quite different. Typically, such people remain outside the system of social security, receive no benefits, and make no direct contributions. But they contribute through general taxes to social security programmes for groups with somewhat higher incomes.

In assessing the role of social security in income redistribution, one has to keep in mind that the redistribution of income between different incomes groups is not the only or even the main purpose of social security. The main purpose, as stated at the beginning of this paper, is to alleviate distress resulting from sickness, old age, unemployment, etc. Redistribution of income from higher to lower income groups is only a part of this broad purpose. Even in the developed countries social security is not the most important instrument for income redistribution, since a much greater vertical redistribution effect is achieved through direct taxation. But the importance of social security in developed countries is that it reaches the lowest income groups and thus usefully supplements other instruments of income redistribution policy.

In the developing countries the situation is quite different. There the members of income groups not covered by social security lose, not only by being excluded from coverage but also as a result of their indirect contributions to the system through general taxation. It is only when we come up the income redistribution scale to the poorest people covered by the social security system that we find a picture similar to that found in developed countries. People in this group, the lowest-paid government employees or industrial workers, benefit from income redistribution from higher income groups and also to some extent from the lowest (non-protected) income groups. Briefly stated, the position is that while income redistribution through social security in developed countries could be represented as a movement from the top to the bottom, in developing countries it resembles more a movement from the top and the bottom to the centre. The first movement is in accordance with the generally accepted feelings about income redistribution, while the second movement is not. What can be done about it? The most obvious solution to this problem is to expand the social security system along the lines commonly found in the developed countries. Such an expansion would correct the adverse redistribution effects of social security in developing countries. But such a course is not feasible, given the circumstances in which most developing countries find themselves. The most that developing countries can do with respect to a more equitable income redistribution is to attempt to develop social security schemes for people other than government employees in order to reduce the impact of government employees' schemes on total social security expenditure.

Within particular social security schemes, the degree of coverage is of paramount importance. The first step in improving the redistribution aspect of social security should be to abolish the exclusion of some of the lowest-paid workers (e.g. domestic servants) from particular schemes. The second step, more important but more difficult, would be to extend the coverage of particular schemes to rural workers and to self-employed persons. There are many different problems to be faced in such an extension, problems that are outside the context of this discussion. However, it might be mentioned that this complex of questions is currently receiving particular attention in the work of the International Labour Organization.

The third step in improving the redistribution effects of social security in developing countries really lies outside the boundaries of social security systems. It concerns the structure of general taxation. To make the global incidence of general taxation in developing countries more progressive would be not only the most important single redistribution step within the power of government but would also greatly increase and improve the income redistribution effect of social security.

23 Leonard Barnes

China Story

Excerpts from Leonard Barnes, *African Renaissance*, Gollancz, 1969, pp. 280–94.

Priority for agriculture

The scale of the Chinese effort has been rightly emphasized by René Dumont in his book *Chine Surpeuplée* (1965), which begins with the observation, 'In the whole history of world agriculture, no peasant countryside has ever changed as much as that of Eastern China between 1955 and 1964.' The purpose of the present sketch is to urge the need for strategists of African development to understand with an open mind the real nature of that change, the grounds on which it was carried through, the mistakes made during its execution, and the measure of its current and prospective success. No intelligent African who reaches that degree of understanding will find it difficult to draw such lessons as may be valid in the conditions of his continent.

In much of our contemporary world, especially in the West, of which this student happens to be a native and an inhabitant, it is regarded as a form of treason to speak of China except in terms of contumely. The attitude is a common one among the ruling cliques of Africa too. He is aware that he throws himself open to that charge in discussing Chinese affairs with politeness and objectivity. It is a risk that he is happy to run, if at the same time he can let in a little genuine light on the baffling problems of African rebirth. The world climax is too close upon us for grown men to allow themselves to be scared by childish bogies. He is comforted at finding himself in Dumont's company here, and proud to acknowledge his debt to Dumont's work.

China's independence came only about ten years ahead of Africa's. The country at that time had been ravaged by twenty years of war, and degraded by a century of colonialism. In point of economic development, the Chinese were among the most retarded nations of the world. China was already a land of endemic famine, sunk, in relation to its current productive capacity, in a terrifying slough of over-population. Its general situation was incalculably worse than that of any tropical African country since 1960, except the Belgian Congo.

The victory in the civil war had, however, been won by a well disciplined Communist Party. The Party leaders, who were also the political rulers, held the U S S R in warm regard as the father of practical communism, whose struggles and achievements afforded the only possible model for China to adopt. They showed no hesitation in stepping briskly out along the trail which the Bolsheviks had blazed over the previous thirty years. The key to Chinese development was to be urban industrialization, with heavy industry as its base, plus the dictatorship of the proletariat.

Experience quickly showed that this pattern did not work in Chinese conditions. No rapid economic expansion took place. The Party, beginning to suspect that growth in China would have to be based on the peasantry, and not on industrial wage-earners, set out to re-think the whole problem of Chinese socialism. The end-result, after many years of intensive deliberation, was a new model which completely set aside the Soviet design. In accordance with Chinese custom, admission of this parting of the ways was a gradual process. It was not until 1964 that Chou En-lai openly and officially declared 'the order of priority is agriculture, light industry, heavy industry'.

By reducing the scope of heavy industry, the planners released large quantities of materials, equipment, and labour, and were therefore able to raise the proportion of investment earmarked for agriculture and for modes of production directly serving it, such as hydro-electric schemes, fertilizers, farm machinery, insecticides.

The People's Communes were originally conceived as the form of organization for carrying out a great leap forward along the whole economic front including heavy industry. Their character and aims naturally shifted with the new primacy accorded to the rural interest. The constitution of the original type of Commune (it was christened Sputnik in honour of the U S S R, rather ironically in view of later events) was published on 7 August 1958. There followed four years of radical experiment and re-adaptation. In

1962 the New Model Commune emerged in a fairly standardized form which gave effect to the special importance of the peasantry. It has undergone only minor structural alterations since.

The Commune, however, remains capable of indefinite organic evolution in harmony with changes in 'the law of the situation'. It is a mistake to suppose, as some enemies of China too readily do, that a phase of ossification is setting in. The official watchword of the future is continuous review, taking time by the forelock. Chen Yi declared in an interview on 12 May 1964: 'At last we know precisely how to proceed. We have made and re-made the Communes, and if necessary we shall re-make them again until perfection is reached.' (Quoted in Dumont, 1965, p. 99.) It is this fluent adaptability of structure, this ease of response to improve design, which should be of special interest in Africa.

Growth of the Commune

The People's Commune did not spring fully armed from the brain of Chairman Mao. It grew naturally from objective and flexible attempts by peasants and Party alike to apply cooperative principles to farm production in Chinese conditions. In this early growth between 1952 and 1957 four main steps can be traced.

Mutual aid teams. These were made up of anything from six to fifteen households working together, at first on a seasonal basis, and chiefly on 'public works' of an environmental rather than a directly productive nature, e.g. roads, drainage, water supplies, conservation, etc. People found that it paid them to make such *ad hoc* arrangements permanent, and to extend them to many tasks of production. Such groups had long been known in China. The Party simply generalized them.

Agricultural producers' cooperatives (lower-grade). As the mutual aid teams became better organized and more universal, difficulties often arose in attempting to mix the collective character of the work with the private control of land, draught animals, implements, etc.

In the USSR nationalization of the land had been one of the very first steps taken by the revolution. In China, on the contrary, the development of the Communes has not so far called for such a policy, and the land is still unnationalized. Instead, the early producer cooperatives met their problem by empowering their management committees to direct the utilization of the land (still *owned* in private) in accordance with an agreed plan. All produce, furthermore, was treated as a unit for distribution. From it was taken first the tax, then the allocations for investment and welfare, the residue finally being apportioned among members according to the work and the land put in by each.

The reforms imparted a new development-momentum to the 'lower-grade' cooperative. Output increased significantly, and with it the earnings of members. The collective investments in turn, by constantly modernizing the infrastructure, further improved the possibilities of production.

As the level rises in this way, new difficulties special to it crop up. Irrigation schemes, for instance, financed by collective investment and serving the holdings of many members, have to be installed on the privately owned land of one or a few. Or again a persistent tendency appears, in the distribution of earnings, for a member contributing more land and less labour to get a larger share than one contributing more labour and less land.

Agricultural producers' cooperatives (higher-grade). It is in resolving difficulties of this sort that the higher-grade cooperatives (later to be called brigades) emerge. In them the land, together with all other productive capital, becomes the collective property of the society as such. The element of land rent is eliminated from the calculation of members' earnings, which henceforward are distributed on the sole basis of work done (with adjustments for variations in the character of the land). At this stage, too, a new feature is introduced in the form of social assistance. 'The five guarantees' are given to member-families who may fall into hardship – nourishment, clothing, shelter, education of children, and decent burial.

Members retain ownership of their houses, their small livestock, and their private allotments (the aggregate of which, however, must not reach ten per cent of the area worked by the cooperative).

The higher-grade cooperative, like the lower-grade, settles its own production plan.

Non-agricultural organs. Complementary to the higher-grade cooperative, and essential for speeding up the rhythm of development, are cooperatives for marketing, supply, credit and thrift, and crafts. In their beginnings these are really local agents, enjoying a considerable measure of autonomy, of the State Plan for sales and purchases. At a later stage they re-enter the scene as autonomous enterprises of the People's Commune. Between them they furnish the ground for a network of small rural business and industries which, as they grow, modernize themselves by whatever means are at hand.

The Commune's main components

Such, in outline, was the position reached by agrarian policy in China by 1958, nine years after victory in the civil war. In that year, as has been mentioned, the formal constitution of the People's Commune (Mark I) was for the first time made public. There immediately began a period of intensive growth and re-shaping of the prototype which lasted for four years. For an account of this complex series of difficulties, advances, retreats, successes, and failures the student is referred to pages 66–82 of Dumont's book, where details are impartially given. By 1962 the New Model commune, like a modern airliner, its development and its tests completed, was ready to go into commercial production.

The changes in design between Mark I and the New Model were made partly in response to the internal needs of the People's Commune considered as a social organism, partly in the light of larger events by which all China was affected. The four-year period includes the great leap forward, and the long black years of 1959–62 which shook the country to the core. It therefore includes the summer of 1960 when the Soviet experts and Soviet technical and financial aid were withdrawn. Thenceforward China was to live, albeit of choice as well as of necessity, by the motto 'By ourselves alone', which applies to the People's Communes just as strictly as to the Chinese State.

By 1965 China completed the repayment of all her indebtedness to the USSR, including the cost of military supplies used in the Korean war. The Soviet offer, made in 1963, to reopen credits and renew the loan of experts was definitively refused, lest these things should be employed as instruments of political pressure.

The New Model commune has four basic components:

1. *The work-teams*. These vary in number from one commune to another. There were seventy of them in one typical commune reported by Dumont (p. 136). Each work-team manages its own affairs by way of a general meeting of all members. Its day-to-day tasks are directed by its elected manager.

2. *The brigades*. These consist of groups of work-teams. Each brigade is managed by a committee to which the work-teams nominate their delegates.

3. *The commune*. The council of the commune is constituted by representatives of the Brigade Committees chosen for two years. The council meets twice yearly. Its General Purposes Committee, having elected a director and a deputy-director, meets once a week. The director is assisted by various administrative sections, for example those concerned with accounts, purchases and sales, crop production, stock raising, works (i.e. buildings, irrigation, electricity), farm mechanization, seed selection and testing.

4. *The science team*. A further component part of some communes, though not yet of all – a feature of great interest and importance – is the science team. In the case of the commune *China-Cuba*, visited by Dumont in 1965, it was made up of thirty-two graduates, forty-three technicians, and three-hundred and sixty peasant members, many of whom were undertaking evening courses of training. Twenty research scientists were testing various possibilities of technical progress.

The commune, for its part, through its personnel and installations, provides the science team with ample means of observation, experiment, and action.

The commune production plan forms, of course, an integral part of the State Plan, and is worked out, after a prolonged flow of two-way consultative traffic, at the level of the district; similarly the brigade production plan is worked out at the level of the commune; and the work-team production plan at the brigade level (though the means of executing the production plan agreed remain the responsibility of the work-team).

The production plan settles:

1. The kinds and amounts of output to be produced in the year;
2. The amounts to be marketed, especially sales to the State;

3. The gross income;
4. Members' earnings;
5. Allocations for investment.

In arriving at operative decisions on these matters, the *Three in One* rule is applied. In other words, on every important issue there must be unanimous agreement between the management (which includes the Party), the technicians, and the work-people, especially the older peasants who represent an indispensable fund of local experience.

In point of size communes vary widely. Dumont reports that the smallest of the twenty-two communes which he visited had ten thousand inhabitants, and the largest had seventy-five thousand, though the latter was by no means typical because it was on the outskirts of the main town of the district. [. . .]

The pillars of the system

Even so brief an outline as the above affords some scope for assessing the first-order significance of the commune system. Four features appear to qualify for this description.

1. China has founded its whole strategy on the farming domain as the crucial point of departure for all balanced social and economic development.

2. Hence it endows the peasant unit of production with political and administrative powers. The commune management, merging as it does with the ground-level organs of the State administration, is responsible for all aspects of affairs within its idea.

Dumont quotes (p. 83) the official definition:

The People's Commune is the basic unit of our socialist social structure, as also of the power structure of our socialist state. It brings together industry, agriculture, commerce, education, and military affairs.

This is an unusual, perhaps a unique, combination of competences to be entrusted to an organ of local government. The long-term consequences of its introduction seem likely to be important not only within China. Some observers, friendly and hostile alike, speak of it almost with bated breath, as if nothing in the world can henceforward be quite the same.

3. China fuses together at all educational levels scholastic work

with manual work. In this way a cultural cleavage between peasants and intelligentsia is sought to be avoided, officialdom to be prevented from hardening into a privileged caste, and the output of neo-mandarins from the school system to be radically curtailed. The Soviet weakness of arrogance among managers and the Cuban weakness of indiscipline among workpeople will both, it is hoped, be by-passed.

An enormous and constant effort of in-training is made, an unresting search for ways of upgrading the performance of workers on the job. Book-keepers, statisticians, 'model-workers' stream through the agronomic institutes, refresher courses are arranged for those in authority, high or low.

Dumont's feeling is clearly that this intense preoccupation with the means to an efficient social and economic order is matched by equal attention to the realm of ends. Every Chinese citizen is urged and helped to reflect as deeply as he can on the motives and the relationships of mutual aid, and on the requirements of the common good. This, in the party jargon, is called raising the level of socialist consciousness. It provides Chinese society, leaders and led, with what is altogether missing from African, a point to march on and to get its bearings by.

The outcome is the spread of an ascetic morality which seeks flexible sophistication in public affairs, yet holds to the child-state in private conduct. As all observers testify, it results in a marked reduction of corruption (in the African sense) in Chinese life. The resolve of Chinese leaders to *rester avec les pauvres* is always evident. *Puisse l'Afrique raisonner ainsi.*

4. China has acknowledged the need to limit population growth, if economic expansion and social growth are to be speeded up. To be sure, there have been some fluctuations in the official line on this thorny issue. For the first six years of the revolution the issue was not faced at all, and was evidently not thought of as having high priority. In 1956–7 contraceptive practices were tentatively recommended by posters, etc., up and down the country. The year 1958 saw a complete *volte-face*, and all birth control steps were harshly condemned, at least in words.

The reversal, it seems, was based on the simplified view that every consumer is, or may be, also a producer. As the Chinese put it, each new mouth is accompanied by two new arms. The arms would increase the food supply in a measure satisfying to the mouth. The magnitude of the problem had been very faultily assessed.

The population growth-rate assumed in the first five-year plan (1952–7) was 2·23 per cent a year. On a total population of six-hundred-and-fifty millions this would mean an annual increase of some 14 millions. It did not take the planners long to find out that any idea of feeding such numbers by stepping up Chinese agriculture was in the long term quite chimerical. Even at six-hundred-and-fifty millions, China was seriously over populated. The real need was to bring the growth rate down below one per cent a year.

China always seeks to know the facts; and once they are known they are decisive. In 1963 the official line was corrected. Thenceforward the emphasis was on the paramount necessity of planned parenthood. Japan has cut its birth rate by half in ten years, mainly by means of generalized abortion. China now discreetly does what it can to terminate unwanted pregnancies in the same way, subject to limits imposed by the distribution of doctors and rural clinics.

It also makes use of an ingenious variety of social and political pressures. The age of marriage is retarded by film propaganda. The allocation of housing is held up, often till the age of thirty for men and twenty-five for women. The private land-holdings of members of work-teams are limited to one third of an acre per head, with a maximum of two acres per household, so that parents cannot acquire an out-size plot by raising an out-size family.

Political discipline in China is such that the State and the Party can, as a serious practical measure, recommend not only the use of contraceptives, but also the observance of general continence. When Chairman Mao proclaims 'It pays better to swat mosquitoes than to make love', he has some assurance that his powerful thoughts will indeed reduce the human as well as the insect population. Numbers of young people, devotees of the revolution, have responded by taking vows of permanent chastity, and their resolve has been warmly praised in public by Chou En-lai. *Puisse l' Afrique raisonner ainsi.*

Some secondary gains

Such are the principles which form the main pillars of the commune system. If the New China is upheld by them, they may have a central significance for African modernization also, as soon as African leaders come to study carefully their bearing on Africa's problems – which, after all, are in essence remarkably similar to China's. Indeed, it seems absurd that Africa should not benefit, and quickly, from the brilliant inventiveness of the Chinese experiments in social and economic organization. Certainly the People's Commune is not a model that African countries can just copy word for word. But its organizing principles can equally certainly be adapted to fit the material and the psycho-social conditions of Africa. For that, no more is needed than a sufficient proportion of Africans with the wit and the motive to grasp fully what those organizing principles are all about.

When this adequate number of adequate Africans at length takes the field, they will be struck by the richness of second-order advantages that flow from the four cardinal points.

For example, the commune, by reason of its scale and scope, paves the way for an ever more sophisticated division of labour and an ever more varied pattern of land use within the farming process itself, by setting up, when occasion arises, special work-teams or brigades for fishing, fruit-growing, forestry, market-gardening, bee-keeping, poultry farming, pig production, dairying, industrial crops, etc. Equally important, it can provide economically a range of workshops and processing plants to service farm production. It can thus gradually bring about the measure of development in light industry that village life needs for full amenity, without allowing its perversion into the wasteful and psychologically perilous disorder of urbanism.

Industry introduced in this way to the heart of the village, even if it pauses temporarily at the craft stage (the level of 'intermediate technology'), transforms the village mentality, deepens its belief in science and progress, diffuses among the rank and file the outlook of the estate manager and improver. At the same time, it offers a kind of preliminary training in the efficient use of tractors, engines, and power-machinery in general.

Again, the commune, in the readjusted and consolidated form now virtually universal in China, well appreciates the need to decentralize responsibility for the day-to-day running of farm work. The most important economic power, that which relates to the daily round and can take account of such vital details as rain or frost or settled sunny weather, is entrusted to the small units, usually the work-teams, sometimes the brigades, especially when 'socialist consciousness' is well advanced in them.

With such necessary decentralization the commune mixes a unified direction wherever it is desirable to maintain this, e.g. in settling of production plans, in planning large-scale construction, in arrangements for deliveries in kind to the State, in the disposal of local grain surpluses and of industrial crops. The mixture makes possible a constant dialogue between base and summit, which is a real exchange of views and not a mere transmission of orders from on high followed too late by remonstrances from below. As the Chinese put it, 'the work-team within the commune is like a fish in water. As the fish, though it holds the initiative, is helpless without the water, so the team without the commune also is helpless.' In economic terms, the work-team contributes the advantages of optimum location, the commune those of scale.

Another of the commune's claims is to have dealt successfully with that bugbear of Africa, the issue of rural investment. The commune is the channel for work-investment at all three levels, team, brigade, and commune itself, and such investment often approaches and sometimes exceeds 10 per cent of all days worked.

More specifically, Dumont lists all sources of investment internal to the commune and gives them a value:

Table 1

Half the land tax	say 4·5 per cent of gross output
The investment funds of work-teams, brigades and communes	say 7·0 per cent of gross output
Work-days earmarked for infrastructure work	say 5·0 per cent of gross output

Thus we get 15–20 per cent of farm output going into rural investment, a rate unknown in Europe before the industrial revolution, and unknown elsewhere in the Third World today. [. . .]

The Chinese evidence is proof, which Africa must surely one day heed, that the sole factor which cannot be dispensed with in social development is an unshakeable reliance on self-help. If that is absent, foreign aid is useless; if that is present, foreign aid is if not otiose, at least very secondary.

Self-help, among many other things, involves putting the whole rural population to productive work the whole year round, as the only possible way of reaching that high rate of productive investment which is everywhere and always the vital fulcrum of generalized growth. Among African peasant farmers, working the whole year round is something that has never and nowhere been known.

Finally, over and above the investment question, the commune system displays an economic sophistication which may well prove decisive for human relations in industry. It has shown how to avoid the more serious defects of agricultural organization in the USSR and Cuba, namely too large work-teams, tax liability which rises with productivity, and earnings not geared to output.

In consequence, it is well on the way to solving the big problem of socialism during the phase of struggle to establish itself alongside a predominant capitalism. This is the problem of working out an incomes policy which, while being fair as between persons and grades, is at the same time the most effective in encouraging individual endeavour within the framework of the collective task.

Reference

DUMONT, R. (1965), *Chine Surpeuplée*, Editions du Seuil, Paris.

Part Four
Ideology and Poverty

It is virtually impossible to discuss any aspect of poverty – measurement techniques, causes, or remedies – without the discussion being strongly affected by political and economic value preferences. While the selections in Parts Two and Three vary in the degree to which such influences are out in the open, the careful reader will not have much difficulty in discerning the political-economic values of any of the authors. Part Four comprises a set of papers in which the role of ideology in relation to poverty is not only explicit but is the major theme.

In the excerpt from 'The Beam in Our Eyes', Gunnar Myrdal discusses the serious consequences of two main sources of bias in Western countries in their dealings with underdeveloped nations. One is the 'predominant role given to considerations of international power relations', exemplified by the preoccupation with saving these nations from communism. The second source of bias is the mechanical application of Western economic development theory to the problems of development in non-Western nations. Myrdal alerts the reader to the fact that concepts of unemployment and underemployment, theories pertaining to markets and prices and to the distribution and use of income rest on assumptions about living standards and institutions that are appropriate for developed lands but not for poor countries. His comments have important implications for many of the papers on 'roots and remedies', appearing in the previous section.

President Johnson's 1968 message to Congress on the Foreign Aid Programme is an excellent illustration of what Myrdal is referring to when he stresses the role of political and military expedience in motivating much of the aid to poor nations and determining the course and consequences of this aid.

Paul Mattick's essay-review of Myrdal's *Asian Drama* summarizes the gist of Myrdal's extraordinarily long and complex 'inquiry into the poverty of nations'. More importantly, for our purposes, it offers a critique of Myrdal's analysis from a Marxist stand-point and conveys a good deal of what would constitute a Marxist approach to the question of the sources and resolution of poverty in underdeveloped lands. Mattick contends that Myrdal is caught up in many contradictions, the basic one being his 'theoretical attempt to combine irreconcilables, namely, a Capitalist market economy with authoritarian controls designed to subject capital production to actual social needs.' One might conclude from Mattick's appraisal that Myrdal himself is constrained by a beam in his eye similar to the one which he so forcibly argues is the trademark of Western economists.

Elinor Graham's early appraisal of America's War on Poverty is that it can best be comprehended as a 'key ingredient in the social and political ideology' of the Johnson administration. She deals with a number of ideological facets of the rediscovery of poverty in the early 1960s and the various schemes launched in an attempt to cope not only with poverty but also with the implications of its presence amid affluence. She contends that poverty became such a politically important issue in 1964 largely because of the increasingly volatile effects of the thwarted civil rights movement. There was a 'need to redefine the racial conflict as a conflict between the "haves" and the "have-nots"'. The ideological differences which Graham indicates are features of the War on Poverty pervade most of the literature on poverty in other nations. Among these are: whether the roots of poverty are basically in the individual or the social system, the competition between liberal and conservative plans for social action or inaction, and the treatment of the poor as participants or pawns in political power struggles.

Richard Titmuss comments on the War on Poverty in the United States from the vantage point of a European. His assessment that the poverty war was launched in the belief that it could be won cheaply and that no significant changes in economic arrangements would occur has proved correct. He believes that the welfare capitalist mentality in Britain as well as in the United States has led to common approaches in both nations which assume that poverty will be eliminated by efficient administration characterized by 'determination' and 'know-how'. Of greater significance is Titmuss' discussion of how the hubbub over poverty has obscured the far more crucial issue of *inequality*. 'To recognize inequality as the problem involves recognizing the need for structural change, for sacrifices by the majority.' He indicates several ideological forces which deflect concern from the fundamental problem of inequality toward a preoccupation with the symptomatic manifestations of poverty.

According to Keith Buchanan, the plight of the Southeast Asian world cannot be remedied by implementing any version of neo-capitalist development planning. Indeed, as he reads the evidence, the 'enterprising' relationship between developed, 'free enterprise' Western nations and their junior underdeveloped partners is the cause of the widening gap between them. The only viable solution is the socialist path, specifically a form of socialism akin to that adopted in North Korea, North Vietnam, and China. Buchanan's championing of this answer to the worsening plight of so many poor lands stands in sharp contrast to even Myrdal's relatively enlightened proposals, not to mention the more conventional remedies flowing from a 'free enterprise' value system.

24 Gunnar Myrdal

The Beam in Our Eyes

Excerpt from Gunnar Myrdal, *Asian Drama: An Inquiry into the Poverty of Nations*, Twentieth Century Fund, 1968; Pantheon Books, 1968; Allen Lane The Penguin Press, 1968; Penguin Books, 1968, pp. 12–23.

Political strategy and diplomacy in research

Impelled by the immense interest at stake, it is natural that the national authorities, the institutions sponsoring and financing research, and, indeed, public opinion in the West all press for studies of the problems of the underdeveloped countries. This clamor for research is entirely justified, as these problems are of increasing political importance to the Western countries themselves. But the studies are also expected to reach opportune conclusions and to appear in a form that is regarded as advantageous, or at least not disadvantageous, to national interests as these are officially and popularly understood. Such community pressure for opportunistic research operates in all Western countries, especially in the larger ones actively involved in the cold war. It operates also, though occasionally in a different direction, in the underdeveloped countries themselves. Their institutions and authorities and their educated class – whose views are commonly referred to as 'public' opinion – are becoming more and more touchy about most questions dealt with in social study.

The most perceptible political influence on the research approach in Western countries to the problems of South Asian countries is the predominant role given to considerations of national power and international power relations. In a world full of perils to national security and survival, this tendency is understandable; it is often asserted to be a more realistic direction of social research. The implication is, however, that studies of the problems of underdeveloped countries are now undertaken, not with a view to the universal and timeless values that are our legacy from the Enlightenment, but with a view to the fortuitous and narrow political or, narrower still, military-strategic interests of one state or bloc of states. All sorts of studies are now justified by, or focused on, their contribution to the 'security' of Western countries. This officious accommodation by the scholarly profession to a new political 'realism' in research often borders on the ridiculous. Even a respectable biologist's compilation of available research on the influence of climatic factors on organisms in the tropics may be introduced by and interspersed with glib and, understandably, inexpert reflections concerning the political effect on the 'free world' of economic development there.

Often this is no more than a confession of faith by a troubled soul. At other times it may be intended to provide a mantle of respectability in an emotional environment dominated by non-professionals. Most of the time it turns out that the political or even the military-strategic interests of one's own country are taken to consist in the preservation of very general values. The 'best interests of the United States', for instance, dictate the establishment and growth in the underdeveloped countries of what many people there themselves strive for: a stable and, where possible, democratic regime in a consolidated nation capable of economic development. This would be an interesting and, we believe, a broadly valid formulation of how American democracy evaluates the underdeveloped countries in the long run. Applied, as it frequently is, to a contemporary short-term perspective on American foreign policy at a time of fluid conflicts and tactical alliances, the proposition is less evidently valid in the policies pursued and is often clearly belied by them. In any case, it is difficult to see the relevance of this assumption about American society, or American interests, to the scientific study of an underdeveloped country's own experiences and problems. If, nevertheless, it *is* given relevance, the door is opened to all sorts of extraneous influences on research approaches, in other words, to biases.

A major source of bias in much economic research on poor countries is thus the endeavour to treat their internal problems from the point of view of the Western political and military interest in saving them from Communism. Sometimes this intention is stated, though not in the form of a reasoned presentation of specific value premises logically related to the definition of the concepts used. More often it remains implicit in the approach, though the study is interspersed with suggestive formulations. This type of reasoning must often make the public and scholars in the underdeveloped countries suspicious and irritated, as they naturally want their problems analysed from the point of view of their own interests and valuations. The taking of an outside view does not in itself constitute a fault in the methodology of scientists whose criterion of validity cannot be the acceptability of approaches and conclusions to the people concerned. What is important is that the practice usually goes hand in hand with a retreat from scientific standards, which permits the entrance of uncontrolled biases – and this, of course, gives substance to the suspicion and irritation in underdeveloped countries.

Consideration of Western political and military interests in saving the underdeveloped countries from Communism invites inhibitions, for instance, about observing and analysing the shortcomings of political regimes in those countries – provided, let it be noted, that they are not friendly with the enemy in the cold war. An indication of such tortuous reasoning, which lends itself to opportunistic arrangement of the facts, is the use even in scholarly writings of labels like 'the free world' or 'the free Asian countries' to denote, not that people are free in the ordinary sense of the word, but the purely negative fact that a country's foreign policy is not aligned to that of the Communist bloc or blocs. This is not an innocent terminological matter; such practice hides shifts in the meaning of concepts. And, as the literature abundantly proves, this kind of reasoning tends to give strength by association to an assortment of loosely argued and inexplicitly stated value preferences even in matters of internal policy – economic policy in regard to foreign trade and exchange, public versus private enterprise, and so on.

This opportunistic approach to a research task is not necessarily, or even ordinarily, egoistic and hard-hearted in its conclusions. A study may have as its purpose to discover better based and politically appealing reasons for giving more generous aid to the underdeveloped countries. The political influences on Western social research do not usually encourage unkind treatment of underdeveloped countries – as long as they are not hopelessly lost to the enemy bloc. On the contrary, what national communities more or less overtly demand from their social scientists are essays in practical diplomacy pleading certain directions of external and internal policy and giving a more solid and scholarly foundation to such pleas. When, as often happens, social scientists resist having their work turned into diplomacy, the pressures on them may nevertheless force them to engage in research on particularly innocuous problems in an underdeveloped country that have less immediate connection with political issues. They become accustomed to bypass facts that raise awkward problems, to conceal them in technical terminology, or to treat them in an 'understanding' and forgiving manner. There are also biases in research. Conditioning that results in omissions rather than commissions nonetheless erodes the basis for objective research. The scholar should not be made to speak with tongue in cheek.

These remarks are not intended to isolate the economic problems of underdeveloped countries from the ideological and power constellations of world politics. The cold war has, of course, considerable bearing on events in the underdeveloped countries of South Asia; and their political allegiance to a power bloc, or their neutrality, is worth studying. Most certainly, the drift of its economy and the social and economic policies it pursues can effect such a country's alignment in the cold war, though this problem is often oversimplified. An underdeveloped country that, for whatever reason, comes under Communist rule will apply Soviet methods of planning for economic development, and this will bring about a major change in the situation under study. In the same way a country's dependence on credits and gifts from the Western bloc may influence its internal policies and thereby affect the social reality we are studying. But to recognize these causal relations is not to say that the Western interest in winning the underdeveloped countries as allies or at least keeping them neutral is an appropriate value premise for the study of their development problems. If it *is* chosen as a value premise, it should be chosen openly and operate in a logical way that does not detract from scientific objectivity. Diplomacy is essential to national policy, but it is disastrous when it dominates the work of social scientists.

The tendency to think and act in a diplomatic manner when dealing with the problems of the underdeveloped countries of South Asia has, in the new era of independence, become a counterpart to the 'white man's burden' in colonial times. No one with any critical sense can be unaware of this trend. I can myself testify that British and American and other Western scholars confess and defend as a principle – when speaking 'among ourselves,' that is, among us who are from the rich and progressive countries – the necessity to 'bend over backwards'. Not only politicians but also scholars, in public appearances, will apologize for making even slightly derogatory remarks and suggest that as foreigners they should not venture to express a view on the matter. In the literature such discretion leads to the avoidance of certain problems and the deliberate understatement of negative findings. I have often heard writers explain that they did this in order not to hurt feelings. A Russian scholar addressing a South Asian audience is equally tactful now that the policy of the Soviet Union has become friendly to the 'bourgeois-nationalist' regimes in the region.

I am here not arguing against diplomacy, except in scientific research. A scholar should work and express himself identically at home and in a foreign country. As a scientist he should, of course, have no loyalty other than that to the truth as he perceives it. When speaking in a wealthy, powerful country like the United States this is easy, as I know from experience. The situation is apparently felt to be different in the underdeveloped countries. But it should be understood that diplomacy of this kind is tantamount to condescension, while to speak frankly is to treat the nationals of these countries as equals. If South Asians realized this, they should be offended by such diplomacy.

An example of how our thinking has become biased in this direction is the escape into terminology that is thought to be more diplomatic than the ordinary usage, as when one or another euphemism is preferred to 'underdeveloped countries'.

Another source of bias:
transference of Western concepts and theories

Another primary source of bias of special importance to the study of the underdeveloped countries of South Asia may appear to be more mechanical, a function merely of the rapidity with which we have undertaken massive research in a previously almost uncultivated field. As research must of necessity start from a theory, a set of analytical preconceptions, it was tempting to use the tools that were forged in the West and that, in the main, served a useful purpose there,[1] without careful consideration of their suitability for South Asia. Thus a Western approach became incorporated into the mainstream of the discussion of development problems in South Asia, both within the region and outside it. Indeed, Western theoretical approaches have assumed the role of master models. For reasons we shall go into at considerable length in the body of the book, a Western approach must be regarded as a biased approach. Let us attempt to understand how this transfer came to pass.

Economic theorists, more than other social scientists, have long been disposed to arrive at general propositions and then postulate them as valid for every time, place, and culture. There is a tendency in contemporary economic theory to follow this path to the extreme. For such confidence in the constructs of economic reasoning, there is no empirical justification. But even apart from this recent tendency, we have inherited from classical economics a treasury of theories that are regularly posited with more general claims than they warrant. The very concepts used in their construction aspire to a universal applicability that they do not in fact possess. As long as their use is restricted to our part of the world this pretense of generality may do little harm. But when theories and concepts designed to fit the special conditions of the Western world – and thus containing the implicit assumptions about social reality by which this fitting was accomplished – are used in the study of underdeveloped countries in South Asia, where they do *not* fit, the consequences are serious.

There is a conservatism of methodology in the social sciences, especially in economics, that undoubtedly has contributed to the adherence to familiar Western theories in the intensive study of underdeveloped countries. Economists operate to a great extent within a framework that developed early in close relationship with the Western philosophies of natural law and utilitarianism and the rationalistic psychology of hedonism. Only with time has this tradition been adapted to changing conditions, and then without

1. Throughout this book I am making the generous assumption that the Western approach is fairly adequate to Western conditions. This might be an overstatement. In any case, this is a book on South Asia, and I have not felt it to be my task to go into a critical analysis of the use of Western concepts and theories outside the region I am studying.

much feeling of need for radical modifications. That economists work within a methodologically conservative tradition is usually not so apparent to the economists themselves, especially as the tradition affords them opportunity to display acumen and learning and, within limits, to be inventive, original, and controversial. Even the heretics remain bound by traditional thought in formulating their heresies. As circumstances, particularly political ones, changed, there was room for a shifting of emphasis and approach. When theoretical innovations lagged far behind events, such adjustments sometimes took on the appearance of definite breaks, as in the so-called Keynesian 'revolution'. The new thoughts were soon integrated into the traditional mold, slightly modified to better suit the environment, the changes in which were themselves largely responsible for inspiring fresh thinking.

Occasionally a breakthrough established new lines of thought that contrasted more sharply with tradition. The most important challenge came, of course, from Marx and his followers. But Marx, at the base of his constructs, retained much of classical economic theory. And gradually economists remaining within the fold incorporated large parts of what was or seemed novel in Marx's approach, not least in regard to the problems of development, as we shall see. For both these reasons we should not be surprised to find that the biases operating on Western economists often tend to converge with those conditioning economists in the Communist countries.

When we economists, working within this tenacious but variegated and flexible tradition of preconceptions that admittedly are not too badly fitted to our own conditions, suddenly turn our attention to countries with radically different conditions, the risk of fundamental error is exceedingly great.[2] This risk is heightened by the dearth of empirical data on social realities in the underdeveloped countries of South Asia, which enables many biases to be perpetuated that might be questioned and corrected if concepts and theories could be exposed to the challenge of concrete facts.

2. 'One ever-present problem is the possibility that a conceptual scheme will imprison the observer, allowing him to see only what the scheme directs him to see and ruling out other interpretations of data. It is readily admitted that this danger is implicit in all *a priori* thinking.' (Snyder and Paige, 1958, p. 358.)

The problem is compounded by another consequence of the Western-biased approach. When new data are assembled, the conceptual categories used are inappropriate to the conditions existing: as, for example, when the underutilization of the labor force in the South Asian countries is analysed according to Western concepts of unemployment, disguised unemployment, and underemployment. The resulting mountains of figures have either no meaning or a meaning other than that imputed to them. Empirical research then becomes faulty and shallow, and, more important in the present context, less valuable for testing the premises latent in the Western concepts that have guided the production of new statistics. The very fact that the researcher gets figures to play with tends to confirm his original, biased approach. Although it is the confrontation with the facts that ultimately will rectify our conceptual apparatus, initially the paucity and flimsiness of data in underdeveloped countries leave ample opportunity for biases, and the continuing collection of data under biased notions only postpones the day when reality can effectively challenge inherited preconceptions.

The danger of bias does not necessarily arise from the fact that students from the rich countries in the West inevitably face the problems of underdeveloped countries in South Asia as strangers. If anything, the outsider's view has advantages in social research. There are two ways of knowing a toothache: as a patient or as a dentist, and the latter is usually not the less objective. The white Southerner's conviction that he, and he alone, 'knows' the American Negroes because of his close association with them has been proved erroneous. The stranger's view may be superficial, it is true, but superficiality is not the monopoly of strangers; it is a matter of the intensity and effectiveness of research. There is thus no necessary connection between superficiality and the extent of bias. Indeed, biases in research have no relation to superficiality *per se*. They emanate from the influences exerted by society, from our personal involvement in what we are studying, and from our tendency to apply approaches with which we are familiar to environments that are radically different. Biases can be present or absent as much when we are strangers to the country we are studying as when we are its nationals and as much when the research undertaken stretches over long periods and is conducted with a huge apparatus as when it is simply a journalist's attempt to put his impressions and reflections in order.

Nor are Western economists uniquely subject to the specific biases emanating from our methodological conservatism. Our *confrères* in the South Asian countries are afflicted as much, if not more, with them. Many have been trained at Western centers of learning or by teachers who acquired their training in the West. All have been thoroughly exposed to the great economic literature in the Western tradition. Familiarity with, and ability to work in accordance with, that tradition is apt to give them status at home. Their motivations for sharing in this bias are fairly independent of their political attitudes. Part of the explanation, as will be shown in the next section, is that application of the Western approach serves both conservative and radical needs for rationalization in the South Asian countries.

That the use of Western theories, models, and concepts in the study of economic problems in the South Asian countries is a cause of bias seriously distorting that study will be a main theme of this book. For the moment a few *obiter dicta* must suffice to outline this general criticism.

The concepts and the theory of unemployment and under-employment rest on assumptions about attitudes and institutions that, though fairly realistic in the developed countries, are unrealistic in the underdeveloped countries.

The neat division of income into two parts, consumption and saving, is realistic in Western societies where the general levels of income and a stratified system of income redistribution by social security policies and other means have largely abrogated any influence of consumption on productivity. This is not the case in the underdeveloped countries.

Marx's assumption, so widely adopted by Western economists, that the effects of industrialization and, indeed, of investment generally – in the final instance Marx's changes in the 'modes of production' – spread quickly to other sectors of the economy and to institutions and attitudes, may be fairly realistic for Western countries, both now and when they started their rapid economic development. But as these 'spread effects' are a function of the level of living and of the general culture, the assumption is not valid for most underdeveloped countries, particularly when the sectors of change are small in comparison with the total community. This should be obvious after many decades of colonial history during which the modern enterprises remained enclaves in a largely stagnating economy, but it is seldom given the recognition it deserves, either in economic analysis or in planning for development.

The lack of mobility and the imperfection of markets in underdeveloped countries rob the analytical method of aggregation of magnitudes – employment, savings, investment, and output – of much of its meaning. This conceptual difficulty is in addition to the statistical one already pointed out: that the data aggregated are frail and imperfect, partly because their categories are unrealistic.

The list could be made much longer, as will be seen in this book. Our main point is that while in the Western world an analysis in 'economic' terms – markets and prices, employment and unemployment, consumption and savings, investment and output – that abstracts from modes and levels of living and from attitudes, institutions, and culture may make sense and lead to valid inferences, an analogous procedure plainly does not in underdeveloped countries. There one cannot make such abstractions; a realistic analysis must deal with the problems in terms that are attitudinal and institutional and take into account the very low levels of living and culture. The newest attempts to analyse education (and health) in terms of 'investment in man' do not even state the problem in a rational way. The 'non-economic' facts do not adjust smoothly to economic changes, but set up inhibitions and obstacles to them, so that often the 'economic' terms cannot even be given a clear meaning. A practical corollary is the much greater need for coordination of planning in the 'economic' and the 'non-economic' fields.[3] Acknowledgment of this important difference is frequently made by way of qualifications and reservations. But the basic approach, not least in regard to the problems of economic planning, has remained a rather simple application of Western concepts and theories.

3. 'For all practical purposes growth and development in the less developed parts of the world seem to depend rather upon the speed and efficiency with which given attitudes and institutions can be and actually are modified and changed. Viewed in its truly dynamic dimension the process of economic growth and development is and always has been a problem of political and socio-cultural change.' (Kapp, 1963, p. 69.)

The Western approach serves deeper inclinations to bias

The temptation to apply the Western approach was said above to be almost mechanical, a function of the speed with which research was begun in a nearly untouched field and our natural inclination to utilize research methods with which we were familiar. The urge to do so was the more impelling as no other kit of tools was available for bringing a semblance of order into the analysis of the complex conditions in South Asian countries. But the matter is not so uncomplicated. The appeal of the Western conceptual approach draws further strength from the fact that it is well fitted to the rationalization of opportunistic interests both in the developed Western countries and among the influential intellectual elite in the underdeveloped countries themselves.

Generally speaking, the Western approach abstracts from most of the conditions that are peculiar to the South Asian countries and are responsible for their underdevelopment and for the special difficulties they meet in developing. These conditions and difficulties are all of a type that South Asians and their foreign well-wishers must desire to forget. They were the features of the social structure that were prominent in the thoughts of the European colonial masters, both in their stereotypes and in their more sophisticated reasonings. Exaggerated emphasis on these impediments to development served their need for rationalization. It explained away their responsibility for the backwardness of colonial peoples and their failure to try to improve matters. Both the post-colonial ideologies and the ideologies of the liberation movements were deeply stamped by protest against that thinking. And so the pendulum of biases swung from one extreme to the other. The intellectuals in these countries want to rationalize in the contrary sense, and it serves their needs to make the abstractions implied by Western economists. Genuine sympathy, in addition to reasons of diplomacy, brought Western economists under the same spell of opportunism. The fact that what they were applying was established theory, which had been successfully used in the Western countries, made the entrance of this systematic bias the easier.

It was an approach that appealed to both radicals and conservatives in South Asia. The radicals, partly under the impact of

Marx's thinking, were prone to exaggerate the rapidity of adjustment of the entire social system to changes in the 'economic' sphere; conservatives, averse to direct policy intervention in modes and levels of living, attitudes, and institutions, welcomed an approach that placed these matters in the shadow. Concerning the radicals, we must also remind ourselves of the similarities, particularly in basic concepts, between Marx's and Western economic theorizing. These have already been referred to and are illustrated in many contests in the ensuing chapters.

There are also differences in approach, however, and it should be clear that certain elements of Marx's economic speculation often seem to fit situations in South Asia much more closely than those in the rich modern welfare states of the West: for instance, the apparent existence of a 'reserve army' of idle, or largely idle, workers; the existence and the increase of a dispossessed proletariat; the often frank exploitation of workers by employers; and the big and widening gap between a few rich individuals or families and the masses of very poor people. It is remarkable that very little fresh analysis of the problems of the region in Marx's terms is forthcoming, while essays in the Western pattern are abundant. We thus often find at the universities in South Asia, economists who are strongly anti-Western in their sympathies and politically far to the left, even avowed Communists or fellow-travellers, but who are yet eager and proud to place the emphasis of their teaching on the latest abstract and formal growth models developed at Cambridge or Yale, and whose ambition is to write articles resembling those in the Western journals and, hopefully, to publish them there.

In attempting to understand this bent of mind of the radicals we must take into account the virtual bombardment of massive Western research on the underdeveloped countries in recent times, while the literary output on their problems in Communist countries has been small, polite, but uninspiring. An additional factor is, however, that pursuit of Marx's particular approach referred to above would inevitably have led to a consideration of 'non-economic' factors. The competitive strength of the Western approach is, at bottom, that its abstractions give an optimistic slant to the thinking about the development problems in the underdeveloped countries of the region.

Optimism, and therefore approaches that make optimism seem more realistic, is itself a natural urge for intellectuals in South Asia. That all planning in the region tends to err on the side of optimism is rather palpably clear.[4] The leaning toward diplomatic forbearance in the Western countries fits equally well with biases toward unwarranted optimism among their economists. In Western countries, especially America, optimism is even prized, as a foundation for enterprise and courage; it is almost part of the inherited cultural pattern – what George F. Kennan once called 'the great American capacity for enthusiasm and self-hypnosis'.[5] In the contest for souls, it is felt to be to the interest of the West that the underdeveloped countries outside the Communist sphere have development and be made to believe in it. In the West there is also a natural wish, and so a temptation to believe, that the underdeveloped countries in South Asia will come to follow policy lines similar to those of the Western countries, and that they will develop into national communities that are politically, socially, and economically like our own. For this reason, too, there is a normal tendency to use a Western approach in studying these countries, as to do so is to play down initial differences and make such development appear more feasible.

The two main sources of bias in the Western countries thus strengthen each other in that their influences tend to converge. As we saw, the international power conflict and the tensions and emotions associated with it have influenced the study of the problems of the underdeveloped countries in South Asia in the general direction of diplomatic kindness and tolerance – again, provided that these countries are not on the wrong side in that conflict. Many of the conditions peculiar to these countries are highly undesirable; indeed, this is what is meant by their being underdeveloped. Therefore, the other source of bias with which we dealt in the last

4. India's First Five Year Plan would seem to be an exception, as it underestimated the growth of output. But the surpassing of estimates was largely due to unexpectedly favorable monsoons and other accidents. The targets in regard to the policy measures actually making up the plan, and in particular the investments, were not met.

5. In the Soviet Union uncritical optimism is programmatic, and realism, when it does not lead to optimistic conclusions, is considered a 'bourgeois' deviation; this constitutes one of the many similarities in cultural situation between the United States and the Soviet Union.

section – the tendency to use the familiar theories and concepts that have been used successfully in the analysis of Western countries – exerts influences in the same direction. For when using the Western approach one can more easily soften the bite of these peculiar and undesirable conditions.

We have wanted to stress the political urges behind these tendencies that affect research on underdeveloped countries in the region. But these tendencies have at their core a compassion that makes them almost irresistible. Quite aside from the cold war and the opportunistic tendencies to bias emerging from it, we of the West are by tradition disposed to be friendly to peoples in distress, once we begin to take an interest in their condition. And it is our earnest hope, apart from all selfish interests, that they will succeed in their development efforts. That we wish them to develop into national communities as similar to our own as possible is a natural ethnocentric impulse that would make itself felt in the calmest world situation. Perhaps it should be stressed again that the concern of the West about the possibility of Communist expansion in underdeveloped countries is also understandable, and from the viewpoint of our own interests valid. And these interests justify using our influence to stop it. Still less can one criticize the human sympathy that characterizes the Western attitude toward these countries.

Nevertheless, we must not let these understandable and genuine feelings influence our perception of the facts. It is the ethos of scientific inquiry that truth and blunt truth-speaking are wholesome and that illusions, including those inspired by charity and good will, are always damaging. Illusions handicap the pursuit of knowledge and they must obstruct efforts to make planning for development fully effective and successful.

References

KAPP, K. W. (1963), *Hindu Culture, Economic Development and Economic Planning in India*, Asia Publishing House, Bombay.
SNYDER, R. C., and PAIGE, G. D. (1958), 'The United States decision to resist aggression in Korea: the application of an analytic scheme', *Admin. Science Q.*, vol. 3, no. 3.

25 President of the United States

Message concerning the Foreign Aid Program

Excerpts from *Message from the President of the United States on Foreign Aid Program, 1969*, House of Representatives, 90th Congress, 2nd Session, 8 February 1968, Document no. 251, pp. 218–19 and 227–8.

To the Congress of the United States:

Peace will never be secure so long as:

Seven out of ten people on earth cannot read or write;

Tens of millions of people each day – most of them children – are maimed and stunted by malnutrition.

Diseases long conquered by science still ravage cities and villages around the world.

If most men can look forward to nothing more than a lifetime of backbreaking toil which only preserves their misery, violence will always beckon, freedom will ever be under siege.

It is only when peace offers hope for a better life that it attracts the hundreds of millions around the world who live in the shadow of despair.

Twenty years ago America resolved to lead the world against the destructive power of man's oldest enemies. We declared war on the hunger, the ignorance, the disease, and the hopelessness which breed violence in human affairs.

We knew then that the job would take many years. We knew then that many trials and many disappointments would test our will.

But we also knew that, in the long run, a single ray of hope – a school, a road, a hybrid seed, a vaccination – can do more to build the peace and guard America from harm than guns and bombs.

This is the great truth upon which all our foreign aid programs are founded. It was valid in 1948 when we helped Greece and Turkey maintain their independence. It was valid in the early fifties when the Marshall Plan helped rebuild a ruined Western Europe into a showcase of freedom. It was valid in the sixties when we helped Taiwan and Iran and Israel take their places in the ranks of free nations able to defend their own independence and moving toward prosperity on their own.

The programs I propose today are as important and as essential to the security of this nation as our military defenses. Victory on the battlefield must be matched by victory in the peaceful struggles which shape men's minds.

In these fateful years, we must not falter. In these decisive times, we dare not fail. [. . .]

America's choice

Foreign aid serves our national interest. It expresses our basic humanity. It may not always be popular, but it is right.

The peoples we seek to help are committed to change. This is an immutable fact of our time. The only questions are whether change will be peaceful or violent, whether it will liberate or enslave, whether it will build a community of free and prosperous nations or sentence the world to endless strife between rich and poor.

Foreign aid is the American answer to this question. It is a commitment to conscience as well as to country. It is a matter of national tradition as well as national security.

Last year some Americans forgot that tradition. My foreign aid request, already the smallest in history, was reduced by almost one-third.

The effects of that cut go much deeper than the fields which lie fallow, the factories not built, or the hospitals without modern equipment.

Our ambassadors all over the developing world report the deep and searching questions they are being asked. Has America resigned her leadership of the cause of freedom? Has she abandoned to fate the weak and the striving who are depending on her help?

This Congress can give a resounding answer to these questions by enacting the full amount I have requested. I do not propose this as a partisan measure. I propose it as an extension of the humane statesmanship of both parties for more than twenty years.

I said in my State of the Union address, that it is not America's resources that are being tested, but her will. This is nowhere more true than in the developing countries where our help is a crucial margin between peaceful change and violent disaster.

I urge the Congress to meet this test.

Lyndon B. Johnson.
The White House, 8 February 1968.

26 Paul Mattick

Gunnar Myrdal's Dilemma

Paul Mattick, 'Gunnar Myrdal's Dilemma', *Science and Society*, vol. 32, 1968, pp. 421–40. (A review of *Asian Drama*.)

I

Professor Myrdal's vast study – the result of a decade of research – deals with the countries of South Asia, with their poverty and their developmental needs. While embracing Pakistan, Ceylon, Burma, Thailand, Malaysia, Indonesia, Laos, Cambodia, South Vietnam, and the Philippines, it concentrates chiefly on India. The regional approach is chosen for comparative purposes and because it was once thought that regional cooperation was a real possibility. In any case, the various countries have enough basic similarities to justify this procedure, particularly because Myrdal's main concern is analytical rather than merely descriptive. It is for this reason also that Myrdal deals extensively with methodological questions within the general text and in a number of appendices.

Economic problems must be studied, according to Myrdal, in their demographic, social, and political settings. While this is a general requirement, it is especially necessary when dealing with underdeveloped nations. This should excuse the length of the book, because the central idea in Myrdal's own 'institutional approach is that history and politics, theories and ideologies, economic structures and levels, social stratification, agriculture and industry, population development, health and education, and so on, must be studied not in isolation but in their mutual relationships' (p. x). It may also be said, however, that the book's extraordinary length is partly due to Myrdal's habit of repeating key statements more often than seems necessary.

In Myrdal's view, a comprehensive institutional approach includes the value premises of the social scientist, determined, as they are, by his relation to his own cultural and social milieu. The long-sustained lack of interest in the problems of underdeveloped countries on the part of the economists, for instance, reflected the more favorable social and economic circumstances of their own conditioning. Now that political changes have led to a real concern with underdevelopment, the bias of modern economics asserts itself, in Myrdal's view, in cold-war considerations which exclude objective research, and in the insistence upon concepts and theories which may have some validity in a Western setting but which remain totally irrelevant as regards the actual problems of the underdeveloped part of the world. Because there is no disinterested social science, Myrdal states his own value premises which are incorporated in suggested particular directions of social change for South Asia's nations. There are the changes also desired, at least verbally, by the articulate elements within these nations, which are supposed to lead to modernization, greater productivity, planned development, higher living standards, social and economic equalization, national independence, political democracy, and to more progressive attitudes and institutions.

The unfolding development, as well as lack of development in South Asia's nations Myrdal sees as a drama, the action of which:

is speeding toward a climax. Tension is mounting: economically, socially, and politically. . . . This drama has its unity in a set of inner conflicts operating on people's minds: between their high-pitched aspirations and the bitter experience of a harsh reality; between the desire for change and improvement and mental reservations and inhibitions about accepting the consequences and paying the price (p. 34).

The main actors in this drama are the educated classes, or intellectual elites, which, while intent on overcoming the general apathy on the part of the masses, are themselves divided in their loyalties.

On the one hand, they are vehicles for the modernization ideas, but on the other hand, they are tied to the privileged groups with vested interests in the *status quo* (p. 117).

In order to find out what must and can be done in this situation, Myrdal turns to the political problems and economic realities that characterize the region. Although nothing new is revealed, the great mass of observed details offered by Myrdal and their integration into a general picture is quite impressive and makes his work one of the most informative in the literature on South Asia.

With the exception of Thailand, all the nations of this region have been colonies and their colonial past has to be taken into consideration in order to appreciate their current aspirations and the difficulties in the way of their realization. Although the process of national emancipation is not as yet complete, Myrdal has no doubts 'that in a few years' time all colonial peoples will be politically independent' (p. 129). This is the more certain, he thinks, because, contrary to what Hilferding, Luxemburg, and Lenin were saying, capitalism has no need for imperialism. This may be so as regards its direct colonial form, but in its neo-colonial indirect form it is still a reality, as Myrdal himself is forced to admit when dealing with the relations between the developed and under-developed countries.

Political independence of the nations of South Asia was itself the result of the dissolution of the colonial power system in the two worldwide imperialistic wars which first provided the opportunities for national liberation movements and which assured their success. The political history of these nations since independence has been determined less by their developmental needs than by their preoccupation with territorial questions. Colonial domination, Myrdal relates, resulted in the creation of larger political entities than those which existed in pre-colonial times. New frontiers were the outcome of the historical interplay of imperial policies and rivalries, and this unfortunate inheritance led to national rivalries between the newly independent countries. While some were trying to regain 'lost' territory, others refused to give up territory bequeathed them by the old colonial powers. And thus, 'while South Asian governments denounce colonialism and all its works, they have formed an intense emotional attachment to one of the most important legacies of colonialism, namely, their own territorial definitions' (p. 186).

Political independence and the national rivalries in its wake did not affect the social relations within the various nations of South Asia. In a country-by-country review, Myrdal shows that real power below the government level is still wielded by peasant landlords, merchants, and moneylenders. What happened in these nations was merely the replacement of foreign by native privileged groups. In contrast to the poverty-stricken Indian masses, for instance, the national political leaders are all members of the privileged upper class. Hierarchical structures of the civil service, with its wide social as well as salary differentials between the higher and lower classes, have been retained. The caste system was left undisturbed, and 'is probably stronger today than it was at the time India became independent' (p. 278). Governments cater to private interests, corruption and nepotism are widespread, politics is considered an avenue to privileges and patronages, and 'the new tax burdens are heaped for the most part on those sections of the populations least able to bear them' (p. 285). There are political and economic differences between the various countries, such as the change from sham parliamentary governments to military dictatorships, the prevalence or absence of plantation industries, the percentage of the landless within the agricultural population, and so forth. But everywhere, 'by leaving real power with the opponents of economic and social change, political stability implies stagnation' (p. 295).

As regards the prevailing economic realities in South Asia, it must first be noted that agriculture is the dominant branch of production. It differs from such production in other parts of the world by a much lower output per unit of arable land. Scrutinizing the many-faceted agricultural problem, Myrdal comes to the conclusion that a raising of living standards would necessitate a higher output per unit of land and only after this has been achieved would it be possible to set labor free for purposes of industrialization. 'Low incomes are only the other side of low labor productivity,' he writes:

a vicious circle makes poverty and low levels of living, or low labor productivity, self-generating. Behind this unfortunate causal mechanism there is, besides the parameter of climate, a social system of institutions and power relations, that is severely inimical to productivity, at the same time as low productivity establishes itself as the norm. And within this social system, both shaped by it and upholding it, are the ingrained attitudes of people in all classes (p. 433).

Tradition-bound and disregarding the population increase, most of the people of South Asia live and work within an agricultural system based on subsistence farming. Although peasant proprietorship has steadily been giving way to tenancy and sharecropping, the surplus thereby produced, falling to the landlords, did not provide incentives for greater productivity. Commercial plantation farming producing tea, rubber, coconut, tobacco, coffee, sugar, and spices were very lucrative, however, and, being based on wage-labor, must be considered capital-intensive industrial enterprises. But plantation farming for exports was mostly in the hands of Western capital and its profits were remitted abroad, so that the 'plantation spurred the industrialization of the Western countries but not of South Asia' (p. 449). The impoverishment of the peasant population was due in part to the systematic destruction of native crafts by the colonizers, which condemned the colonies to become producers of exportable raw materials and importers of industrially manufactured goods. But even the extension of *laissez-faire* policies to the colonies worked in favor of the colonizers, for their different economic and technological levels are a 'natural mechanism tending toward greater inequality' (p. 456).

The poverty of the nations of South Asia is too obvious to require statistical proof. What economic data exist, Myrdal finds 'so unreliable that not much importance can be attached to them' (p. 498), not only because of the crudeness of statistical procedures, but also because 'large sections of the economy are non-monetized and without much of a link with any markets' (p. 477). However, and for whatever it may be worth, Myrdal utilizes some data with respect to national output, or income, and to the structure of the economies as determined by agriculture, industry, and types of manufacturing establishments. We learn that workers are largely employed in cottage industry, that private manufacturing firms are quite small, and that, with the exception of India, 'heavy industry, producing consumer durable or producers' goods, is conspicuously absent' (p. 521). Incomes are not only extremely low but show increasing inequality with respect to both the rural and urban populations.

Although Myrdal seems convinced that the expenses of empire exceeded the gains so that the end of colonization was a blessing for colonizers and colonized alike, the structures of the South Asian economies are nonetheless 'the product of international economic and political relationships developed over the past century' (p. 581). Being largely producers of primary products, these countries suffer from a decreasing demand for their traditional exports. If development is to occur, in Myrdal's view, it will come not as a response to foreign demand, but must be internally based 'since the spontaneous growth-inducing stimulus of a relatively free and expanding international trade is no longer present' (p. 583). Development must proceed in relative independence of the world market and together with a stimulation of intraregional trade. But while there is little hope for larger exports, there is a growing need for imports. Development thus depends on the 'ability to attract adequate amounts of foreign capital on reasonable terms' (p. 612). Thus far, however, and with the United States as the leading exporter of capital, little has been done in this respect. The 'inflow of fresh private capital from abroad . . . exceeded the repatriation of capital by only negligible amounts' (p. 622). Capital from public sources has flowed in somewhat more rapidly, but, reflecting strategic and political cold-war considerations, it did not stimulate economic development.

Because the nations of South Asia must increase their exports in order to cover their import requirements, and since this cannot be done in traditional ways, Myrdal suggests a diversification of production as well as alternative markets, such as may be found in Communist countries and the underdeveloped nations of Latin America and Africa. But even so, he realizes that 'export prospects . . . do not appear promising' (p. 661). And neither does the influx of capital in the form of credits, as the 'debt service is becoming an increasing burden' (p. 665), absorbing as it does a growing portion of export earnings. Loans should be replaced by grants, 'but the trend has been, and is, in the opposite direction' (p. 666). All in all, it is a dismal picture, which appears the more hopeless as the whole Western approach to the development of underdeveloped nations is basically wrong because of the dominant idea that such development will be a mere replica of that of the now-advanced nations. But Myrdal insists that the initial conditions prevailing in the underdeveloped countries are so different and of 'such a nature as to prohibit a pattern of growth analogous to that experienced in the developed Western countries' (p. 674).

II

Myrdal traces this idea on the part of modern economists to their unacknowledged acceptance of the Marxian proposition that 'the country that is more developed industrially only shows the less developed the image of its own future' (p. 674). He does not seem to realize that Marx was speaking here of Continental Europe, and particularly of Germany, but not of the world at large.[1] Referring to a Russian critic, Marx once pointed out that although entering the stage of capitalist development means that a good part of the peasantry must be turned into proletarians, his 'historical sketch of the genesis of capitalism in Western Europe [must not be changed] into an historico-philosophical theory of the general path every people is fated to tread' (Marx and Engels, 1942, p. 379). It is true, of course, that in Marx's view capitalist colonialism involved 'the annihilation of the old Asiatic society and the laying of the material foundations of Western society in Asia' (Marx, n.d., p. 34), but this did not mean that its further development would follow the definite historical path of the old capitalist nations. For Marx, 'the specific task of bourgeois society is the establishment of the world market, at least in outline, and of production based upon this world market' (Marx and Engels, 1942, p. 134). This task was accomplished, as Myrdal himself points out in his descriptions of the economic relationships between the colonies and the capitalist nations.

Capital accumulation determines the character of the world market. Just as its concentration and centralization tendencies imply the polarization of rich and poor in each capitalist nation, so they imply the division of the world into poor and rich countries. Industrialization and modernization can proceed only insofar as this is compatible with the accumulation requirements of the dominating capitals. Their own development is based, in part, on the lack of development of countries subjected to their exploitation. On the basis of his own theory, it could not enter Marx's mind that all nations would some day become fully-

1. In *Capital*, vol. 1, p. 13, Kerr ed., Marx wrote: 'I have to examine the capitalist mode of production, and the conditions of production and exchange corresponding to that mode. Up to the present time, their classic ground is England. That is the reason why England is used as the chief illustration in the development of my theoretical ideas. If, however, the German reader shrugs his shoulders at the conditions of the English industrial and agricultural laborers, or in optimistic fashion comforts himself with the thought that in Germany things are not nearly so bad, I must plainly tell him, "*De te fabula narratur!*"'

developed capitalist nations, even though all would be part of the monopolistic capitalist world market.

While Myrdal's argument does not apply to Marx, it does fit the so-called growth theories of bourgeois economy which see the historically limited and *fetishistic* categories of capital production as universally valid and eternal economic categories. Economics as a positive science allows the economists both to abstract from the real socio-economic relations and to suit their theories to the specific, and mostly apologetic, needs of capitalist society. From their point of view, the underdeveloped nations can only repeat that development which leads to the formation of capital. Myrdal, too, sees development as capitalization, but he feels that 'the modern approach tends to overlook or minimize the factors that make development so difficult in the underdeveloped countries or, conversely, that should necessitate radical and comprehensive policy measures' (p. 1853). Things omitted in the fashionable model-building for development, such as climate, population, health, education, attitudes, and so forth, he believes, must be brought back into the analysis, so as to enable the formulation of more realistic policies for the underdeveloped nations. Development, moreover, cannot be awaited as a process of natural evolution, but must be planned and hastened by 'a telescoping of change as the only alternative not only to continued stagnation but to regression' (p. 700).

An appendix, prepared by Professor Streeten, goes somewhat deeper into the question of the usefulness of economic models for planning in South Asia. He admits that the separation of 'economic' from 'non-economic' factors makes some sense in the West, where 'people's attitudes and social institutions have been rationalized and standardized and are therefore either adapted or adaptable to economic progress' (p. 1942). But this is not true for South Asia, he says, where attempts to change attitudes and institutions meet with strong opposition from vested interests and other obstacles and inhibitions. Streeten also admits that Marx did not accept the isolation of 'economic' from 'noneconomic' factors; yet 'Marxism', he says, 'fell into the opposite error of assuming that the required adjustments in the parameters – attitudes and institutions – occur inevitably and rather rapidly' (p. 1942) – a position which bases itself, as Myrdal believes, on the

Marxian proposition that 'the whole culture is a superstructure erected on the modes of production' (p. 1864).

Because 'economic development is much more than industrialization' (p. 1842), Myrdal finds it necessary to treat each South Asian country 'as a *social system*, consisting of a great number of *conditions* that are causally interrelated, in that a change in one will cause changes in others' (p. 1860). That this is not so, however, is made clear in his own text, which bewails the fact, for instance, that the achievement in political independence and the new ideology of planning and modernization altered nothing in traditional social and economic relations. Obviously some things can change while others remain the same; the persistence of some conditions in the face of changes in others should indicate that among 'the great number of conditions which are causally interrelated' some are more important than others. This is only another way of saying that there are basic social relationships which underlie all other social relationships and for that reason must have priority in any social analysis.

For Marx, too, 'economic development is more than industrialization', even though it is by way of industrialization that capital accumulates rapidly. Political economy – not to speak of 'economics' – is a bourgeois 'science,' which Marx criticized on the ground, among others, that it changed social into economic categories. These categories have meaning only for bourgeois society, wherein the actual social relations between peoples and classes appear as economic relations. As such, they have to be attended to in order to detect capitalism's developmental tendencies, but they must also be recognized as social class relations. Social attitudes and institutions cannot really contradict the mode of production, that is, the relations of production as capital-labor relations. If they did, capitalism could not exist. And so long as they do not seriously contradict the mode of production, an analysis of the latter is at once an analysis of the ruling attitudes and institutions.

A definite mode of production can, however, accommodate a variety of attitudes and institutions, or institutions and attitudes may change without affecting any change in the mode of production. A change from political democracy to fascism, or from *laissez-faire* to a mixed economy, for instance, will change the 'superstructure', but the result remains the 'superstructure' of the untouched basic social production relations. It is for this reason that the analysis of capital production can, and even must, abstract from the 'superstructure'. This is not a question of the isolation of 'economic' from 'noneconomic' factors and neglect of the latter. In the Marxian view, the apparently 'economic' factors and the apparently separate 'noneconomic' factors both find their determination in the underlying social relations of production, which are totally disregarded by bourgeois economy and by Myrdal as well.

Neither is this a question of the tempo of the 'adjustments' of attitudes and institutions to economic change. For Marx, it is the impossibility of such 'adjustments' which makes for revolutionary change. For Streeten and Myrdal, however, change and development seem mainly a problem for underdeveloped countries. In the developed nations, 'economic progress' leads to more or less automatic adjustments of attitudes and institutions, and changes in the latter do not impair further economic development. In other words, although the 'superstructure's' determination by the mode of production is denied, a developed capitalism, in their views, tends to bring the 'economic' and 'noneconomic' factors into equilibrium, thus allowing for a relative disregard of the 'superstructure,' or of the 'noneconomic' factors, of social life. It is, then, only in the underdeveloped countries that economic progress requires a deliberate change of attitudes and institutions and therewith political activities which affect the whole of society.

Actually, even in highly developed capitalism only some attitudes and institutions 'adapt' themselves to economic change, or, vice versa, economic change to altered attitudes and institutions. Changes that occur 'automatically', or are evolutionary, do not disturb the class-conditioned mode of production, nor do they affect the immanent developmental tendencies of the given mode of production. They can thus be disregarded in its analysis. To alter the mode of production requires a situation wherein attitudes and institutions prevent a necessary change in the mode of production, and where the actualization of such change demands different attitudes and institutions such as correspond, that is, to another mode of production. It is clear, then, that the Marxian distinction between base and superstructure implies just as much a difference as an identity, which finds its mediation in the social revolution. Neither 'economic' nor 'noneconomic' factors as such, not both in combination, are responsible for stagnation or social change. Whether one or the other of these conditions prevails depends on the struggle of social classes in defense of, or in opposition to, a given mode of production and on the outcome of these struggles.

Myrdal differentiates himself from 'modern economics' by his recognition of the necessity of political revolutions and social change in underdeveloped countries. Marxists do not deny this necessity. The Marxist analysis of capital production is that, however, of an established capitalist system. As such, it is not directly applicable to the countries of South Asia, which to an overwhelming extent find themselves in a precapitalist state of arrested development. A Marxian analysis of South Asia would have to deal with different modes of production and with different social forces trying to maintain or to change them. This does not hinder but encourages considerations of attitudes and institutions, just as the Marxist analysis of capital production does not prevent but fosters a concern with general social issues.

Because the existing conditions, attitudes, and institutions in South Asia are codetermined by those existing in the capitalistically-developed nations, a Marxian analysis would have to deal with the relationships of South Asian nations to modern capitalism as an imperialist world-market system. To estimate the chances of their development requires not only a thorough grasp of their particular socio-economic conditions, but also an understanding of capitalism's general developmental tendencies. But while Myrdal recognizes that the development of South Asia depends also 'on the commercial and foreign exchange policies pursued by other countries, even their domestic policies and their rates of growth, and, more generally, on structural changes in world demand and supply' (p. 1897), he pays no attention to the exploitative character of capitalism and to its increasing need to subordinate development to its own specific profit requirements. These may prove to be a greater hindrance to the development of underdeveloped countries than their own stationary or regressive attitudes and institutions. And thus, while the analysis of capital production cannot supplant an analysis of the modes of production prevalent in South Asia, it is nonetheless a prerequisite for a realistic comprehension of the region and of its possible future.

III

The capitalist mode of production, that is, relations of production as capital-labor relations, identifies progress with the accumulation of capital, which determines and limits the volume and direction of industrial development, and gives social attitudes and institutions their peculiar capitalistic characteristics. So long as this system expands without effective opposition, it may appear, at any rate to its beneficiaries, as the ideal economic system. Because all that matters in this system is the formation of capital; the latter is generally treated 'as the strategic variable . . . juxtaposed to output as the dependent one.' And since in the capitalistically-advanced countries output has been growing roughly in proportion to capital input, growth models have largely been based on the theory of a constant capital/output ratio. These growth models are held to be equally useful for the developmental plans in under-developed countries. Myrdal and Streeten find them unrealistically abstract, because 'rational planning in South Asia has to be a coordinated system of policies directed at a very large number of conditions that must be changed to engender development. The approach to planning represented by the capital/output model tends to conceal this fact and provides no useful theoretical framework for this type of planning' (p. 1956).

Myrdal's institutional analysis is also an abstraction of course, but with a claim to greater realism. With the mistaken assertion that 'in the social system there is no up and down, no primary and secondary, and economic conditions do not have precedence over others,' Myrdal classifies the causally interrelated social conditions in six broad categories: 'Output and income; conditions of production; levels of living; attitudes toward life and work; institutions; and policies' (p. 1860). These, and their various subdivisions, have to be considered in planned development, and planning there must be to have development at all. 'The basic principle in the ideology of economic planning', Myrdal writes, 'is that the state takes an active, indeed the decisive, role in the economy: by its own acts of investment and enterprise, and by its various controls – inducements and restrictions – over the private sector, the state shall initiate, spur and steer economic development' (p. 709).

The ideology of state planning, which, according to Myrdal, must be counted among the social facts that determine policies, stems from the Communist countries as well as from the West. However, insofar as it can be traced to the West, it implies no more than state interventions in the otherwise private-enterprise economy. When Myrdal says that 'all Western governments as well as business people are supporters of state planning in South Asia' (p. 728), they are so only in this particular and limited sense. Actually, there is no planning in the West; although governments intervene, the economies remain subject to the vicissitudes of uncontrollable market events. Neither is there planning in South Asia. Here, as Myrdal complains, 'the planners remain in their paradoxical position: on a general and non-committal level they freely and almost passionately proclaim the need for radical social and economic change, whereas in planning their policies they tread most warily in order not to disrupt the traditional social order' (p. 117). Yet, because state planning exists as an ideology, all that seems necessary to Myrdal is that the planners should lose their inhibitions and begin practicing what they preach.

As in the West, the development plans in South Asia are essentially nothing but fiscal policies for public investments, which make it possible, as Myrdal says, 'to have a plan without planning, to create an appearance without reality' (p. 2008); particularly so, because fiscal budgets are here such a small part of the total economy. Real planning, for Myrdal, would have to embrace the private sector of the economy as well, and would require interventions in market relations by planned pricing policies. This, too, would not suffice, because 'the bulk of the marketable surplus of agricultural produce is not provided by a market process but is exacted as tribute from sharecroppers and other peasants by the landlords and moneylenders on whom they depend' (p. 913). It is for these and other reasons, that 'a plan that conveys what it purports must be based on some kind of physical factors, goods, and services in the various sectors of the economy' (p. 1919).

What Myrdal has in mind is a planned system such as exists in Russia, but modified to suit the mixed economy under the conditions that prevail in South Asia. While, on the one hand, he appreciates the Russian government's ability 'to free resources for investment by a consumption squeeze in such a way as to combine suppression in some directions with rapid and substantial increase in others, as dictated by the requirements of growth' (p. 1918), on the other hand, as far as South Asia is concerned, he seems to prefer a less rigorous planning system, wherein 'it is part of the function of the plan to assist in striking compromises and bargains between conflicting interests and to construct a framework within which conflicts of convictions and interests can be thrashed out' (p. 1891).

It is, then, not a definite plan which Myrdal proposes, but rather a political program, in which planning is itself an evolving process to assure the 'upward movement of the entire social system.' Only those changes in the social structure that would assure an increase in production and productivity would be required. More is needed than a planning approach which sees in investments the sole strategic factor; particularly, because capital inflow from abroad can never be more than supplementary; so that provisions for development must be internally created. The *given* conditions must first be improved, which demands a greater emphasis 'on agriculture, and on raising the levels of education and health, on increasing the volume of labor input, and on improving labor efficiency in the economy as a whole' (p. 1842).

Myrdal believes that even without investments, but through longer and more efficient work, agricultural yields could be raised substantially. Usually it is argued that there are too many people living on the land, which implies the underutilization of their labor, described as disguised unemployment, and that some must be removed through employment-providing industrial development. Myrdal shows, however, that these supposedly superfluous peasants have no inclination to go anywhere, and if they had, would have no place to go to. But neither are they inclined to work harder – the result of insufficient incentives and a generally prevailing antipathy toward work, especially wage-labor. 'The scale of values determining social ranking in rural South Asia,' Myrdal points out, 'continues to be a pre-capitalist one. To own land is the highest mark of social esteem; to perform manual labor, the lowest' (p. 1057), which induces even the poorest of

landowners to prefer a miserable existence to any form of employment. The actual cultivators of the soil do not have the physical
and mental stamina to increase their labor productivity because of
ill health, nutritional deficiencies, lack of education, and general
attitudes toward life and work 'as determined by climate, levels of
living, customs and institutions' (p. 1016). Yet, with a decisive
change in these latter conditions, Myrdal still thinks it possible
to overcome the self-defeating vicious circle of poverty and low
labor productivity provided the population growth can be stem-
med. The introduction of Western biochemical medicine reduced
mortality rates, and with fertility rates remaining what they were,
led to a 'population explosion' which now threatens not only any
economic advance, but stagnation and even deterioration. It has
to be coped with through government-directed educational cam-
paigns popularizing birth control methods, and through agricultural policies which raise the productivity of the increasing labor
force.

While nothing can be done directly about climate, its possibly
debilitating effects can be reduced through the productivity-raising
effects of education, health, and better consumption. But all this
presupposes institutional changes and governments able and
willing to carry them out. Unfortunately, according to Myrdal,
the main characteristic of the countries of South Asia is the existence of 'soft states', which 'require extraordinarily little of their
citizens' (p. 896). They rely on voluntariness when what is actually
needed, in Myrdal's view, is the enforcement of greater social
discipline.

The 'soft state' is, of course, the state which corresponds to the
social structure of South Asia's nations. It cannot be expected to
engage in activities contrary to its own interests, which, as Myrdal
shows so exhaustively, are those of the ruling classes. Apparently,
Myrdal deems it possible to have a state which stands above class
interests and carries out policies benefiting the nation as a whole.
But the 'soft state' is such only *vis-à-vis* the class it represents; it is
quite 'hard' in its dealings with the oppressed classes simply by not
interfering in the traditional production relations. To have another
state would mean to have another society, which requires far more
than a mere ideological commitment to the general welfare. Myrdal
finds it neither possible, nor necessary, however, to change

existing social relations. All he proposes is greater efficiency and more production.

What is the state to do to bring this about? Until now, its policies benefited not the poor but the rich, and its economic controls worked mostly 'in favor of established business, and particularly big business' (p. 738). As regards agriculture, government policies are allegedly oriented toward land and tenancy reforms. Actually, however, 'in none of the countries of the region have reforms brought any direct benefits to landless laborers' (p. 1319). Because the demand for land is acute, landowners are able to claim half and more than half of the gross output of their sharecroppers, and in view of the rapid growth of the labor force, all 'attempts to decrease land rents while allowing landowners to remain as owners ... are foredoomed to fail' (p. 1311). While a radical land distribution may increase production by increasing incentives, Myrdal thinks that nationalization would be an even better procedure for a more rational utilization of the land. He is convinced, however, that neither the one nor the other of these policies is feasible at the present time.

There is simply 'no enthusiasm for a radical expropriation among a peasantry that jealously guards its private title to even the smallest plot of land ... nor is support for such measures likely to be found among the landless; their aspirations are for a plot of their own rather than for participating in collective ventures' (p. 1376). Under these conditions it would be best to develop agriculture on capitalist lines. 'The indigenous agricultural practice in South Asia,' Myrdal writes, 'is typically a form of quasi-capitalism combining the least favorable features of capitalist and feudal pattern of economic organization' (p. 1370). A genuinely capitalist agriculture would be a step forward as it would not tolerate passive and parasitic landownership, which saps the surplus but does nothing to enlarge production. The elimination of this type of ownership, Myrdal holds, could be accomplished through a tax system that places severe penalties on the income of nonparticipatory landowners and through laws prohibiting the future transfer of titles to nonfarming residents. This reform, Myrdal emphasizes, 'would not take anything from anybody, but would outlaw purchases of land by persons who are not prepared to become cultivators' (p. 1380).

This, again, would presuppose the existence of governments not bound to 'passive and parasitic landownership' and, in the absence of such, Myrdal's suggestions can only fall on deaf ears. He is aware of this for he sees it as an indication of the real power situation in South Asian countries that such suggestions are not even seriously debated. Still, they may find a hearing at some other time. Myrdal admits that a capitalist pattern of agriculture could lead to a reduction in the demand for labor and could thus impede the fuller utilization of the rapidly growing labor force; for instance, through the introduction of mechanized processes. But if this is the case, it should be the job of the government, he says, to check the use of labor-saving devices. In other words, Myrdal does not really want capitalist farming, determined, as it is, by the profit motive. What he suggests is capitalist agriculture fitted to a planned economy which is not determined by the principles of capital production.

With Myrdal's 'genuine agricultural entrepreneur' goes the agricultural wage-laborer, to whom 'should be given a respectable place in the capitalist agricultural system' (p. 1382). How 're-spectable' this place can be under the best circumstances may be surmised from the conditions of agricultural wage-workers in the most developed capitalist nation, namely, the United States. What this 'respectability' amounts to in South Asia is clearly demonstrated by the agricultural wage-labor extant in this region. Still, Myrdal is convinced that whatever the present situation, 'long-term advance in agricultural output and efficiency can only be achieved if South Asian people can be brought to accept the fact that wage-employment is a normal and healthy feature of progressive economies' (p. 1383). It is also the way to a social system that would 'gradually acquire the characteristics of welfare capitalism' (p. 1382). And thus, Myrdal concludes, it may be just as well to scrap all the current ideological nonsense about egalitarianism and even socialism, not only because it has failed to lead to effective reforms, but also because it stands in the way of realistic and pragmatic solutions to South Asia's problems.

This, essentially, is the message of Myrdal's enormous book. It is, of course, an adaptation of the Marxian concept that feudalism makes room for capitalism by a change of the mode of production, involving the capitalization of agriculture. 'An industrial revolution,' Myrdal writes, 'depends on a prior, or at least concurrent, agricultural revolution' (p. 1249). But neither of these revolutions is a clean-cut affair. Because capitalist and noncapitalist modes of production intermingle in underdeveloped countries, Myrdal calls the economies of South Asia 'quasi-capitalist' systems. He suggests that they be turned into genuine capitalist systems, starting with agriculture and ending up with modern welfare capitalism.

In Marxian theory, capitalism implies the transformation of labor into wage-labor. As regards agriculture, this metamorphosis has not been complete in even the most developed capitalist nations, even though there is no longer subsistence farming but production for the market. However, the individual farmer is steadily displaced by industrial farming based on wage-labor. Like all capitalist production, capitalist agriculture is competitive production for profit and becomes increasingly more capital-intensive. While at first it frees agricultural labor for industrial production, at a later stage it frees industrial workers from any kind of production by turning them into unemployables. This is the 'final' result of the production relations as capital-labor relations under *laissez-faire* conditions as well as in welfare capitalism.

It took a long period of development to reach modern welfare capitalism. For the South Asia nations to get there, Myrdal suggests, as a first step, capitalist farming, that is, a repetition of that process described by Marx as part of the transformation from feudalism to capitalism. Yet, in Myrdal's view, Marx was in error in assuming that all noncapitalist nations would have to follow the path trod by the first capitalist countries. Although this is an erroneous interpretation of Marx's position, it becomes nonetheless Myrdal's own vision of South Asia's development. It must be added, however, that this envisioned development differentiates itself from capitalism's historical development by the new factor of government planning, which was absent during capitalism's early days. Supposedly, this makes all the difference by suspending the immanent laws of capital production, as, for instance – to speak in Marxian terms – increasing relative surplus value by way of technological development. According to Myrdal, governments could prevent this from happening by restricting development to the mere increase of absolute surplus value, i.e.

through longer working-days and greater labor intensity. Not the search for profitability should be the determining element in production, but an overall plan, the existence of which would presumably turn capitalist into 'progressive economies'.

While Myrdal rejects both Marxism and 'pure economics', his own analysis of the manifold and interrelated social conditions that constitute a 'social system' also proceeds from an 'economic angle'. He claims, of course, that an approach from any other 'angle', would have done just as well; still, in his programmatic conclusions he acknowledges the overruling importance of society's economic base. For Myrdal, everything depends on raising the productivity of labor and the growth of production. This requires a mode of production different from the prevailing one, and this, in turn, requires policies which bring the change about. To approach the problem from another 'angle' – the political, for instance – could only mean that policies must change so as to bring about a change in the mode of production in order to make possible an increase in production and productivity, which is absolutely necessary in order to have development instead of decay. Whether one starts from the economic or the political 'angle', in either case what finally matters is the mode of production as the determinant of social production and productivity.

Myrdal's institutional approach to development does not prevent him from quite often coming close to a Marxian position. This may explain his uneasy fascination with Marxian theory, displayed throughout his work. He appears profoundly disturbed by a recognition of the need for revolutionary change and a simultaneous desire to have such change stop short of revolution. Moreover, he seems convinced, though not completely, that 'Marx's simplistic theory about the class struggle and the proletarian revolution' is not applicable in the nations of South Asia, and he looks with 'profound skepticism' upon the idea 'that the increasing impoverishment of the masses in underdeveloped countries will lead to political revolts'. It is perfectly possible, he writes, 'that the lower strata in the Indian villages would remain supine in their shackles of inequality even if living standards were to deteriorate still further' (p. 796). He rather pins his hopes on the emergence of governments willing and able to sacrifice special interests to the general social welfare.

Although Myrdal deprecates the possibility of revolutionary actions on the part of the impoverished masses, his sympathies are nonetheless on their side. It is to lift them out of their state of misery and ignorance that the system must be altered and its course set toward development. It is to this end that agriculture must assume a capitalist pattern and, by doing so, mitigate existing social inequalities. Myrdal's reasoning seems rather surprising on this point, for the division between entrepreneur and wage-worker is no less unequal than that between tenant and landlord. But Myrdal explains himself by pointing out that, generally, 'the conventional Western approach is predisposed to view reductions in inequalities as more likely to discourage than to encourage expansion in production' (p. 1368). This argument, he says, is not valid for South Asia because, while 'the Western economic discussion is normally restricted to the analysis of inequalities in the distribution of income, in South Asia, the inequalities relevant to prospects for economic advance are more deep-seated. They concern not only differences in income, but more important, differences in status and in control over productive resources' (p. 1369). Since wage-workers are what they are because they have no control over productive resources, the equality of which Myrdal speaks is that of landlord, capitalist peasant, and other entrepreneurs – in short, the achievement of bourgeois equality in South Asia, the completion of the delayed bourgeois revolution by non-revolutionary means.

Such an achievement would, of course, differ widely from the earlier results of bourgeois revolutions because of the planning factor which, according to Myrdal, assures a new type of development leading into welfare capitalism. Planning itself requires government domination over the whole of society even though it is to remain a private-enterprise society. Under its auspices, prices, for example, would no longer be market-determined but planned, that is, 'would be *prices* that, under all existing conditions including the full range of government policies, would give entrepreneurs and, more generally, producers, traders, consumers, and savers incentives to act according to a particular development plan' (p. 2037).

This is quite a tall order. It has never before been suggested or attempted in even the highly developed welfare capitalism. To be sure, there is a lot of price-fixing in the latter; not to support planned development, however, but to maintain the profitability of specific enterprises. There is also indirect price manipulation by monetary and fiscal means on the part of central authorities to combat depression and secure a necessary degree of social stability. These policies, however, find their definite limits in the profit requirements of capital production. It is the latter which determines the character and extent of government interventions – as the conditions in the various welfare economies currently demonstrate – unless, of course, it is assumed that they 'plan' their own economic difficulties. But this kind of pseudo-planning presupposes highly advanced industrial systems able to afford, if only for a time, engaging in nonprofitable production in order to bring total social production up to a higher level. This is the only 'planning' possible in the 'mixed economy' in response to a declining demand resulting from a decreasing rate of capital formation. It has no relevance whatever for the impoverished nations of South Asia, which must increase the supply in order to accumulate capital. A 'planning' fitted to the conditions of underdeveloped market economies would require policies radically different from those that would offer 'incentives' to all social layers to induce them to adapt their behavior to the exigencies of a particular development plan.

Myrdal's dilemma, then, is his theoretical attempt to combine irreconcilables, namely, a capitalist market economy with authoritarian controls designed to subject capital production to actual social needs. This forces him to misunderstand both capitalism and socialism, and to provide them with features they do not possess. It induces him also to assume that it is actually possible to treat the development problems of South Asia in relative isolation from the problems of the capitalist world economy. Although he shows in great detail in what particular manner American capitalism subordinates development in the Philippines to its own specific interests, and though he objects to American imperialism in Vietnam and the whole of Southeast Asia, he still imagines that the capitalist, and therewith imperialist, nations, could be genuinely interested in the development of underdeveloped countries for the sheer sake of development. He suggests that the capitalist nations initiate policies aiding this development, without asking himself whether or not this is actually possible in view of their needs for continuous expansion to secure their own privileged positions. It does not occur to him that it may be far too late to have any kind of progressive development under the auspices of capital production, and that the development of South Asia, most of all, might depend on a further non-capitalist development of the advanced nations.

References

MARX, K., and ENGELS, F. (1942), *Selected Correspondence*, Moscow.
MARX, K. (n.d.), *The First Indian War of Independence*, Moscow.
MARX, K. (1926), *Capital*, Moscow.
MYRDAL, G. (1968), *Asian Drama: An Inquiry into the Poverty of Nations*, Twentieth Century Fund, Pantheon Books. Penguin, 1969.

27 Elinor Graham

The Politics of Poverty

Excerpts from Elinor Graham, 'The Politics of Poverty', in Ben B. Seligman (ed.), *Poverty as a Public Issue*, Free Press, 1965, pp. 213–49.

In January 1964, a man familiar to congressional surroundings delivered his first address to a joint session of Congress in his new role as President of the United States. As he presented his presidential program to Congress, Lyndon Johnson called for an 'unconditional war on poverty', a government commitment 'not only to relieve the symptoms of poverty, but to cure it; and above all, to prevent it'.

The complex of ideological themes and political programs officially recognized and initiated by this address – all under the slogan of a War on Poverty – is the topic of this paper. The analysis developed here views this 'war' as a key ingredient in the social and political ideology embraced by President Johnson, his administrative officials, and his advisers. As part of an ideology, it is designed to motivate elements in the society to political action. The language of the War on Poverty and the form of its accompanying social-welfare programs are set within the boundaries of traditional social beliefs, arise from the pressure of political needs, and are molded by the nature of those groups seeking action, as well as by the official bodies from which they must receive approval.

Poverty, consequently, is now a major preoccupation of hundreds of public officials, statisticians and social planners across the nation. In less than a year it has been thrust dramatically into the center of governmental programing on local, regional, and national levels. President Johnson (1964) has called for 'total victory' in a national War on Poverty – 'a total commitment by the President, and this Congress, and this Nation, to pursue victory over the most ancient of mankind's enemies'. Joining the administration forces and local and state governments, private social-welfare organizations and institutions normally engaged in non-welfare activities have increasingly indicated an awareness of possibilities and a willingness, to engage their organizational resources in 'extra-institutional' activities aimed at the alleviation of poverty. Colleges, churches, and corporations have plunged into a *por-pourri* of activities designed to provide 'opportunities' for deserving members of low-income groups in forms, and to an extent, that welfare workers could previously conceive only in their wildest dreams.

Given an 'understanding of the enemy' which emphasizes the special characteristics of certain low-income groups that cannot easily be integrated into the market economy, what 'strategy of attack' is advocated by the national policy-makers? The 'war on poverty' proposed in 1964 consisted of a ten-point attack which strikingly resembled the President's entire domestic program: income tax cuts, a civil rights bill, Appalachian regional development, urban and rural community rehabilitation, youth programs, teenage and adult vocational training and basic educational programs, and hospital insurance for the aged. A special 'anti-poverty package was introduced – the Economic Opportunity Act of 1964. The Office of Economic Opportunity created by this legislation was to be the headquarters for the new 'war'.

Administration of the Economic Opportunity Act and supporting programs, as well as plans for future expansion, indicate that the War on Poverty seeks to mobilize the social services of the nation along three major lines: youth education and employment programs, planned regional and community redevelopment, and vocational training and retraining under the beginnings of a national manpower policy.

Under this 'strategy of attack', aid to the poor is, in theory, provided in the nature of a new and expanded 'opportunity environment'. Such aid is primarily directed toward the youth and employable heads of poor families; it will not reach the really critical poverty categories – the aged, female heads of families, and poor farm families – except in the form of improvements in the surrounding physical and economic environments or the administration of welfare and health services. As the Council of Economic Advisers noted in their 1964 report, the proposed programs are designed 'to equip and to permit the poor of the Nation to produce and to earn ... the American standard of living by their own efforts and contributions'. Those Americans who are not in a physical or family position which allows them to earn their way out of poverty will not be immediately aided by the programs under the War on Poverty. This situation simply illustrates the difference between social needs defined in a statistical manner and a political designation of poverty. It does not indicate that the War on Poverty is a political hoax or a hollow slogan to attract votes; on the contrary, its ideology and programs respond to social and political needs of a very real, although very different, nature, than those of poverty *per se*.

The sociology of poverty programs

It is useful to locate welfare-state programs on two scales, vertically and horizontally, in order to visualize the range and nature of programs open to government planners in formulating the War on Poverty and to understand the implications of the particular path chosen. The vertical scale of our imaginary axes indicates at one end whether the poverty-stricken are singled out of the total society as objects for special aid or, at the opposite pole, social services and income payments are provided to all as a right of citizenship. The latter method is followed in most of the Swedish welfare programs. Family payments, old-age pensions, and health services are provided for all members of the society regardless of their financial position. Most United States welfare programs, including those proposed under the War on Poverty, are located at the opposite pole: programs are focused at a particular low-income category and need must be proven in order to receive aid. The second (and horizontal) scale indicates at one end that aid may be provided in the form of direct income payments and at the other extreme through social services. The major portion of the welfare activities in the United States, and particularly those connected with the War on Poverty, are found in the service category, even though, as was argued above, the nature of American poverty in the sixties indicates an urgent need for consideration of direct income payments to critical poverty-stricken groups.

Certain important implications follow from the need-based and service-oriented nature of the War on Poverty programs. First, separation of the poor from the rest of the society by means of needs requirements, increases the visibility of the low-income earners. This is a 'war' *on poverty* – the very nature of such a proposal requires an exposure of 'the enemy' in its human form. In addition, separation of the poor creates a donor-donee relationship whether it exists between the income-tax-paying middle and upper classes and the low-income earners, or the social worker and his client. In the context of American social philosophy, such a situation enhances the self-image of the well-to-do and places a stigma of failure and dependency upon aid recipients. Above all, it is 'the American way' to approach social-welfare issues, for it places the burden of responsibility upon the individual and not upon the socio-economic system. Social services are preferred to income payments in an ideological atmosphere which abhors 'handouts'.

Second, a focus upon *poverty* allows for a redefinition of the racial clash into the politically understandable and useful terms of a conflict between the 'haves' and the 'have-nots'. The donor-donee relationship, sharply cast into relief by the poverty label, reasserts and stabilizes the power of the political elite, whose positions have been threatened by enfranchisement of the Negro.

Third, the social-service orientation, particularly the stress upon the 'reorganization' and 'total mobilization' of existing programs, is strongly supported by the nature of the experimental programs started during the Kennedy years. These programs and, of more importance, the ideas and 'method of attack' which they initiated, are vigorously advocated by a well-organized and sophisticated lobby within the administrative branch.

Fourth, the social-service orientation of the War on Poverty is activity- and job-creating for the middle and upper classes. Provision of social services, as opposed to income payments, requires the formation of new organizations and institutions which in turn are the source of activities and income-paying roles for the nation's expanding number of college-educated individuals. The War on Poverty, its programs and ideology, are a response to the demands of an educated 'new class': it provides a legitimate outlet for the energies of a group that poses a greater threat to the political system and moral fabric of the society than the inadequately educated poor who are the official objects of aid.

Ideology and poverty

A nation which confidently points to its unparalleled level of wealth, the 'magnificent abundance' of the American way of life, has been suddenly and surprisingly engaged in the public unveiling of the impoverished degradation of one-fifth of its population. Affluence and poverty confront each other, and the shock of the encounter is reflected in the phrase that acknowledges the 'stranger's' presence: a 'paradox' – the 'paradox of poverty in the midst of plenty'. This mysterious stranger is apparently inconsistent with the nation's vision of itself and particularly with its moral notions of equality.

One supposes that there is an element of honest surprise and, with many, disbelief, for they *know* that if you work hard and take advantage of all of the opportunities available, you *can* climb out of poverty and reach the top – well, perhaps not *the* top, but certainly a comfortable level of living. It is axiomatic. Numerous individuals will tediously cite their own life experiences as examples of this general law of dynamics of American society. The following account was provided by a retired educator who sought to establish his qualification to talk about poverty in the sixties:

I was born in a homestead in the lowland swamps of Louisiana. There were no schools. We lived off the land. And, since I have viewed the very sections of the underprivileged and poor people in the Appalachian highland, I decided I must have been very poor, because those children there have much more now than I had. We lived from game, and we had no electric light. We got food if there were plenty of ducks and geese and rabbits ... I was a drop-in at school when they finally got a little one- or two-room school. I mean, I dropped in when there were no potatoes to plant or corn to pull, or something of that sort. I have three college degrees from standard universities, and I never spent a day on a college campus during regular session. I belong to the old school. I took correspondence; I did some summer terms, and I did extension work, traveling sometimes a hundred miles each weekend to take it. So I think I know what it means to get an education the hard way. . . . I understand the phase in our help to the underprivileged (House Hearings, 1964, p. 1120–21).

Everyone who is over thirty will say that they know what it is like to be poor because they lived during the Great Depression; that is taken as automatic qualification. When attacked by his

Democratic 'bretheren' for a lack of understanding of the complexities of the problem, Representative Griffin (Republican – Michigan) responded with, 'my father worked most of his life in a plant; and I worked my way through school, and I believe I do know a little bit about poverty' (House Hearings, 1964, p. 854–5). Without denying the achievements of the poor boy from the swamps of Louisiana who is now a distinguished educator, or the son of a worker holding the office of US congressman, such accounts and their implications for the 'struggling young men' from present-day poor families reflect a general confusion of the income and social-class mobility of an individual with a rising national standard of living. The American dream is substituted for the American reality and evidence drawn from the second is said to be proof of the first.

President Johnson intertwined the two concepts when he declared in his 1964 War on Poverty message that:

With the growth of our country has come opportunity for our people – opportunity to educate our children, to use our energies, in productive work, to increase our leisure – opportunity for almost every American to hope that through work and talent he could create a better life for himself and his family (Johnson, 1964).

Traditional themes of the bright boy attaining entrance to the world of wealth through 'work and talent' are intermingled with the profit figures of economic growth. In suggesting that the benefits of a rising standard of living include increased opportunity for bettering income and even social-class position, two distinct and different concepts are equated for ideological purposes.

Fusion of dream and actuality in the national vision has been strongly influenced by the American business creed and its image of the relationship between the economic system and the individual. Benefits derived from the economic growth of the nation are not conceived as social products. The idealized 'free-enterprise' system produces the national wealth through the efforts of atomized individuals operating within a 'free competitive market system with individual freedom'. A guarantee of the rights of the individual to insure his freedom and free opportunity are thus essential. Since mythology need not correspond to reality (particularly if believed in strongly enough), equality of opportunity is assumed and is 'proved' through the individual success stories which abound in the popular literature. Such 'proof' is, however, subject to a great deal of doubt. Citing several sociological studies, the authors of *The American Business Creed* observe that a survey of the overall statistical situation 'might well lead to more tempered conclusions about American freedom of opportunity' (Sutton, 1956, p. 26).

With an image of itself that denies the possibility of widespread poverty, a nation bent on 'recognizing realities' must squeeze the poor in through the basement window. We are told that we are not faced with extensive conditions of poverty (as are other less fortunate nations). Poverty in the United States is 'grinding poverty', found only in 'pockets of poverty' and has defied all laws of genetics to acquire an hereditary quality exhibited in the 'ruthless pattern' and 'cycle of poverty'. This is not a case of good old-fashioned poverty, it is a special and uniquely American–1964 brand.

A particularly vivid exposition of this version of poverty can be found in the explanation of the Economic Opportunity Act prepared by Sargent Shriver's office for the first congressional hearings (OEO, 1964). Much of the credit for the modern version of poverty expounded within its covers must go to the influence of John Kenneth Galbraith's writings. He broke the poor into two groups – those afflicted with *case* poverty and those who are victims of *insular* poverty. Characteristics of the individual afflicted with case poverty prevent him from mastering his environment, while the environment proves to be the handicapping factor for those living in 'islands of poverty'. In both situations an hereditary factor is introduced either in fact (as a physical tendency toward poor health or mental deficiency) or in effect through the deficiencies of the social environment (as with poor schools, lack of job opportunities, lack of motivation and direction from parents) (Galbraith, 1958, p. 251). Whether or not such a view corresponds to reality, it should be recognized that when one maintains that the society is affluent, poverty can hardly be tolerated as a widespread phenomenon and must be of a very special and individual variety. With such a thesis, one is not likely to observe that an average American family with an income of $5665 – the median for all families in 1960 – may not feel particularly affluent at this 'modest but adequate' level.

Where, then, are the roots of poverty in an affluent society? Few combatants in the war of ideologies argue that the fault underlies the American landscape and may be lodged in the economic system. The principle according to which the wealth of the society is divided is left unscathed. On official levels, voices do not openly suggest that a system which distributes economic goods solely upon the basis of the individual's present or past functional role within the economy may be at the source of American poverty now and increasingly so in the future. Although not reflecting official opinion, the statement of the *Ad Hoc* Committee on the Triple Revolution was a notable exception. This group of distinguished educators, labor leaders, economists, and critics suggested in part that:

The economy of abundance can sustain all citizens in comfort and economic security whether or not they engage in what is commonly reckoned as work. ... We urge, therefore, that society through its appropriate legal and governmental institutions undertake an unqualified commitment to provide every individual in every family with an adequate income as a matter of right (Committee on Triple Revolution, 1964).

Right-wing reaction is clear and quite predictable when the legitimacy of the American economic system is questioned in any context. There was no doubt in the mind of Representative Martin (Republican, Nebraska) that the suggestions of the committee were of 'the same kind of plan worked out in Communist nations' (House Hearings, 1964, p. 747). Such a reaction hardly leaves room for political debate.

Where questions regarding 'the system' are taboo, those focusing upon the individual are welcome and quite comprehensible to the political protagonists. In acceptable political circles, the causes of poverty are sought in the process through which individuals acquire qualities enabling them to succeed and share in the national wealth. Conservatives argue that the fault lies with the poor for being lazy or stupid and not taking advantage of opportunities to obtain education, good health, a marketable skill, and a stable family life. 'The fact is that most people who have no skill, have had no education for the same reason – low intelligence or low ambition!' says Barry Goldwater (1964). On the other hand liberals maintain that something is wrong with the present means provided for individuals to obtain these desirable attributes – in short, the society is at fault: the poor are the 'have-not people of America. They are denied, deprived, disadvantaged, and they are discriminated against', argues Walter Reuther of the United Auto Workers (House Hearings, 1964, Part I, p. 429). President Johnson and Sargent Shriver, commander of the poverty forces, bow to both groups. They maintain that it is first necessary to change the attitudes of the poor – to give them achievement motivations by changing 'indifference to interest, ignorance to awareness, resignation to ambition, and an attitude of withdrawal to one of participation' (OEO, 1964, p. 43). At the same time, present education, social-welfare, and job-training programs sponsored at all levels of government and in both the public and private sectors of society, must be coordinated, consolidated and expanded to provide a new 'opportunity environment' for the poor.

The emphasis is upon the process by which Americans attain the attributes necessary to achieve economic success rather than the legitimacy of the system to distribute the national wealth. This view is enhanced by the assumption that Americans, and poor Americans in particular, must earn and 'want to earn' any social or economic benefits they receive. In our society, states former Senator Goldwater, one receives rewards by 'merit and not by fiat' – essentially, you earn your keep or you get out (or stay out):

I strongly believe that all people are entitled to an opportunity . . . to get an education and to earn a living *in keeping with the value of their work* (emphasis supplied). . . . But I do not believe that the mere fact of having little money entitles everybody, regardless of circumstance, to be permanently maintained by the taxpayers at an average or comfortable standard of living (Goldwater, 1964).

Conservatives make no effort to conceal their reliance on this basic assumption; they quite frankly do not want to change the present distribution of wealth, or potential advantages they may have in gaining a greater future share. They are successful because they deserve to be successful, while others are poor because they are innately incapable of doing any better. This assumption about human nature is an integral part of the business creed, for the idealized economic system is dependent upon the 'achievement motivations' of the individual. These crucial motivations could easily be destroyed if people became dependent upon government doles. If this happened, the greatest welfare system of all, the 'free-enterprise system', would be destroyed. As the witness from the Chamber of Commerce explained to Representative Edith Green during the House antipoverty hearings, the Chamber does not support 'programs for people' because:

economic measures to improve the efficiency of production and thus to get a larger output for our people from the same input of materials and manpower and capital goods is one of the greatest contributions to wealth that has ever been discovered in the history of mankind and the United States excels among all nations of the world in providing this kind of welfare (House Hearings, 1964, Part I, p. 707).

Despite conservative denunciations, President Johnson eagerly reserves a benevolent role for the federal government, and particularly on an ideological level. He counters conservative views by adding a second act to the drama of the poor struggling young man working his way to the top in the 'free-enterprise system'. A magnanimous millionaire, glowing with compassion and wisdom, stretches out a benevolent helping hand to enable 'Ragged Dick' to make good in the final panel of the American dream. Evoking an image of a goddess of peace and plenty rather than lanky Uncle Sam, Johnson declares (1964b) that both at home and abroad, 'We will extend the helping hand of a just nation to the poor and helpless and the oppressed.' In the American reality, however, 'we' take care to see that the 'helping hand' doesn't contain money or tangible goods – just opportunities to earn a better way of life and opportunities to *learn* to 'want to earn' in the American way.

Such a sense of *noblesse oblige* is not inherent in the actual programs and techniques proposed in the War on Poverty, but it plays a part in the language which is inevitably used to describe them (and which is perhaps latent within our 'progressive' attitudes toward social welfare). It is also the result of the effective control and administration of the government by the affluent and educated classes. In short, the official government attitude toward poverty should be expected to reflect the views arising from the life-situations of those who have formulated it. In speaking of poverty, no one bothers to deny or to hide the fact that the federal government is an instrumentality of the successful classes. This is assumed. The poor are recognized as not having a significant political voice. The entire War on Poverty was created, inspired, and will be carried out by the affluent. Action by the upper classes and all superior groups is urged on moral grounds, because it is right, because, as Senator Robert Kennedy stated simply, 'those of us who are better off, who do not have that problem have a responsibility to our fellow citizens who do' (House Hearings, 1964, p. 330).

Without an economic crisis which affects the upper-income groups as well as the poor, the social philosophy of the federal antipoverty programs will necessarily contain this strong moral emphasis. Caught between the language of American social mythology and the attitudes generated by the existing social and political realities of a wealthy nation ruled by a distinct class of successful men, the public debate generated by the proposed 'war' can only reveal our poverty of ideology. Conservatives balk at action because the poor are 'getting what they deserve', and liberals cannot seem to act without assuming the 'white man's burden'. The militants of the new 'war' look for the enemy and find him all too often in the personal attributes of the poor. The remedy offered for poverty amounts to a middle-class success formula (and, perhaps it *is* the route to success in American society): education, a stable family life, and above all, the proper attitudes. In short, there appears to be justification for the charge that the War on Poverty can be more accurately characterized as a 'war on the poor' (Jencks, 1964).

The politics of poverty and race

Confronted with a social ideology which easily obscures the existence of poverty, and lacking a thunderous economic crisis that directly threatens the middle and upper classes, the public concern with poverty of a traditionally reactive government is most remarkable. Why did poverty become a politically important issue in 1964?

When asked the reasons for a War on Poverty, President Johnson and Sargent Shriver presented themselves as puppets of the American people who 'are interested in the Government and in themselves making a focused or concentrated effort to attack poverty' (House Hearings, 1964, p. 99). A public demand for the elimination of poverty, did not, however, exist before it was deliberately made into an issue by the Johnson Administration in 1964. Government programs were not a response to public protests against conditions of poverty for one-fifth of a nation. [. . .]

Political power-needs, rather than an articulated public demand, were at the source of the sudden resolution to recognize poverty in 1964. Briefly, the most plausible occasion for the urgency and publicity devoted to poverty by the Executive Office can be found in the political and emotionally disrupting effects of the civil-rights movement, especially in regard to white morality and the white power structure. Emotionally, the nation needed to redefine the racial conflict as a conflict between the 'haves' and the 'have-nots'. Politically, a transmutation of the civil-rights movement secured the threatened power position of whites as whites, and further eased the agonies of the slow political death of the south. The latter, with its implications for the composition of the national political parties, has held special meaning for Johnson in his struggle to unify the Democratic Party and attain congressional compliance with presidential programs. In practical terms, the War on Poverty and its implications for opening a new field of jobs and social status, is the means by which American society will expand to accommodate the Negroes' demands for integration. [. . .]

Suddenly in the sixties, the Negro has become a political power; he has become a 'new' Negro who won't fit into the old images. This forced racial confrontation has caught the white off-guard. He does not possess a cultural reservoir that would allow him to interact – or avoid interaction – easily and unemotionally. Political protests, in short, have resulted in a social dislocation of the Negro and have created a necessity for both races to become aware of themselves and their inter-projective images. Politically, this awareness and the knowledge it can bring, is both necessary and beneficial. But this is an inconvenience for the white, an inconvenience requiring extra effort that may result in heightened tension as well as awareness.

The task of knowing is greatly simplified for the white American

if he substitutes 'poverty' for 'race'. He can more easily understand the frustrations of job hunting or unemployment than what it
means to possess a black skin. 'Poverty' has a comfortable sound
to it, it makes 'sense' and is not emotionally upsetting. Politically
speaking, to *re-define* race and civil rights as a manifestation of
conditions of poverty, opens a path for action. Where race and
nationalism are vivid, emotion-based issues, not easily resolved
through reason and logic, conflict between the 'haves' and the
'have-nots' is well understood. The Western world has a supply
of practical tools and intellectual theories with which this persistent enemy can be explained and controlled. Marxian ideology,
liberal benevolence, or a religious morality all allow for practical
political action that is denied when confronted by race in and
of itself. Whether or not the civil-rights movement dramatized
existing conditions of poverty, white Americans had to raise the
poverty issue to relieve the emotional tension and political *im-
passe* created by the racial confrontation. The dollar costs of a
War on Poverty are exchanged for the high emotional price-tag
attached to race. [...]

Reaction to the race riots of previous summers provides ample
illustration of the ideological function of an anti-poverty slogan
and the practical role of its accompanying programs. Immediately
after the 1964 riots in New York City, Wagner made a special trip
to Washington to see if more antipoverty projects and other federal
money could be directed toward the slum areas of the city. As
the *New York Times* (1964) interpreted the visit:

It would be highly surprising if Mr Wagner – Mayor of the city where
the present epidemic of racial disturbances began – did not mean, as
part of his mission, to remind members of the House of the intimate
connection between the battle against poverty and the battle against
riots. ... The anti-poverty bill, in the new perspective given by the
disturbances of this long, hot summer, is also an anti-riot bill. The
members of the House of Representatives will do well to bear that in
mind when the time comes for a vote.

[...] Not only has the President's War on Poverty provided evidence
of sincere efforts to alleviate some of the needs of the low-income
Negro ghettos, but it also provided white society with a defense
against charges of overt racism. Poverty and racism have joined

hands to create the Negro's hell – the effects of one cannot be separated easily from the other. When given the choice, however, white society prefers to attribute the source of Negro resentment and protests to poverty. The *New York Times* (1964) employed this defense when it maintained that the race riots were 'as much demonstrations against Negro poverty as against discrimination and what some call "police brutality"'. In this respect, we should note the extent to which right-wing politicians ignore the racial aspect of the Negro protest and refer to it almost exclusively as a conflict between the 'haves' and the 'have-nots'. They simply make it clear that they are on the side of the 'haves'. Morally there may be something wrong with denying privileges on the basis of race, but within the right-wing ideology, there is 'nothing wrong' with defending your own property and privileges from someone who is not as successful.

For reasons of a less than morally commendable nature, white America has responded to the Negroes' demands for an integrated society with an antipoverty movement: a response slow in coming and pitifully inadequate at first, but still a response. In terms of realistic social dynamics, integration is not, and will not be an interpretation of the old by the new, but will be a process of *expansion* and then assimilation. Societies expand and contract; they do not blend except with passing of generations, and that cannot even be predicted with assurance. Those who are within the socioeconomic structure will not give up their positions to Negroes seeking entrance. New roles must be added to the job structure and new status rungs created in the social ladder.

Such is the function of the War on Poverty. As was pointed out, it is a service-oriented welfare measure. The activity- and job-creating nature of its programs are presently opening and shaping new fields in the social services, a process that is certain to increase its range in the future. New professional positions in community organization and social planning, as well as the clerical and blue-collar jobs created to staff the research institutions and service organizations of the 'antipoverty' projects, are particularly accessible to the Negro. This is true, above all, for the now small but increasing ranks of the college educated and professionally trained Negro. The politically dangerous energies of the Negro elite can be molded into socially legitimate channels through the creation of roles in an entirely new area of the nation's job structure.

References

COMMITTEE ON THE TRIPLE REVOLUTION (1964), *Report of the Ad Hoc Committee*, April.

GALBRAITH, J. K. (1958), *The Affluent Society*, Houghton Mifflin.

GOLDWATER, B. (1964), Quoted in the *New York Times*, 16 January.

HOUSE HEARINGS (1964), Economic Opportunity Act of 1964, Subcommittee on the War on Poverty Programme of the Committee on Education and Labor, Housing Representatives, Congress, 2nd Session.

JENCKS, C. (1964), 'Johnson v. Poverty', *New Republic*, 28 March.

JOHNSON, L. B. (1964a), President's Message on Poverty to the Congress, March 16.

JOHNSON, L. B. (1964b), Quoted in the *New York Times*, 23 September.

NEW YORK TIMES (1964), Editorial: 'Riots and Poverty', 4 August.

OFFICE OF ECONOMIC OPPORTUNITY (1964), *The War on Poverty: A Congressional Presentation*, March 17.

SUTTON, F. X., *et al* (1956), *The American Business Creed*, Harvard University Press.

28 Richard Titmuss

Poverty versus Inequality

Richard Titmuss, 'Poverty versus Inequality: Diagnosis', *Nation*, vol. 200, 1965, pp. 130–33.

Not for the first time in the modern history of Western nations, poverty has been rediscovered and reapproved as a socially acceptable subject for public debate. Britain and the United States have recently put behind them, at least for a season, the thought – expressed so well by Bagehot, the typical nineteenth-century organization man – that 'the character of the poor is an unfit topic for continuous art'.

In the United States, Michael Harrington, for one has helped to shift opinion in favour of the poor. The civil rights movement constitutes an increasingly powerful force in the same direction, as does fear of juvenile violence – perhaps the political equivalent in the twentieth century of working-class revolution in the nineteenth-century. In Britain, the rediscovery of poverty has mainly come from respectable Labour intellectuals, not from the extreme Left; it has come from a nascent understanding of the limits of conventional welfare, and from a growing sense that after thirteen years of Conservative rule Britain is still a deeply class-divided society.

Both countries have now elected governments committed to act on the poverty question. There are, of course, large differences in approach, in the definition of what constitutes poverty in the second half of the twentieth century, in the identification of 'the poor', and in the remedies proposed. In broad comparative terms, American public concern seems to be dominated by the issues of unemployment – particularly among the young, the Negroes and the casualties of technological change. In Britain, where it is much more broadly agreed that full employment is a responsibility of government and where color is numerically a smaller problem, the emphasis is different and less clear-cut. Poverty is being seen here in individual and environmental terms. There is the poverty of the aged, of fatherless families and of other minority groups. There is the poverty of an educational system that denies opportunity for a substantial proportion of the nation's children and allows them to leave school at fifteen, illiterate, unskilled, deprived. There is the poverty of housing and a grim and sordid physical inheritance from the industrial revolution.

But underlying these different public views on the priorities for an attack on poverty, certain general and often unstated assumptions seem to prevail in both countries – or so it appears to a British student of welfare who has visited the United States on four occasions since 1957, and has learned much from American friends and colleagues in the fields of social policy and social work. Politically speaking, there has been in both countries a shift away from the naïve belief of the middle-fifties that poverty would gracefully succumb to economic growth. There is less facile talk now of dwindling 'pockets of poverty'; more awareness that the problem is larger, many-sided and formidable.

This new realism was symbolized in a message sent to Congress in March, 1964, and published with the Economic Opportunity Act ('The War on Poverty' programme):

there remains an unseen America, a land of limited opportunity and restricted choice. In it live nearly 10 million families who try to find shelter, feed and clothe their children, stave off disease and malnutrition, and somehow build a better life on less than $60 a week. Almost two-thirds of these families struggle to get along on less than $40 a week. These are the people behind the American looking glass. There are nearly 35 million of them. Being poor is not a choice for these millions; it is a rigid way of life. It is handed down from generation to generation in a cycle of inadequate education, inadequate homes, inadequate jobs, and stunted ambitions.

This was no narrow, pathological definition of poverty. It was a challenge to action involving values, institutions and policies.

However, despite the *élan* of this diagnosis and of similar, though less arresting, restatements in Britain, another general assumption prevails in both countries: the poverty war can be painlessly won provided there is sufficient political and administrative determination. It is not a matter of values or of conflict over fundamental changes in a market economy. It is more a matter of the administrative, organizational and manipulative skills of those waging the war. Since we have decided that there is still a problem of poverty, let us determine to solve it; all we need is activity, efficiency and programs that change the attitudes, motivations and employability of the poor.

In the American Job Corps programme, for example, the task of the conservation camps is 'to do far more than provide basic education, skill training, and work experience; they must change indifference to interest, ignorance to awareness, resignation to ambition, and an attitude of withdrawal to one of participation'. Hence, those with 'serious emotional or psychological disorders' will not be eligible for the Job Corps. In effect, they will be rejected for reasons of work motivation (on what criteria?); they will be classed as ineligible to participate in American values. This categorizing of the poor by their personal characteristics is faintly reminiscent of the attempt by framers of the New Poor Law of 1834 in England to distinguish between the 'deserving' poor and an 'undeserving' pauper under class.

One appreciates the real, practical difficulties that face those who will run these programs. Indeed, they are so frighteningly complex that one is led to ask whether the diagnosis is correct, although at the same time one understands how it was reached. If the 'culture of poverty' is to blame, then, logically, the social and economic system is blameless. It follows from such an assumption that one of the central questions for social policy today can be set aside; that is, *how to continually invest proportionately more resources in the 'poor' than the 'non-poor' without stigmatizing the poor by their personal characteristics and circumstances.* Separate and differential programmes for the poor as a definable class must involve some test of poverty and, because such minority programmes cannot escape the need to be 'success oriented' (which means selection), they inevitably involve a test of personality and potential merit.

For more than 100 years the poor law was hated by the poor of England because it branded them. Whether the Labour government, with its proposals for an income guarantee in old age, will solve this problem remains as yet uncertain.

What is certain is that the political alternative to separate, deprecating programmes for the poor is to channel more resources to them through established, socially approved, 'normal' institutions: social security, tax deductions, education and training, medical care, housing and other acceptable routes. But what we are then discussing is something more fundamental: we are not defining 'poverty' and devising separate laws for the poor, but embarking on a dialogue about inequality and measures to redistribute resources.

But it is poverty that has been rediscovered in the West, not inequality. To recognize inequality as the problem involves recognizing the need for structural change, for sacrifices by the majority. It involves approving categories of public welfare we have hitherto disapproved of. In short, it means a painful war. Our societies have not yet begun to understand the immense complexities and the political implications in a market economy of a realistic attack on the problems of underprivilege and inequality. Poverty, said Voltaire in 1759, weakens the courage of the poor: poverty programs in 1965 may weaken the courage of democrats to face industrial and technological change.

Those political commentators, economists and sociologists on both sides of the Atlantic, who in recent years have been proclaiming the end of political ideology in the West, imply, directly or indirectly, that inequality is no longer an issue for our societies. Incrementalism in social welfare is approved: small-scale programmes for small-scale problems. These observers of the scene do not raise questions about values and goals: indeed, they deny the need for basic change. So the concern is to find better means whereby administrators, psychologists and social workers can help and counsel the minority poor to abandon the 'culture of poverty'.

Seymour Lipset in *Political Man* spoke for many when he declared that 'the ideological issues dividing left and right [have] been reduced to a little more or a little less government ownership and economic planning'; and there was general agreement that it really makes little difference 'which political party controls the domestic policies of individual nations'. With minor disagreements, parties of the Right and of the Left will both be concerned to alleviate those social injustices that still remain.

To quote Lipset again (though writers in a similar vein could equally be cited in England, France and Germany):

the fundamental political problems of the industrial revolution have been solved: the workers have achieved industrial and political citizenship, the conservatives have accepted the welfare state, and the democratic left has recognized that an increase in overall state power carries with it more dangers to freedom than solutions for economic problems. This very triumph of the democratic social revolution in the West ends domestic politics for those intellectuals who must have ideologies or utopias to motivate them to political action.

It is conceivable that this statement may serve historians as a summing up of majority opinion in the 1950s, but from the perspective of 1965 it is, to say the least, a dubious proposition.

First, it is unhistorical. Implicit in the thesis is the assumption that the 'industrial revolution' was a once-and-for-all affair. Thus, it ignores the evidence concerning the trend toward monopolistic concentrations of economic power, the role of the corporation as private government with taxing powers, the problems of social disorganization and cultural deprivation, and the growing impact of automation and new techniques of production and distribution in economically advanced societies. If the first phase of the so-called revolution was to force all men to work, the phase we are now entering may be to force many men not to work. Without a major shift in values, only an impoverishment in social living can result.

Second, it is a misuse of language to imply that membership in a trade union is synonymous with 'industrial citizenship'. Conceptions of what constitutes 'citizenship' for the worker must be related to what we now know about man's potential and his basic social and psychological needs; they cannot be compared with conditions of industrial slavery in the nineteenth century.

Third, the thesis implies that the problem of the distribution of income and wealth has either been solved or is now of insignificant proportions in Western society. In any event, such disparities as do exist are justified on grounds of individual differences and the need for economic incentives, and present no threat to democratic values.

In 1960, 1 per cent of the British population owned 42 per cent of all personal net capital and 5 per cent owned 75 per cent. Even these proportions are underestimates, for the figures exclude pension funds and trusts (which have grown enormously in recent years), and do not take into account the increasing tendency of large owners of property to distribute their wealth among their families, to spread it over time, to send it abroad, and to transform it in other ways.

This degree of concentration of wealth is nearly twice as great as it was in the United States in 1954, and far higher than in the early 1920s era of rampant American capitalism. But since about 1949, inequality of wealth has become more pronounced in the United States, the rate of increase being more than twice as fast as the rate of decline between 1922 and 1949. Measured in terms of the increase in the percentage of wealth held by the top 1 per cent, the growth of inequality during 1949–56 was more striking than at any time during at least the past forty years.

Not unexpectedly, the distribution of income also appears to have become more lopsided in recent years, affecting most adversely the one-fifth to one-quarter of the United States population living below the currently defined 'poverty line'. These are not all Negroes; 80 per cent of the American poor are white, and only one-fifth receive welfare aid. Economic growth in the richest society in the world had not been guided by any automatic equalizer. Crime is the modern form of acquisitive social mobility for the lower classes, particularly the unemployed youth.

There is no evidence to suggest that Britain has been following a different path since the end of the 1940s. It is even possible that inequality in the ownership of wealth (particularly in terms of family holdings) has increased more rapidly in Britain than in the United States since 1949. The British system of taxation is almost unique among Western nations in its generous treatment of the rich in respect of settlements, trusts, gifts and other arrangements for redistributing and rearranging income and wealth. This is reflected in the remarkable fact that in the mid-1950s the tendency for wealth to be concentrated in a few hands was most marked in the young-adult age group.

Such evidence as this is ignored by those who proclaim the end of political ideology. More than a quarter-century of political upheaval, global war, 'welfare statism', managed economics and economic growth have made little impression on the holdings of great fortunes in at least two of the largest industrial nations, the United States and Britain, and similar trends are probably in operation in de Gaulle's France and Erhard's Germany. Wealth still bestows political and economic power, more power than income, though today it is probably exercised differently and with more respect for public opinion than was the fashion in the nineteenth century.

How can these great disparities in the private ownership of wealth and in the exercise of economic power be made to fit into the thesis that we have reached the end of political dialogue? No political utopia since Plato has envisaged such degrees of economic inequality as permanent and desirable states for men. Socialists do not protest at such disparities because of envy; they do so because, as Tawney argued, they are fundamentally immoral. History suggests that human nature is not strong enough to maintain itself in true community where great disparities of income and wealth persist.

Fourth, and finally, there is in the thesis expressed by Professor Lipset an assumption that the establishment of social welfare necessarily and inevitably contributes to the spread of humanism and the eradication of poverty. The reverse can be true. Welfare can serve different masters. A multitude of sins may be committed in its appealing name. It can be used as a form of social control. It can be used as an instrument of economic growth which, by benefiting a minority, indirectly promotes greater inequality. Education is an example. We may educate the young to compete more efficiently as economic men in the private market, or we may educate them to be more capable of freedom, more capable of fulfilling their different potentialities, irrespective of income, class, religion and race.

Welfare may be used to serve military and racial ends – as in Hitler's Germany. More medical care was provided by state and voluntary agencies not because of a belief in every man's uniqueness but because of a hatred of men. Welfare may be used to narrow allegiances, not to diffuse them – as in employers' fringe benefit systems. Individual gain and political quietism, fostered by the new feudalism of the corporation, may substitute for the sense of common humanity nourished by systems of non-discriminatory mutual aid.

What matter, then, what indeed are fundamental to the health of welfare, are the objectives toward which its face is set: to universalize humanistic ethics and the social rights of citizenship or to divide, discriminate and compete.

In the past we have distributed resources according to success and failure in economic competition; in the future we must decide whether it is morally right to continue on this basis in an economy of abundance. To distribute services according to needs and not according to productivity will help us to discover equality in our neighbors. 'Awareness of equality,' wrote Daniel Jenkins, 'always arises in personal relationships and nearly always confronts us as a challenge, for it means placing a greater value upon our neighbor than we had previously been disposed to do. We are all ready to love ourselves. The discovery of equality might be defined as the discovery that we have indeed to love our neighbours as ourselves.'

And so we have to ask: 'What are we to do with our wealth?' This is today a more relevant question than are those that seek to find more effective ways of punishing criminals, preventing abuse of public assistance, motivating men to work without creating jobs or providing adequate incomes, compelling them to save for old age when they cannot feed their children properly, shifting them out of subsidized housing, inventing cheap technological substitutes for their education, and charging them more for access to medical care.

Science and technology, in alliance with other structural and demographic changes under way in our societies, call for a major shift in values; for new incentives and new forms of reward unrelated to the productivity principle; for new criteria applied to the distribution of resources which are not tied to individual 'success' as a measure; for new forms of socially approved 'assistance'. They will make the conventional criteria of capitalism largely irrelevant.

Many years ago Keynes foresaw that the time would come when changes in values would be needed. When that time comes:

we shall be able to rid ourselves of many of the pseudo-moral principles which have hag-ridden us for two hundred years, by which we have exalted some of the most distasteful of human qualities into the position of the highest virtues. ... All kinds of social customs and economic practices affecting the distribution of wealth and of economic rewards and penalties, which we now maintain at all costs, we shall then be free to discard.

We shall need different rules to live by; more examples of

altruism to look up to. Indeed, our societies in Britain and the United States are already in need of them. In no other way will it be possible for us to prevent the deprived and the unable from becoming more deprived and unable; more cast down in a pool of apathy, frustration, crime, rootlessness and tawdry poverty.

In all this, social policy will have a central role to play. If this role is defined at all it will have to be defined in the language of equality and change. Here it is that ethics will have to be reunited to politics. The answers will not come and, indeed, logically cannot come from those who now proclaim 'the end of political ideology'; those who would elevate the principle of pecuniary gain and extend it to social service by equating education and medical care with refrigerators and mink coats: those who advocate that more and more people should 'contract out' of the public services and create for themselves new areas of privilege and discrimination; and those who think they can painlessly solve the problems of change by rehabilitating the poor.

29 Keith Buchanan

Contours of the Future

Excerpts from Keith Buchanan, *The Southeast Asian World: An Introductory Essay*, Taplinger Publishing Co., 1967, pp. 154–61.

South-east Asian peoples have been exposed to widely differing colonial influences and have emerged as independent nations with widely differing political systems, many of which are still in a state of experimentation and change. Moreover, like small nations all over the world, they have been drawn into, or affected to varying degrees by, the global strategies of the two great power blocs. And, alongside these factors of diversity, there are strong elements of unity. All the countries of Southeast Asia are impoverished by comparison with the countries of the West and of the European Soviet bloc and this impoverishment is increasing in relative terms. The poverty is due to the warping of their economic structures during the colonial period; more specifically, it was due to 'the intrusion of capitalism into a society within which a minority, indigenous or foreign, took advantage of the crippling of indigenous society to confer upon itself exorbitant political, economic and social powers'; the depredations of this group are a major factor limiting the development of an internal market, impeding modernization, and prolonging the dependence of the economy on foreign markets. Under such conditions the economies (with the exception of North Vietnam) remain heavily agrarian in their emphasis; underemployment in the rural areas is a direct outcome of lack of modernization and of change in the economic and social structure; a rapid expansion of population aggravates an already difficult situation. These are the conditions facing most Southeast Asian countries and being confronted with uneven effectiveness by their governments; it is out of these conditions that the future political and social geography of the region will grow.

In their drive towards a better life (which means for most of these peoples not only 'to have more' but 'to *be* more') two alternative roads are open to them, the liberal or free enterprise road and the socialist road. The first of these is the road being followed by most of the emerging nations. This is partly because the free enterprise system was the economic system bequeathed by the former colonial power, partly because it is the system that best serves the interests of the governing elite, and partly because, in dispensing aid, the United States tends to favour countries whose regimes support free enterprise – and the United States is the greatest donor of aid and without aid the economies and governments of many of the emergent states would crumple. The free enterprise system may be able to achieve a modest rate of economic growth in some emergent countries but has signally failed in many countries. And where it seems to have achieved some measure of success this is often more apparent than real; what at first sight seems an impressive economic advance may, on closer inspection, be due largely to the rapid expansion of export-oriented 'enclave economies', an expansion which conceals the stagnation of the countryside as a whole. In Southeast Asia both Malaya and Thailand illustrate this uneven development, this widening margin between the prospering 'poles of development' (such as the West coast of Malaya or the Bangkok region in Thailand) and the stagnation of large sectors of the back-country. Given the preoccupation of the system with profits this could hardly be otherwise; investment, and especially overseas investment, flows inevitably to those sectors of the economy and to those regions which offer the prospects of the highest and most certain return on investment; there is little prospect of it flowing towards the peasant sector which accounts for some four-fifths of the employment. Just as, on a global scale, the free enterprise system contributes to the widening gap between the affluent nations and the 'have-not' nations, so, too, at the national level does it contribute to the widening of the gap between the elite and the masses, between the restricted areas where modern and diversified economies have been built up and the remainder of the country which remains stagnant economically and little touched by modernization. And in these economic inequalities, which become increasingly glaring with the passage of time, we may find the major cause of the social and political ferment which is involving many of the underdeveloped countries.

The limited success of the free enterprise system (or of capitalism) is not hard to understand; it arises from the fact that many of the conditions which contributed to the success of the system in the Atlantic world are lacking elsewhere. The class of entrepreneurs, of businessmen, who played a major role in creating the economic structures of Western Europe and North America has no counterpart in Southeast Asia[1] or other parts of the Third World. The abstention from spending, the investment in long-term development projects, which provided the momentum for the industrialization of the West in the eighteenth and nineteenth centuries, are largely lacking in an area such as Southeast Asia, where investment in land or in commerce offers more immediate and more lucrative returns than investment in secondary industry. And in countries where the large land-owner is still a powerful force the social structure is a major limiting factor to real development; high rents leave the peasant impoverished and thus severely reduce the purchasing power of the great mass of the population while the wealth thus diverted from the peasantry is channeled into either luxury spending by the land-owning group or into the accumulation of yet more land. ... As the history of Western Europe illustrates, agrarian reform, is an essential prerequisite for successful industrialization – and, as the example of South Vietnam today shows, the possibilities of implementing a *real* agrarian reform are limited in some of the Western-aligned countries. The situation is different in North Vietnam which carried out a drastic land reform in the early years of the communist regime; in Cambodia the favourable man/land ratio and the limited extent of tenant farming means that the agrarian problem is not of major importance.

The socialist path has been chosen by North Vietnam, and, in the form of a 'Buddhist socialism', by Burma and Cambodia. It involves the establishment of an overall plan for the national economy; such a plan makes it possible to allocate scarce resources, such as skilled manpower, capital or equipment, to those economic sectors where the need is greatest. Concerned with the development of the country's economy in the interests of the people as a whole rather than with maximizing profits, it can

1. The Chinese of Southeast Asia are possibly an exception to this generalization.

achieve a more balanced distribution of development than under the system of economic liberalism; above all, it can bring about a narrowing of the gap between various classes, or between the developed regions of the State territory and the backward regions. It demands a programme which will arouse the enthusiasm of the masses and this may necessitate a restructuring of society through agricultural reform and the active involvement of the people, the medium of state-controlled enterprise, in the non-agricultural sectors of the economy. And, given this enthusiasm, it is perhaps the only system which can mobilize the greatest hidden wealth of the region – its underemployed or unemployed masses; by so doing, it converts what had been a problem, in the shape of heavy population pressure, into a factor for progress. And while it calls for discipline and austerity, i.e. for the control of consumption so that the resources necessary for the diversification of the economy can be slowly built up, such discipline and austerity have been shown to be essential if an 'underdeveloped' region such as Southeast Asia is to move to the point of self-sustaining economic growth. A French expert has referred to the 'illusion of foreign aid', by which he means the widespread but erroneous belief that large injections of foreign aid can initiate real economic development. Few areas illustrate the truth of his verdict as clearly as Southeast Asia; within Southeast Asia a comparison of, say, South Vietnam which has received hundreds of millions of dollars of aid (or Laos, where the aid per capita was among the highest in the world) with North Vietnam, where ten years of uphill struggle, and limited aid from the Sino-Soviet bloc, have created the beginnings of a modern and diversified economy, puts this truth into even clearer focus.

Looking to the future, the trend towards more radical types of political and economic structure may be expected to continue. This will not be because of propaganda or subversion but because the 'liberal' – or free-enterprise – alternative not only fails to 'deliver the goods' in a Third World context but also because it fails to create a decent society; in other words, it not only fails to create the conditions in which men may *have* more but also the conditions in which they may *be* more. This prospect of a leftward shift is one which many in the West regard with fear and suspicion; indeed, at the moment a bloody and ruinous war is being fought to arrest this trend in South Vietnam. Yet even a perfunctory – but objective – examination of conditions in Southeast Asia, in other parts of the Third World, will drive home the fact that for these countries *there is no other solution* to the gigantic problems that face them, that, for the peoples of Southeast Asia, the examples of China, of North Vietnam and above all North Korea provide an object lesson whose significance is becoming increasingly obvious – and relevant. If this is true, then many of the existing Southeast Asian regimes may prove to be transitional phenomena, whose continuing existence is made possible only by massive external support which maintains the regimes in power without at the same time solving the economic problems which beset them. And with mounting population pressure these problems grow inexorably more acute.

The comments above are not meant to imply, as some Western politicians appear to believe, that the whole of this region faces the prospect of integration or absorption into a monolithic communist bloc. The strength of local nationalisms – well illustrated by Cambodia or Vietnam – is likely to be sufficient to make this a remote possibility; what *is* much more likely is the emergence of a wide spectrum of left-wing regimes each coloured by the specific social and cultural characteristics of the various Southeast Asian peoples. Some of these traditions will be religious, as in the Buddhist countries of the mainland, or Islamic, as in the Greater Indonesian world; yet others will draw on the traditions of former greatness (as in the case of Cambodia and the Khmer Empire) or on the intensity of feelings forged by long centuries of struggle against a powerful neighbour (as in the case of Vietnam). Under such conditions, the unity of these lands will arise from the common fashion in which they confront the common problems posed by poverty and rapidly expanding populations.

These considerations may seem far removed from the earlier discussion of the geography of the area, but it is a removal in appearance only. One of the most striking features of the postwar period has been the increasing role of political and social factors as agents of geographic differentiation; this, in turn, is linked with the emergence of a series of socialist regimes whose techniques and patterns of economic development show sharp contrasts with those of the capitalist regimes which had hitherto dominated the whole of the globe except the Soviet Union. The influence of the political factor can be seen in particularly striking fashion in countries which have been partitioned and in which one part of the former state continues under a traditional 'liberal' economy (using the term liberal in an economic sense) while the other part has developed on socialist lines. In Asia the outstanding examples of this are provided by North and South Korea and North and South Vietnam. The boundaries between such divided countries separate not only different political systems but also widely differing social and economic systems and, since the social and economic system plays a major role in shaping the geography of a country, these boundaries now separate regions with sharply contrasting geographies. Thus, among the impressions on the cultural landscape of a socialist system are the beginning of territory-wide modernization and diversification of the economy; the development of a series of dispersed industrial complexes; urban growth on a controlled rather than *laissez-faire* basis; the reshaping of the social and economic structure of the rural areas through agrarian reform, a re-shaping which, by releasing 'hidden resources' of labour, makes possible the physical transformation of the countryside through irrigation development; finally, the attempts to integrate fully into the country's life minority groups who had formerly been relegated to the category of second-grade citizens. Such developments stand in sharp contrast to the widening gap in levels of modernization and standards of life which separates the 'poles of development' in non-socialist societies from the stagnating back country.

The hesitant but increasingly inevitable penetration of the Southeast Asian world by socialist concepts of planning and development will, in the years ahead, result in a geography very different from the contemporary geography of Southeast Asia. Part of the inspiration for the ideas which shape this new world will be derived from the ancient and luminous cultures of the area, part from the lessons drawn from the experience of the other Asian socialist states. In this process of development many of the glaring contrasts in levels of living and economic opportunity (between classes or between areas) will be progressively eliminated in Southeast Asia and, what is even more important, the rise of modern and diversified economies will make it possible for the peoples of the region to begin, first to arrest, then to narrow, the widening economic differential between themselves and the affluent nations of the Atlantic world.

Further Reading*

Part One

C. Booth, *Life and Labour of the People in London*, First Series: *Poverty*, Macmillan, 1902, 3rd edn.

Citizen's Board of Inquiry into Hunger and Malnutrition in the US, *Hunger, USA*, Beacon Press, 1968.

J. de Castro, *Of Men and Crabs*, Vanguard, 1970.

F. Engels, *The Conditions of the Working Class in England*, Allen and Unwin, 1892.

O. Lewis, *La Vida*, Random House, 1966.

J. Lopreato, 'How would you like to be a peasant?', *Human Organization*, vol. 24, 1965, pp. 298–307.

M. Meltzer, *Brother Can You Spare a Dime*, Knopf, 1969.

J. Riis, *Battle with the Slum*, Macmillan, 1902.

R. Segal, *The Anguish of India*, Stein and Day, 1965.

Part Two

J. Bhagwati, *The Economics of Underdeveloped Countries*, World University Library, 1966.

W. Beckerman, *International Comparisons of Real Incomes*, Organization for Economic Cooperation and Development, 1966.

S. Kuznets, *Modern Economic Growth*, Yale University Press, 1966.

S. Lens, *Poverty: America's Enduring Paradox*, Crowell, 1969.

J. Marchal and B. Ducros (eds.), *The Distribution of National Income*, Macmillan, 1968.

* The United Nations has addressed itself to the problem of world poverty and related issues since its inception. The reports of various UN study commissions are excellent sources of information. For the general reader, *Ceres*, a monthly publication summarizes, in non-technical language, much of the UN's work. Other more technical releases include *World Economic Survey*, *Demographic Yearbook*, and the *Economic Bulletins* and *Economic Commission Reports* for Europe, Africa, Asia and the Far East, and Latin America.

J. May, *The Ecology of Malnutrition in Five Countries of Eastern and Central Europe*, Hafner, 1968.

S. M. Miller, and P. Roby, *The Future of Inequality*, Basic Books, 1970, chap. 2.

Ministry of Social Security, *Circumstances of Families*, Her Majesty's Stationery Office, 1967.

M. Orshansky, 'How poverty is measured', *Monthly Labor Review*, vol. 92, 1969, pp. 37–41.

W. E. Mann, (ed.) *Poverty and Social Policy in Canada*, Copp Clark, 1970.

'The anatomy of Indian poverty', *Monthly Commentary on Indian Economic Conditions*, vol. 10, 1968, pp. 1–154.

D. Simpson, 'The dimensions of world poverty', *Scientific American*, vol. 219, no. 5, pp. 3–11.

P. Townsend, (ed.), *The Concept of Poverty*, Heinemann, 1970.

M. Woodis, 'Some problems of poverty in Britain today', *Marxism Today*, vol. 11, 1967, pp. 357–63.

L. J. Zimmerman, *Poor Lands, Rich Lands: The Widening Gap*, Random House, 1964.

Part Three

G. Arroba, 'Social Security Schemes and the National Economy in the Developing Countries', *International Social Service Review*, vol. 22, 1969, pp. 26–60.

T. Balogh, *The Economics of Poverty*, Macmillan, 1966.

C. Bettelheim, *India Independent*, Monthly Review Press, 1968.

W. Birmingham, and A. G. Ford (eds.), *Planning and Growth in Rich and Poor Countries*, Praeger, 1966.

F. Castro, 'The shame will be welcome', speech of 26 July 1970, *New York Review of Books*, vol. 15, 24 September 1970, pp. 21–33.

S. Child, *Poverty and Affluence*, Schocken, 1970.

C. Clark, *Starvation or Plenty*, Taplinger, 1970.

P. Cutright, 'The distribution and redistribution of income', in Warner Bloomberg Jr, and H. J. Schmandt (eds.), *Power, Poverty and Urban Policy*, Sage, 1968.

R. Dumont, *False Start in Africa*, Praeger, 1969.

A. G. Frank, *Latin America: Underdevelopment or Revolution*, Monthly Review Press, 1970.

J. Galtung, *Development in Three Villages of Sicily*, Columbia University Press, 1970.

R. Green and A. Seidman, *Unity or Poverty: The Economics of Pan-Africanism*, Penguin, 1970.

W. A. Hance, *Population, Migration and Urbanization in Africa*, Columbia University Press, 1970.

S. Levitan, *The Great Society's Poor Law*, The Johns Hopkins Press, 1969.

G. Myrdal, *Asian Drama*, Pantheon, 1968, Allen Lane Penguin Press; 1968, Penguin 1969.

G. D. Ness, *The Sociology of Economic Development*, Harper and Row, 1970.

L. R. Pearson, *Partners in Development*, Praeger, 1969.

S. Pflanczer, 'Poverty, urban policy and the mature welfare states of Europe', in W. J. Bloomberg Jr and H. J. Schmandt (eds), *Power, Poverty and Urban Policy*, Sage, 1968.

G. Rimlinger, 'Social security and society: An East-West comparison', *Social Science Quarterly*, vol. 50, 1969, pp. 494–506.

P. Streeten, and M. Lipton, *The Crisis of Indian Planning*, Oxford University Press, 1968.

The State of Food and Agriculture, 1969, Rome: Food and Agriculture Organization of the United Nations, 1969.

B. Ward, 'The poor world's cities', *Economist*, vol. 233, 1969, pp. 56–62.

Part Four

P. A. Baran, *The Political Economy of Growth*, Monthly Review Press, 1957.

J. Bosch, 'The impoverishment of Latin America', *Review of International Affairs*, vol. 449, 1968, pp. 6–8.

B. Cavala, and A. Wildavsky, 'The political feasibility of income by right', *Public Policy*, vol. 18, 1970, pp. 321–54.

P. J. Eldridge, *The Politics of Foreign Aid in India*, Schocken, 1970.

P. Jalée, *The Pillage of the Third World*, Monthly Review Press, 1968.

H. Lumer, *Poverty: Its Roots and its Future*, International Publishers, 1965.

K. Moody, 'Poverty and politics', *New Politics*, vol. 6, 1968, pp. 37–42.

J. D. Montgomery, 'Programs and poverty: federal aid in the domestic and international systems', *Public Policy*, vol. 18, 1970, pp. 517–37.

Proceedings of the International Peace Research Association: Second Conference. Poverty, Development and Peace. N. V. Assen: Van Gorcum and Co., 1968.

B. B. Seligman, (ed.), *Poverty as a Public Issue*, Free Press, 1965.

H. G. Shaffer, and J. S. Prybyla (eds.), *From Underdevelopment to Affluence*, Appleton-Century-Crofts, 1968.

R. M. Titmuss, *Essays on the Welfare State*, Unwin, 1963, rev. edn.

J. Woodis, *Africa, The Way Ahead*, International Publishers, 1963.

Acknowledgements

Permission to reproduce the Readings in this volume is acknowledged to the following sources:

1 Houghton Mifflin Co. and A. P. Watt & Son
2 Beacon Press and Hodder & Stoughton
3 New American Library Inc.
4 New American Library Inc.
5 Grossman Publishing and Granada Publishing Co.
7 Routledge & Kegan Paul and London School of Economics
8 Oxford University Press
9 *Monthly Labor Review*
11 University of Chicago Press
12 London School of Economics
14 Praeger Publishers Inc.
15 Royal Institute of International affairs
16 Food and Agriculture Organization of the United Nations
17 Food and Agriculture Organization of the United Nations
18 Macmillan Co. and Georg Borgstrom
19 University of Illinois Bulletin and Philip Hauser
20 *Outlook*
22 International Labour Review
23 Bobbs-Merrill Co. Inc. and Gollancz
24 The Twentieth Century Fund
25 *Science and Society*
27 Free Press
28 The Nation Associates
29 Taplinger Publishing Co. Inc. and G. Bell and Son

Author Index

Subject Index